JAPANESE CULTURAL POLICIES IN
SOUTHEAST ASIA DURING WORLD WAR 2

Japanese Cultural Policies in Southeast Asia during World War 2

Edited by
Grant K. Goodman

Professor Emeritus of History, University of Kansas, and Visiting Professor, International Center for Research in Japanese Studies, Kyoto

St. Martin's Press   New York

All rights reserved. For information, write:
Scholarly and Reference Division,
St. Martin's Press, Inc., 175 Fifth Avenue,
New York, N.Y. 10010

First published in the United States of America in 1991

Printed in Hong Kong

ISBN 0–312–05243–X

Library of Congress Cataloging-in-Publication Data
Japanese cultural policies in Southeast Asia during World War 2
   edited by Grant K. Goodman.
      p.   cm.
   Includes index.
   ISBN 0–312–05243–X
   1. Asia, Southeastern—Relations—Japan.   2. Japan—Relations–
–Asia, Southeastern.   3. Japan—Cultural policy.   4. World War,
1939–1945—Social aspects—Asia, Southeastern.   I. Goodman, Grant
Kohn, 1924–
DS525.9.J3J37   1991
303.48'252059—dc20   90–39913
                                                                CIP

For Paul.

Contents

List of Tables

Acknowledgments

The editor would like to acknowledge the generous support and assistance of the International Center for Research in Japanese Studies, Kyoto, Japan.

Professor E. Bruce Reynolds wishes to express appreciation to the East-West Center, the Crown Prince Akihito Scholarship Committee, the Japan–U.S. Education Foundation, the Department of Education Fulbright Program, the Robert Sakai Travel Fund, the University of Hawaii Japan Studies Endowment (funded by a grant from the Japanese government), the Northeast Asia Council of the Association for Asian Studies, and the San Jose State University Foundation for financial support of his research on Japanese–Thai relations over the past seven years.

Permission has been granted to draw on aspects of an earlier version of Aiko Kurasawa's essay on Java, entitled "Propaganda Media on Java under the Japanese, 1942–45," which appeared in the journal *Indonesia*, October 1987.

GRANT K. GOODMAN

ix

Notes on the Contributors

Yoji Akashi received his M. A. and Ph.D. degrees from Georgetown University. He is currently Professor of the History of International Relations at Nanzan University, Nagoya and is President of the Japan Association of Southeast Asian History. His important publications include *Nanyang Chinese Anti-Japanese Boycott and the National Salvation Movement, 1937–1941* and "The Japanese Occupation of Malaya, Interruption or Transformation."

Grant K. Goodman received his Ph.D. degree from the University of Michigan and is Professor Emeritus of History at the University of Kansas and Visiting Professor at the International Research Center for Japanese Studies in Kyoto. His publications relevant to Japan–Southeast Asian relations are *An Experiment in Wartime Intercultural Relations: Philippine Students in Wartime Japan, 1943–1944, Davao: A Case Study in Japanese–Philippine Relations, Four Aspects of Philippine–Japanese Relations, 1930–1940* and *24 in '44: Filipino Students in Wartime Japan.*

Kenichi Goto graduated from the Faculty of Political Science and Economics, Waseda University, Tokyo in 1965. He received the M. A. degree from Cornell University in 1970 and is currently Professor, Institute of Social Sciences, Waseda University. His recent major publications include *Shōwaki Nippon to Indonesia* (Japan and Indonesia in the Prewar Shōwa Period), *Haraguchi Takejirō Nampō Chōsa no Senku* (Haraguchi Takejirō, A Pioneer of Southeast Asian Studies) and *Kindai Nippon to Indonesia* (Modern Japan and Indonesia).

Aiko Kurasawa studied International Relations at the Graduate School of Tokyo University and received her Ph.D. in History from Cornell University in 1988. Her dissertation "Mobilization and Control: A Study of Social Change in Rural Java, 1942–1945" will be published shortly in both Jakarta and Tokyo. She is presently on the Faculty of International Language and Culture, Setsunan University, Osaka.

E. Bruce Reynolds received his M. A. degree from Central Missouri State University and his Ph.D. degree from the University of Hawaii in 1988. His dissertation research focused on Japanese–Thai relations during World War 2. A lecturer in the Faculty of Arts, Chulalongkorn University, Bangkok from 1979–1982, he is currently Assistant Professor of History at San Jose State University.

Motoe Terami-Wada received her B. A. degree from Kwansei Gakuin University in Nishinomiya, Japan and has two M. A. degrees: in Asian Studies from the University of Hawaii at Manoa and in Philippine Studies from the University of the Philippines. She is currently Professorial Lecturer at the De La Salle University, Manila and is completing her Ph.D. in History at the University of the Philippines.

Introduction
Grant K. Goodman

In 1988 Prof. E. Bruce Reynolds, one of the five distinguished contributors to this volume, proposed that I organize and chair a panel on Japanese cultural policies in Southeast Asia during World War 2 at the annual meeting of the Association for Asian Studies the following year. Like myself, Prof. Reynolds has academic interests encompassing both Japanese and Southeast Asian history and wanted to develop an appropriate forum where this combination of skills might be best evidenced. Since he quite correctly believed that a study of Japanese cultural programs in Southeast Asia during the wartime period was long overdue, I enthusiastically agreed to try to assemble a group of outstanding specialists whose combined scholarly abilities would provide an attractive and stimulating session at the next AAS meeting. In Washington in 1989 the panelists presented their papers: Mrs Terami-Wada on the Philippines, Prof. Akashi on Malaya and Singapore, Prof. Goto on Indonesia and Prof. Reynolds on Thailand.

Finding the contents of the four papers enriching and rewarding, Mr Simon Winder of St Martin's Press suggested to me that I edit a book on the same topic utilizing the same specialists, a proposal which I very willingly accepted. With the subsequent addition of Prof. Aiko Kurasawa, who has done a superb study of film under the Japanese on Java, the present volume has now very happily reached publication.

Clearly there are certain aspects of Japan's cultural activities in Southeast Asia which are uniformly apparent throughout all the contributions which follow. And there are equally certain nagging questions which remain even after reading these fine essays. This is undoubtedly because there are matters which require the observer to speculate extensively, something which careful historians are understandably loath to do. In the few paragraphs which I have at my disposal, I shall try both to identify certain unifying themes in this volume and to put forward some ideas about the impact or lack thereof of Japanese cultural efforts in Southeast Asia during World War 2.

As one reads the chapters in this book, one is confronted over and over by the remarkable lack of preparation by the Japanese for the

1

tremendous obligations which they suddenly found themselves assuming after their lightning-like victorious sweep through Southeast Asia after December 8, 1941. Several reasons for this can be suggested: (1) until 1940 the possibility of a military move to the south had not been seriously contemplated by most Japanese political or military leaders; (2) Japan had, since at least World War 1, by dealing almost exclusively with colonial officials and Chinese merchants, a relatively profitable trading relationship with most of Southeast Asia and, despite a variety of occasional irritants with the colonial powers in the region, had developed reasonable access to Southeast Asian raw materials and markets; (3) given Japan's Sinic cultural heritage, historic fear of Russia (and more recently of Russian communism as well) and its modern imperial ambitions, Japanese political, military and cultural energies had been heavily focused on Northeast Asia whose peoples, languages, religions etc. were, accordingly, quite well known in Japan; (4) before World War 2, in contrast to the prestige given to the study of Chinese language and culture in Japan, there was literally no academic study of Southeast Asian languages and cultures.

Indeed, what knowledge of Southeast Asia there was in prewar Japan was largely based on infrequent Japanese translations of English, French, Dutch or American books. There were, of course, a few eyewitness accounts by immigrants, journalists or even the occasional scholar, but these had only minimal currency and were certainly not such as to arouse deeper Japanese interest in or consideration of the region. In short, as can be seen well from the contributions in this book, whatever cultural policies and programs were devised for Southeast Asia were of necessity almost entirely *ad hoc*. As the authors herein point out, a propaganda corps was organized and educational programs were devised for occupied Southeast Asia. However, as they also carefully describe, this was done either practically "on the eve" of invasion or after the conquering Japanese armies had established full local control. Moreover, cultural activities were directed by an officer corps flush with victory and fully convinced of Japanese moral and "spiritual" superiority to the subject Southeast Asians. Thus, the programs put into place were based largely on the model of Nazi German propaganda plus experience gained in such Japanese colonies as Korea, Taiwan and Manchuria or in previously militarily occupied areas of China.

Perhaps the major innovation of the Japanese cultural propaganda campaign throughout Southeast Asia was the recruitment, mobilization and utilization of hundreds of *bunkajin* ("men of culture" or intellectuals) to be sent to Southeast Asia to "reeducate" the populace in order to bring them docilely into Japan's cultural orbit. These writers, artists, professors, musicians etc. were indeed "the best and the brightest" of 1930s and 1940s Japan, and the decision to make use of their talents in Japan's cultural enterprise in Southeast Asia was on the face of it a most prescient one.

However, neither the military officers who directed cultural propaganda nor the *bunkajin* themselves, for the most part, had any prior acquaintance with Southeast Asia nor any prior experience in the region. For example, they knew no indigenous Southeast Asian languages (and, in fact, almost no Dutch or French), so paradoxically, while Japanese *gunseikanbu* (military government) officials were urging Southeast Asians to rid themselves of all vestiges of "Anglo-American" imperialism, especially the English language, those very exhortations were almost entirely written in English! Similarly, while widespread campaigns were under way everywhere in Southeast Asia to make the subject population learn the Japanese language, the occupying authorities apparently saw no analogy between their propagation of their own language and the prior spread of English which they so bitterly condemned.

Clearly one more paradox which should be noted is that, despite the Japanese intent, frequently reiterated, to depict themselves as "liberators" of Southeast Asia, in fact it would seem that they "out-colonialed" the colonials from whom they were supposedly freeing the colonized. From its inception in the 1930s the *Daitōa Kyōeiken* (Greater East Asia Co-Prosperity Sphere) had been for the Japanese a kind of economic blueprint for Japan's intensive campaign to bring all of Southeast Asia's natural resources and markets more firmly under Japanese economic hegemony. Such a "plan" was exceedingly opportunistic, of course, and reflected a growing conviction at the highest levels of Japanese leadership that the "wave of the future" lay with Japan's Axis partners, Hitlerian Germany and Mussolinian Italy, and that the anticipated death of the "flabby" democracies of Western Europe and North America foretold the termination of their Southeast Asian colonial stewardship.

When in 1940 and 1941 the Greater East Asia Co-Prosperity Sphere took on an additional distinctly political coloration, it became evident that the overriding goal of a Japanese physical presence in Southeast Asia would be to secure its resources for Japan itself and, accordingly, to deny them "forever" to the former colonial powers.

In this context, then, cultural policies had, of necessity to serve that primary Japanese purpose. To that end, "Japanization" of the indigenous populace meant the development of programs of education and indoctrination which would keep the locals subservient and acquiescent in order to assure Japan the fullest access to the natural resources it had always coveted and now, more than ever, required for its war effort.

The implicit as well as explicit result of such a program was to sustain a proto-colonial, superior–inferior relationship between the Japanese and the occupied peoples. Most of the Japanese had little or no respect for the Southeast Asians who were looked upon as "uncultured" and were generally viewed by the Japanese as lazy, cowardly, backward people whose servile condition had been severely worsened under Euro-American colonial domination. Thus, as the Japanese saw it, the only way to "save" these benighted beings was to bring them into the superior world of Japanese values which would, incidentally, at the same time also make more secure Japan's control of the region.

The Japanese decision to utilize *bunkajin* to spearhead their cultural program was surely a logical one. However, the *bunkajin* hardly proved to be miracle workers: (1) the *bunkajin* were from the outset under the aegis of career military officers committed to the Japanese ultranationalist shibboleths of *Kōdō* (way of the Emperor) and *Hakkō Ichiu* (eight corners of the world under one roof); (2) as several of the contributors to this volume demonstrate, the *bunkajin* too were seemingly committed to the same shibboleths thus lacking the kind of intellectual sensitivity which ideally they might have brought to their assignments; (3) the emphasis on "Japanization" of the indigenous population, no matter how idealistically motivated it may have been, was clearly based on a universal Japanese presumption that Southeast Asians either had no culture of their own or that whatever culture they did have lacked the "sophistication" which the superior Japanese culture had attained. These attitudes, not entirely dissimilar to those of Nazi Germany in occupied Europe, were, of course, in the end self-defeating. Practically no vestiges of Japan's wartime cultural program remain in Southeast Asia today.

Yet, there is one very important exception to all of this, one to which Professors Akashi and Goto give their close attention. Certainly the *Nanpō Tokubetsu Ryūgakusei* (Special Overseas Students from the Southern Region) program was an outstanding success for Japan and an almost uniformly positive experience for the young

Southeast Asians who benefited from it. From the selection of the students who were to be sent to Japan to study, through the preliminary training programs both in Southeast Asia and in Japan, to the education of these youths in the best Japanese institutions of higher education, this enterprise was impressively organized and carried out. Interestingly too, this program was uniquely based on a detailed preliminary study done in 1941 before the war started, which was carefully reexamined in detail again in 1942, and on the foundation of which the actual program was begun in 1943.

Not surprisingly this program, too, was essentially to further the "Japanization" of Southeast Asia by training future leaders who would be indoctrinated in Japan with *Yamato damashii* (Japanese spirit) and who, on returning home, would help to mold their fellow countrymen into ideal participants in the Greater East Asia Co-Prosperity Sphere. To try to achieve this result, despite all of the wartime hardships that were endemic in Japan by 1943, the Japanese gave these young men the best that they had in training and education, provided them with opportunities for travel and sightseeing in Japan and, most importantly, made it possible for them to meet and to know Japanese families who welcomed these Southeast Asians into their midst with warmth, consideration and real friendship.

The *Nanpō Tokubetsu Ryūgakusei* program was truly a singular achievement which stands out starkly against the background of so many much less successful wartime cultural efforts. The surviving "products" of that experience are to this day among the fastest friends of Japan throughout Southeast Asia. It is to be hoped, accordingly, that some Japanese who read the story of the *Nantoku* (or *Nantokusei* as they were also commonly called) as included in this volume will recognize both the long-range significance of that remarkable program and the possible lessons which such an impressively successful cultural undertaking may have for Japan today.

Finally, there have been certain voices, especially in Japan itself, which have argued that Japan's general lack of success in its wartime cultural policies in Southeast Asia was entirely due to the brevity of the Japanese presence. In other words, these critics ask how one can judge policies which were in place for such a short historical moment. The answer to such contentions must, I think, be that the time factor surely should be taken into account but that it is probably of only secondary importance. The "theoretical" premises of Japan's conquest of Southeast Asia – *Daitōa Kyōeiken, Kōdō, Hakkō Ichiu* – gave rise to a cultural program of "Japanization" which, in turn, generated a Japanese neo-colonialism. Such policies, whether Nazi German, Soviet Russian or Imperial Japanese, can only lead to disaster for their progenitors and to an extreme backlash from their unwilling recipients.

Yet, as historians we need to know what was done, who did it and how it was done as well as why it was done. I believe that in this volume Professors Akashi, Goto, Kurasawa and Reynolds and Mrs Terami-Wada have done exactly that. I thank them all for their sterling scholarship, and I heartily commend their work to you in the pages that follow.

1 "Bright Legacy" or "Abortive Flower": Indonesian Students in Japan during World War 2

Kenichi Goto

INTRODUCTION

Throughout the entire course of the "Greater East Asia War," Japan's objectives in occupied Southern Asia, including Indonesia, were based on three principles of military administration: (1) maintenance of peace and security in the area, (2) acquisition of important raw materials, and (3) local self-sustenance. In other words, Japanese authorities concerned with the occupation tended to put heavy emphasis on the military, political, and socio-economic aspects giving only secondary attention to the cultural policies toward the local population except for pacification activities. Their lack of interest in cultural affairs was indicated by the weakness of the organization and staff who were assigned to the execution of cultural policies.[1]

Thus, despite progress in studies on Indonesia during the Japanese occupation period in various countries, most researchers' attention has been directed toward political, military and socio-economic fields with cultural aspects being usually omitted from their perspectives. No substantial studies have been made as to what sort of cultural policies Japan drew up and put into effect, and what impact, if any, they had on the Indonesian side.[2]

One reason for this lack of interest may be found in the fact that few cultural policies of dramatic significance were introduced into wartime Indonesia. In contrast with the broad impress which Japan's political, military and economic policies seem to have had, some of which are still observable in Indonesia, cultural policies of the Japanese military administration have had relatively limited effects in postwar Indonesian society.

7

Another significant reason for the seeming lack of cultural research is the apparent dearth of official and non-official data and materials in this field. It is the writer's hope that in view of the situation described above, this contribution on the program for "Special Overseas Students from the Southern Regions," *Nanpō Tokubetsu Ryūgakusei* in Japanese (and often abbreviated as *Nantoku*), which was one of the few systematic cultural policies planned and executed throughout the occupied southern regions, may throw some light on the cultural policies of the Japanese military administration.[3]

CONCEPTION AND ORGANIZATION OF *NANTOKU*

It was in the mid-1930s that the Japanese government took a positive step forward in receiving Southeast Asian students into schools in Japan. A definitive milestone was the formation of the International Students' Institute (*Kokusai Gakuyūkai*) under the jurisdiction of the Foreign Ministry in December, 1935.[4]

After Japan's formal withdrawal from the League of Nations in March 1933, under the banner of "Back to Asia," the Japanese recognized the potential propaganda value of inviting to Japan students from Southeast Asia, where, with the exception of Thailand, all political entities were colonies of the Western powers. Heretofore, most Southeast Asian students who studied in Japan did so at their own expense or with financial assistance from some Japanese individuals. No Japanese government agencies provided scholarships or helped them to enter Japanese schools.

However, the *Nantoku* program which was put into effect in 1943 and 1944 was officially integrated from the very beginning into the overall cultural policies of the Japanese government and was placed under the jurisdiction of the so-called Greater East Asia Ministry. On February 21, 1942, two-and-a-half months after the outbreak of the Greater East Asia War, the government installed the Greater East Asia Establishment Council which was to report directly to the cabinet. It was a deliberative organ presided over personally by the Premier, Army General Tōjō Hideki, and was composed of 45 important members from various fields, with the president of the Planning Board, Army Lt. General Suzuki Teiichi serving as the secretary general. Its function was to "investigate into and deliberate on important matters (except those related to military and diplomatic policies) bearing upon the establishment of Greater East Asia, in response to queries from the Prime Minister of the Cabinet under whose supervision it belonged."[5]

Among the reports submitted to its President was one entitled "Cultural–educational Policies concerning the Establishment of Greater East Asia" drawn up on May 21, 1943. This report was a highly important proposal outlining the basic principles of educational and cultural policies for the various regions of Southeast Asia placed under Japanese military administration. The basic principle of "cultural–educational policies for the Southern peoples" was stipulated as follows: "The principal emphasis in education and all cultural–educational policies should be on having those peoples discard all the remnants of Anglo-American ideas and having them achieve a full appreciation of being peoples of East Asia so that they will recognize and understand that the Greater East Asia War is a Holy War for the liberation of East Asia, and also for the noble ideal of the establishment of the Greater East Asia Co-Prosperity Sphere."[6]

Inauguration of foreign student programs was felt to be urgent as a part of the concrete measures designed to effect such basic policies. However, it must be pointed out that this was not the first time that the question of inviting Southeast Asian students to Japan was brought up within government circles. Half a year before the outbreak of the war, the Education Minister had taken the initiative in discussing a government scholarship program for Asian students. A glimpse into the specific contents of the Education Ministry-proposed Southeast Asian student program can be obtained from a report of a meeting of the "Liaison Committee on Foreign Students" held one week before the war and participated in by concerned officials from various ministries. At this meeting the committee discussed the draft of an "Outline of Guidance for Foreign Students in Japan" which was drawn up by the Higher Education Bureau of the Education Ministry. The basic objective of foreign students' education was stated as follows: "to have promising young people from various regions of the world, with major emphasis on the Orient, come to our country for study . . . not only to learn of our excellent academic and artistic achievements but also to come into direct contact with the essence of our national character so they will perceive that the realization of Japan's ideals of a New Order is the best way for their own motherlands as well and so that they will come forward to cooperate with us."[7]

Here we see the clear manifestation of Japanese expectations that these students would learn of "our excellent culture" and that they would realize that a Japan-sponsored New Order and their country's "supreme way" were inseparable and that they would serve as a bridge between the two entities.

Putting it more concretely, this draft of the Education Ministry stipulated that the students must be selected from among young men of superior capabilities; that they must be exposed to intense indoctrination about Japan's national features; that when they arrived in Japan, they would be given a certain period of orientation as preparatory to starting schooling in Japan; that during the above preparatory period in Japan they would be given "experience in group living according to their place of origin as a matter of principle;" and that the students would be "distributed widely to local schools under a preplanned guideline avoiding undue concentration in Tokyo." It is noteworthy that most of these recommendations were, in fact, put into practice in the later wartime programs for Southern students.

Originally, as explained, the Southern student program had been developing under the leadership of the Education Ministry, but after the spring of 1942 when virtually the whole Southern area was put under Japanese rule, the Southern student program became a matter of realistic urgency, and other government agencies – the Foreign Ministry, the Information Bureau, and even some organs of the military – came to be actively involved in this program, each with its own viewpoints and interests.

Indeed, some of the various government agencies concerned were in open rivalry with each other regarding the proposed program for foreign students. The Foreign Ministry saw the plan as part of its overall cultural exchange policy giving a cold shoulder to the Education Ministry which, in the view of the Foreign Ministry, lacked experience in this field. The Foreign Ministry also criticized the Information Bureau stating, "[This program] is not something that can be dealt with half-heartedly by an amateur organization that knows little about cultural–educational affairs".[8]

It was at the 8th directors' meeting on April 13, 1943 that the ISI (International Students' Institute) formally decided to receive and take care of the Southern regions' special students. An ISI report on the activities of 1942 (April 1942–March 1943) presented at the meeting explained that "following the February 1943 directive of the Greater East Asia Ministry, the Institute has undertaken the education of the students from various Southern regions during a preparatory period in order to help foster special leaders for Southern cultural operations."[9]

Also at this directors' meeting it was reported that the purpose of the special Southern regions' student program was to "foster in as short a period as possible" the education of future leaders who would, upon their return home, "willingly cooperate in leading the native populace in the establishment of the Greater East Asia Co-Prosperity Sphere." According to Kanazawa Hitoshi, who played a central role in the ISI's *Nantoku* program, the initial title of the program was "Project to Foster Special Leaders in Southern Cultural Operations" but "Cultural Operations" was later dropped, and it was called simply the "Special Southern Students Program."[10]

INDONESIAN RESPONSE TO THE *NANTOKU* PROGRAM

While preparation was under way in Japan, in Java, which was under the jurisdiction of the 16th Army of the Southern Forces, on April 1, 1943 an announcement appeared from the Japanese military administration on the "despatch to Japan of 20 native students" the very next month. Two examinations were administered to 72 applicants from various provinces, and 24 successful applicants were identified on the 29th of the same month (April 29 being the Emperor's birthday).[11]

In short, this first group of the *Nantoku* was selected only 4 weeks after the initial announcement of the plan, and the fast action reflected the eagerness on the part of Japan to foster "as soon as possible" personal ties between the military administration authorities and the local populace. A general outline of the reactions and views of the Indonesian *Nantoku* students will be attempted below, based on memoirs and notes of some former *Nantoku* students, and also on interviews with those who participated in a symposium held in Tokyo in December, 1983 to commemorate the 40th anniversary of *Nantoku*.

These young men came to know of the new program by means of various Indonesian newspapers, through teachers of the schools they were attending or from which they had graduated, or through government officials with whom they were personally acquainted. There was a considerable number of families who thought it would be advantageous to send their children to Japan for education in view of the possible prolongation of Japanese rule, especially since many of the applicants were in their late teens and were anxious about their own future and that of their motherland. Though with complex sentiments, they decided to apply for the chance to "study in Japan at government expense," to pursue "further studies which were otherwise unavailable," or "to make parents' wishes come true."[12]

It seems that the decisions were entirely their own and that there was no particular political or social motivation in their desire to study in Japan. According to the recollections of Sam Soehaedi, a student from Bandung, for example, the initial 19 applicants from his province were reduced to five after the first examination, and these five students were then screened together with 72 young men from other provinces, leaving a total of 24 successful candidates. These same 24 students received preliminary training in Indonesia and then departed for Japan in June, 1943.[13] The preliminary training camps were set up at Jakarta in Java, Bukittingi in Sumatra, and Makassar (now Ujung Padang) in the region of Indonesia administered by the Japanese Navy. These camps were under the supervision of the officers in charge of education under the respective military governments. The students awakened early, had marathon running practice, gymnastics and took lessons in Japanese martial arts such as judo, sumo, and Japanese fencing (kendo). Academic emphasis was focused on Japanese language, geography and history. The students lived under strict paramilitary discipline in sub-groups with the students alternatively taking leadership. This group living was designed to strengthen their morale and to engender a spiritual outlook on life.

Table 1.1 shows the number of students selected from the different Southern regions and compares the various numbers as percentages of the total *Nantoku* student population. Several important features of the Indonesian group can be discerned from this table:

1. Among the first Southeast Asian students who came to Japan in 1943, 44.8 percent, namely nearly half of the total figure, were from Indonesia, and among those Indonesian students 46 percent were from Java (about 20 percent of the total). These percentages quite equitably represented the then population distribution of the Southern regions as a whole.

2. However, in the second group of 1944 the ratio of Indonesians drastically decreased, while the number of Burmese and Philippine students increased to 62.1 percent from the 38 percent of the previous year. This is probably due to the fact that both Burma and the Philippines were granted "independence" in August and October, 1943, respectively, when the two countries concluded pacts of alliance with Japan.

Table 1.1   Number of *Nantoku* students[14]

Place of Origin	1943 Number	%*	1944 Number	%*	Total	%
Indonesia**	52	44.8	29	23.3	81	39.9
Java	(24)	(20.7)	(20)	(23.0)	(44)	(21.7)
Sumatra	(7)	(6.0)	(9)	(16.0)	(16)	(7.9)
Sulawesi, etc.	(21)	(18.1)	(0)	(0)	(21)	(10.3)
Malaya	8	6.9	4	4.6	12	5.9
Burma	17	14.7	30	34.5	47	23.2
Philippines	27	23.3	24	27.6	51	25.1
Thailand	12	10.3	0	0	12	5.9
Total	116	100	87	100	203	100

 * % means % of total student group for that year.
** Indonesia was divided into three administrative areas.
Calculations based on the *Nantoku* file of the ISI.

3. Another significant aspect in the second year is the suspension of the dispatch to Japan of students from the Indonesian area under naval administration and from Thailand. The area of naval control including Sulawesi sent a relatively large share (18.1 percent) in the first year despite its small population, and its drop to zero in the second year certainly contributed to the lowered Indonesian ratio. In the case of Thailand, it is important to point out the absence from the Assembly of Greater East Asian Nations in Tokyo in November, 1943 of the Thai Premier Phibun Songkhram. It was quite likely that the Thai government judged the war situation to be unfavorable to Japan and was hesitant about sending more students to Japan.

With a general picture of the *Nantoku* in mind, significant features of the Indonesian students from three localities of Java, Sumatra, and the Navy-occupied area consisting of Celebes (Sulawesi), Borneo (Kalimantan) and East Indonesia, can be investigated. (In considering this question, the writer is much obliged to ISI for their permission to use such basic materials as academic records and the like.)

Students from Java

Table 1.2 A Breakdown of the Students from Java

	1943 (a total of 24 students)		1944 (a total of 20 students)	
	Number	% of the total	Number	% of the total
Holder of Aristocratic Titles	10	41.6	12	60
Father as Government Official	12	50.0	8	40
Place of Origin				
Jakarta	1	4.2	5	25
West Java	7	29.2	1	5
Central Java	5	20.8	5	25
East Java	8	33.3	0	0
Unknown	3	12.5	9	45
Foreign Languages				
Dutch	21	87.5	20	100
English	20	83.8	3	15
German	11	45.8	2	10
Major				
Engineering	6	25.0	7	35
Medical Sciences	4	16.67	2	10
Agriculture	4	16.67	0	0
Japanology	3	12.5	0	0
Army Military Academy	0	0	9	45
Education	2	8.34	0	0
Economics	1	4.16	0	0
Police Training School	1	4.16	0	0
Unknown	3	12.5	2	10
Location of School				
Kurume	7	29.2	0	0
Hiroshima	7	29.2	1	5
Miyazaki	5	20.8	0	0
Kumamoto	3	12.5	1	5
Tokyo	2	8.3	9	45
Tokushima	0	0	4	20
Kyoto	0	0	3	15
Unknown	0	0	2	10
Year of Return to Indonesia				
1945	0	0	1	5
1946	1	4.16	0	0
1947	10	41.67	2	10
1948	0	0	2	10
1949	0	0	0	0
1950	1	4.16	4	20
1951	4	16.67	2	10
1952	1	4.16	3	15
Unknown	7	29.18	6	30

1. Among the two major ethnic groups of Java, namely Javanese and Sundanese, it was customary to place a certain traditional title in front of their name to show that they were of the former aristocracy (*prijaji* in Java and *manak* in Sunda). Indonesian students from Java with such titles amounted to a high 41.6 percent in the first year and a higher 60 percent in the second year. This seems to be closely connected to their fathers' occupation as government officials, in the first group 50 percent, and in the second 40 percent. The Japanese adopted a policy of maintaining and utilizing the existing bureaucracy as much as possible, and this may have had relevance to the high percentage of government officials among the students' fathers.

2. A majority of the students in both years came from East Java which is farthest from Jakarta, and many of them came from small local towns such as Malang and Blitar rather than from a major city like Surabaya. However, as Surabaya was the center in East Java of European-style education, many of the students had attended schools in Surabaya.

3. The overwhelming majority of the students had received Dutch-style elementary and middle-school education. Although the Japanese aim was to "eradicate the residue of Anglo-American ideas," the Japanese authorities had to give due weight to basic scholastic achievements acquired through Dutch education in selecting the *Nantoku* students who were being groomed as future leaders of a Japanese-led Asia. Their European educational background is revealed by the fact that 87.5 percent of the first group and 100 percent of the second group of the *Nantoku* were well-versed in the Dutch language. In any case, their exposure to European schooling in their early youth seemed to prevent them from being indoctrinated in Japanese ways as was intended by the Japanese authorities. Rather, they appear to have had sufficient maturity to be able to observe war-time Japan from an objective standpoint.

4. As to the fields of specialization which they chose in Japan, the most popular was engineering, followed by agriculture and medical science. It is clear that they were attracted by more practical studies. However, among the second group of students, some 45 percent went to the Japanese Military Academy. It is quite likely that those young men were inspired by the inauguration and development in Java of the PETA (Army for the Defense of the Fatherland), the formation of which appealed greatly to their patriotic spirit to "defend the fatherland." Probably they saw the chance to study in Japan as an

opportune way to acquire more sophisticated military knowledge and training.

According to the memoirs of Kanazawa Hitoshi, cited above, from the outset a considerable number of the *Nantoku* students desired military training, but the Japanese Army refused to accept them. The Army changed this attitude abruptly in March, 1945 and agreed to accept *Nantoku* students. When the ISI informed the *Nantoku* students scattered in various localities asking them if they would like to change their course and enter the Military Academy, more than 30 students expressed a desire to do so. Kanazawa attributed the Army's sudden turnabout in policy to its opportunism. He stated that the Army was reluctant in the beginning to accept those students because they feared that time was too short to train "good assistants" for the administration of occupied areas, but that later they came to realize that it could be more advantageous to train those military-minded students for a few months at the Military Academy, and send them back home secretly by submarines to use them as guerrilla fighters.[15]

5. The *Nantoku* students received Japanese language and other training at ISI for a half year following their arrival in Japan, and they were to enter higher educational institutions of their chosen specialized field in the following April. Of the first group, more than three-fourths of the total studied at Kurume Technical College, Hiroshima Teachers' College or Miyazaki Agricultural–Forestry College. Of the second group, the greatest proportion (45 percent) studied at Tokyo (mainly Military Academy), followed by Tokushima Civil Engineering College and Kyoto Imperial University.

6. *Nantoku* were initially to study in Japan for at least three years, but Japan's defeat in August, 1945, of course, placed them in serious jeopardy. Nevertheless, about one-third of them managed to overcome obvious financial and psychological difficulties and continued to remain in Japan to further their studies by some means or other. According to the files of the ISI, of the first group of the students 33.3 percent, and of the second group 35 percent, graduated from their schools. The first large group (41.7 percent) returned home in 1947 after four years in Japan, and the majority of the second group remained in Japan until the 1950s.

Students from Sumatra

Table 1.3   A Breakdown of the Students from Sumatra

	1943 (a total of 7 students)		1944 (a total of 9 students)*	
	Number	% of the total	Number	% of the total
Father as Government Official	3	42.9	6	75
Foreign Languages				
Dutch	6	85.7	8	100.0
English	7	100.0	7	87.5
German	7	100.0	1	12.5
Major**				
Engineering	2	28.6	3	37.5
Agriculture	1	14.3	1	12.5
Education	3	42.9	1	12.5
Police ('43)/Army Military Academy ('44)	1	14.3	3	37.5
Location of School				
Yokohama	1	14.3	0	0
Hiroshima	3	42.9	1	12.5
Kurume	3	42.9	0	0
Fukuoka	0	0	1	12.5
Gifu	0	0	1	12.5
Tokushima	0	0	2	25.0
Tokyo	0	0	3	37.5
Year of Return to Sumatra				
1947	3	42.9	3	37.5
1948	2	28.6	1	12.5
1951	2	28.6	1	12.5
1952	0	0	2	25.0
1955	0	0	1	12.5

* Data are available for 8 students.
** Judged from the schools they attended.

1. As in the case of Javanese students, there were many government officials among the students' fathers. Sumatrans did not use aristocratic titles as frequently as Javanese, reflecting the absence of long-standing "traditional" dynasties there, but two of the seven first-group students from Sumatra had a title which evidenced their aristocratic status.

2. Here also the overwhelming majority had received elementary and secondary schooling in the Dutch language and were well-versed both in Dutch and English.

3. Of the seven students in the first group, three specialized in education and two in engineering, and of the second group, judging from the schools they entered, three students specialized in engineering and three others entered the Military Academy. The popularity of the engineering field and the high application rate for the Military Academy paralleled the example of Java.

4. Distribution of the schools they entered in Japan was similar also to that of Javanese students. Of the first group of Sumatrans, about 85 percent went to Hiroshima or Kurume, and of the second group 37.5 percent studied in Tokyo (mainly the Military Academy) and 25 percent in Tokushima.

5. In most cases the year of return to Indonesia is not clear. However, it is assumed that they went home in the year of graduation or the last year they were at school, which was available from the ISI records. The first big wave of returnees occurred in 1947 for both groups (approximately 40 percent) followed by those in the early 1950s (about 35 percent).

Students from the Navy-occupied Area of Indonesia

Table 1.4   A Breakdown of the Students from Navy-occupied Areas

| | 1943 (a total of 21 students) | |
	Number	% of the total
Father as Government Official	8	38.1
Foreign Languages		
Dutch	16	76.2
English	16	76.2
French	2	9.5
Major		
Engineering	6	28.6
Medical Sciences	7	33.3
Agriculture	7	33.3
Unknown	1	4.8
Location of School		
Tokyo	14	66.7
Yokohama	4	19.0
Omiya	3	14.3

Table 1.4 *continued*

| | 1943 (a total of 21 students) | |
	Number	% of the total
Year of Return to Navy-occupied Areas		
1947	18	85.7
Still in Japan	2	9.5
Unknown	1	4.8

1. Twenty-one students came to Japan in the first year only. Their social standing is unknown because no aristocratic titles are given, unlike in Java and Sumatra, but nearly 40 percent of the students had fathers who were government officials.
2. Their familiarity with foreign languages seems rather low compared with students from Java and Sumatra, but more than three-fourths of the total gave Dutch and English as foreign languages they could use.
3. There is not much difference from other areas in their choices of specialization except that medicine and agriculture were preferred to engineering.
4. Their abodes in Japan were centered around the Tokyo metropolitan area with 66.7 percent remaining in Tokyo, followed in order by Yokohama and Omiya. Furthermore, they did not enter universities. Many of them were first assigned to a Police Training School at Yokohama as well as to government-established research institutes, regardless of their preference. (However, later on, transfer to Gifu and Yamaguchi prefectures was approved.) Probably underlying this situation was the Navy's basic policy of stressing the acquisition of skills, and not education *per se*, so that under naval supervision the *Nantoku* could be used for practical purposes upon their return to Indonesia. It is also conceivable that the naval administration authorities at Makassar were wary that young men from their area might be affected by "bad influence" by coming into contact with the youth from Java and Sumatra who had relatively high nationalistic sentiments. In this regard, the fact that the Navy-occupied areas of Indonesia were, from the beginning, intended to be placed under permanent Japanese rule should be noted.
5. Whereas only 40 percent of the young men from Java and Sumatra returned home aboard the first repatriation ships in 1947, as many as

85.7 percent of the students from Navy-administered areas returned home in February, March and May of the same year. This would reflect the situation in their native districts: in Java and Sumatra the fight for independence was intensifying, while a limited degree of Dutch rule was restored in the old Japanese Navy-occupied area. At the same time, many of the students from the former Navy-controlled area, who had been sent to study at places against their will were ready to give up studies in Japan when the general situation changed.

NANTOKU STUDENTS' JAPAN EXPERIENCE

Group Living and Discipline

The first group of 21 students from Java and Sumatra arrived at Moji, Kyushu, together with 8 Malayan students and 15 Burmese students on June 28, 1943, and they arrived at Tokyo station on June 30. (Students from the naval-controlled area came in September.) They had short-cropped hair, wore the "national uniform" with short-sleeved khaki colored shirts, and responded in groups to the calls in Japanese of sub-group leaders.

Kanazawa Hitoshi of ISI, who met them at the Tokyo station, observed, in contrast to the satisfied smiles on the faces of Japanese Army personnel who found delight in such militaristic behavior, "There was no bright light of hope in the eyes of the youth who seemed a little afraid and nervous . . . What a burden we have agreed to take."[16]

Such was Kanazawa's first impression. Probably he was afraid that the paramilitary training they had received would not be in tune with the "liberal" air of the ISI which was to be their first stop in Japan. However, the guiding principle of the ISI covering the *Nantoku* was basically aimed at group living sustained by dormitory life with much emphasis on discipline and "spiritual force" as could be seen in the "Outline of Guidance for the Foreign Students in Japan" mentioned earlier.

Upon their arrival in Tokyo they were taken immediately to the Imperial Palace ground to salute and to shout three *Banzais* to the Emperor at the direction of the accompanying Japanese official. Then, before their entrance to the ISI's Japanese Language School, they were also taken to pay homage at the Meiji Shrine and the Yasukuni Shrine. Thus, the Japanese took every opportunity to force

Japanese values on the *Nantoku* students. "Cultural frictions" emerging from such "contacts" were perhaps unavoidable since in Japan the *Nantoku* were under pressure to eradicate the Anglo-American type of "leisurely study" and to "imbibe the Japanese spirit through their daily life." In the case of the Indonesian students, however, there arose scarcely any serious trouble regarding Japanese guidelines in comparison with the Philippine students, for example, who were reported to have confronted the Japanese authorities with serious protests.[17]

Course of Study

For the *Nantoku* students the matter of greatest concern naturally was whether they would be able to pursue the studies of their choice after completing the "preliminary period" that included study of the Japanese language coupled with group living in the city of Tokyo. The Japanese, concerned with the *Nantoku*, had begun deliberations on this matter based on the cabinet decision on September 10, 1943, "Basic Principles for Guiding the Foreign Students in Japan."[18] At a meeting held at the Education Ministry on January 15, 1944, the decision was taken to apply to the foreign students the "comprehensive test system" that had been just put into force for Japanese middle-school applicants. Accordingly, all the foreign student examinees were to be assembled at one place to take an entrance examination administered by the Education Ministry. Those who passed the examination would be sent to appropriate schools in consideration of the students' own wishes and in accord with the desires of the authorities of the three regions under Japanese rule.

The January 15 conference was attended by 35 people concerned including officials of the Ministries of Education and of Greater East Asia, representatives of 15 higher schools with experience in having foreign students, and officers from the Manchukuo Embassy in Japan, the Japan-China Society and the ISI all of whom were involved in the guidance of students from various parts of the "Greater East Asia Co-Prosperity Sphere." The basic principles in determining the academic courses for the Asian students drawn up at this important meeting were as follows:[19] (1) the foreign students' entrance to schools would be determined by the Education Ministry uniformly instead of leaving the matter in the hands of the schools concerned; (2) when admitting them to schools, they would be treated as foreigners making it easier for them to pass the examinations; (3) foreign applicants would be admitted outside the fixed number to enable as many of them as possible to enter the schools of their choice.[20]

Japan's Defeat and the *Nantoku* Students

Most of the Japanese people were kept in the dark as to the deteriorating war situation. It was not surprising that most of the *Nantoku* students did not anticipate Japan's defeat as they listened to and believed the announcements of the Imperial Headquarters. The following statement of Abdul Razak, a Malayan student in the second year group enrolled in Hiroshima Higher Normal School, seems an accurate expression of their feeling at the time: "We did not think that Japan would lose until the very end of the war. However, the number of Japanese planes flying toward the enemy planes decreased day by day. So I asked my teacher why it was. The teacher replied, 'We have changed tactics and now the Japanese side is letting the enemy planes come nearer so that we can cause a fatal crash at a single stroke.' Is that the idea? I thought. Silly, wasn't I?"[21]

Japan's defeat became reality, and the students from the Southern countries had to face a serious dilemma. In the Philippines and Burma, their former suzerain countries, the U.S. and the U.K. had already regained their power and the schedule for independence of the former colonies was already worked out. As a result, students from these two countries could make a relatively smooth homecoming. The Filipinos returned home at the directive of the U.S. Occupation Forces in Japan in three groups on August 21, October 7, and October 31, 1945 respectively, while the 47 Burmese students departed from Yokohama on September 23, 1945.[22]

The Dutch government, on the other hand, had no attention to spare for Indonesian students stranded in Japan, as their attempt at colonizing Indonesia again after the war was met with strong resistance from the Indonesian Republic that declared independence on August 17, 1945. After the dissolution of the Greater East Asia Ministry, the Foreign Ministry tried to contact the Dutch concerning the repatriation of the Indonesian students in Japan, but could get no definite replies.

In the meantime, a GHQ memorandum was issued in 1947 calling on those students who wanted to return home to submit their names, adding that this would be the only chance for their return and that those who opted to remain in Japan must do so at their own risk.[23] A total of 36 students availed themselves of this opportunity to go home in 1947. There were 12 from Java, 6 from Sumatra and 18 from the Japanese Navy-occupied area.

It is not easy to ascertain the motives of those who returned and those who decided to stay on in Japan. But one thing seems clear. It is that those who had desired to come to Japan to study of their own free will would not go home to cooperate with the Dutch who were setting up puppet regimes in various localities with the intention of colonizing Indonesia again. Considering the situation in 1947 when the Dutch forces were making a military offensive, it is more likely that the students who chose to return then did so out of a patriotic spirit and in order to join the ranks of national liberation forces. The fact that 4 out of 12 Javanese returnees of 1947 had been enrolled in the Military Academy of Japan would make this hypothesis more likely.[24]

Why did some students choose to remain in war-torn Japan? Some were so deeply involved in their studies that they hated to give them up midway; some were absorbed in making money in the social upheavals of the defeated nation;[25] some others were heartily opposed to the conditions the Dutch laid down in helping them return home. It was reported that the students must negate the new-born Indonesian Republic and must acquire Netherlands citizenship if they wished to return home.[26]

Some students were perhaps concerned that they might be accused of or be slandered as being "Japan cooperators," because they had studied in Japan. In the new Republic immediately following independence, Sutan Sjahrir, who became the first Premier in November, 1945, and other political leaders were reported to have severely criticized "Japan cooperators" as the "running dogs of Fascism." Indeed, the Indonesian students in Japan were likely to have heard of such a situation in their home country. In fact, since the 1930s, Sjahrir had spoken about the threat of "Japanese fascism" and in one of his prewar books he had stated, "To put sympathy with Japan is a reverse of Asiatic inferiority complex that finds a substitute in Japan's glory."[27]

Now that the *Nantoku* students were deprived of any financial support from the Japanese government they had to make their own way in postwar Japan. By this time, however, most of the remaining students had mastered the Japanese language to a considerable degree in addition to English and Dutch with which they were familiar since their childhood. So many of them got employment with various GHQ SCAP organs working as interpreters, translators, and the like. For example, Arifin Bey of Sumatra who came to Japan in the second group came up to Tokyo from Hiroshima where he was a student of the Hiroshima University of Science and Literature. He was employed as an interpreter for the U.S. Forces, and, while working, he attended the English language course provided by the Army College Education Center to brush up his English. He recalled that he had nothing to worry about as far as food, clothing and housing were concerned since he had access to U.S. military facilities. "Thanks to my good luck, I could grow out of the post-atomic bomb ailment very soon," he said with a sort of nostalgia for the easy life he had had.[28]

It is interesting to learn that three *Nantoku* students including Bey were employed at the U.S. Information Section in Okinawa from the late 1940s through the early 1950s, monitoring Dutch and Indonesian language broadcasts and translating them into English. It must be pointed out in this connection that they had no official contacts with the Dutch representatives in Japan who were there as members of the Allied Forces.

NANTOKU STUDENTS AND INDEPENDENCE

Naturally the former *Nantoku* students were keenly concerned with the political situation of their now "independent" country where fighting for independence against the Netherlands was going on. For the first group of *Nantoku* who came to Japan in June and August, 1943, the exchange visits of Premier Tōjō to Java in July 1943 and of three influential Indonesian political leaders – Soekarno, Hatta and Ki Bagus Hadikusumo – to Japan in the autumn of the same year were taken as a sign of the importance Japan attached to their home country. Probably the students were favorably impressed by these developments. Although Indonesian criticism and discontent concerning Japanese military administration were gradually rising in various parts of Indonesia, they were as yet at a low ebb as Japan's exploitation of both personnel and natural resources was not on as full a scale as in 1944 and 1945. To the *Nantoku* in 1943, extension of Indonesian political participation, establishment of the *Chūo Sangi-in* (Central Advisory Council), and of the PETA Army were the tidings from home that certainly made a favorable impression on their young minds.

However, "independence" granted to Burma in August 1943 immediately after the students' arrival in Japan, and the granting of similar status to the Philippines in October must have had an impact on the feelings of Indonesian students in Japan. The following passage from the diary of Leocadio de Asis, a Filipino student in Japan, seems to reveal the intricate sentiments of the Indonesian and Malayan students who were bystanders to these events: "October 10, Thursday. We made a placard of the declaration of Philippine Independence and put it up on the school's bulletin board. We were so noisily excited and overjoyed that the attentions of all the teachers and students on the campus were turned to us. They all said, 'Congratulations!' and we were given bouquets from every foreign student group at school."[29]

In early November, soon after Philippine independence, the Assembly of Greater East Asian Nations was held in Tokyo. Premier Tōjō invited the leaders of five "independent" countries in the Sphere, namely Manchukuo, Republic of China, Thailand, Burma and the Philippines. Burmese and Philippine students were elated to meet Premier Ba Maw and President Jose P. Laurel in Tokyo, and de Asis wrote as follows on November 6: "I think this is a historic conference designed to uplift the morale of the one billion people of East Asia. They were dignified and restrained and looked superb. President Laurel's eloquent speech was very encouraging and greatly impressed the Japanese audience."[30]

De Asis added that President Laurel was the only speaker who referred to the "saddening status of the peoples of Java, Sumatra and Malaya who are still under oppression," and that this speech was highly evaluated by the "Annamese" students. Obviously the same feelings were shared by the *Nantoku* students from Indonesia.

The Indonesian students must have felt left out among the jubilant students from Burma and the Philippines who were excited over their "independence," whether nominal or real. So it must have been a relief and joy for them to meet the three leaders from their own country who were invited to visit Japan soon after the Assembly of the Greater East Asian Nations.

As the war situation gradually deteriorated for Japan in the latter part of 1944, the newly established Koiso Cabinet was obliged to pronounce the "granting of independence to the East Indies in the near future" as a means of concession to prevent alienation and to secure the further cooperation of Indonesia that was the greatest supply base for Japan's military forces. The so-called "Koiso statement" of September 7, 1944 did not give any specific date of the said independence and carefully avoided, as before, the use of the term "Indonesia."

However, the new policy line was received as a step forward by the Indonesian students in Japan as well as by the people in Indonesia. Although it was in the midst of the Muslim Month of Fasting, 65 Indonesian students planned and carried out a "meeting to appreciate the Koiso Statement" at the Greater East Asia Hall on the 19th, the date that marked the end of their Month of Fasting. They proudly sang their national song "Indonesian Raya" for the first time in two-and-a-half years since it was banned, and, representing the whole group, Omar Barach, a Waseda student, who had been in Japan since before the war, presented a resolution to "cooperate with fighting Japan with all our heart and soul."[31]

To the students from Indonesia who were very much concerned with the independence of their homeland, the Declaration of Independence that came two days after Japan's defeat was the realization of their much-awaited, long-cherished desire. Whether they chose to continue their studies in Japan or to return home immediately did not make much difference. One way or another, the tacit understanding among the young Indonesians in their early twenties was to devote themselves to the development of their newly free Indonesia.

Those *Nantoku* students who chose to remain in Japan for furthering their studies got together in the *Sarekat Indonesia*, the Association of Indonesian Students in Japan, which was originally organized in 1933 but suspended activities during the war period. Under the guidance of students from the prewar period like Umaryadi, a student at Hitotsubashi University who later became the Secretary General of ASEAN in the 1970s, and Suwanto, a school teacher who studied in Yamaguchi, the remaining *Nantoku* made efforts in reestablishing the *Sarekat Indonesia*, and they began their PR campaign to give support to Indonesian independence. The first of such activities was the rally held at Hibiya Park on November 4, 1945 under the name of "Rally to Achieve Independence of Our Fatherland." Students from Indonesia and Vietnam, which also declared its independence on September 2, formed the core of the rally that was participated in by students from Korea, China, the Philippines and Turkey. After the meeting, they paraded through the streets of central Tokyo raising high the national flags of their native lands.[32]

After this event, the Indonesian students continued to make frequent appeals to the Japanese and to international public opinion on such occasions as their Independence Day on August 17, while keenly watching the course of the War of Independence which their compatriots were fighting against the Dutch forces. The highlight of their activities was the great rally held at Hibiya Park on January 19, 1949. About one month before, on December 19, 1948, the Dutch arrested in Jogjakarta, the then capital, leaders of the young republic including President Soekarno, Vice-President Hatta and Foreign Minister H. Agus Salim, and confined them at Prapat at Lake Toba in North Sumatra.

The rally was held in protest of this incident. The students made a protest march to the Dutch Embassy together with some 300 Japanese sympathizers and other Asian students, shouting "Merdeka" (freedom) and singing "Indonesia Raya."[33] At the rally, Hitotsubashi University student Umaryadi made a vehement speech denouncing the Netherlands, and Arifin Bey and Abdullah Karim of Sophia University drew up a public statement. Prior to this rally, a petition was sent to the United Nations in the name of *Sarekat Indonesia* dated January 4, 1949. The petition signed by Sudarmo Mertonegoro and Dairam Hassan demanded: (1) denunciation by the U.N. of the Dutch military invasion of Indonesia, and ousting of the Netherlands from the U.N. and (2) unconditional recognition by the U.N. of the Republic of Indonesia.[34]

The Indonesian students in Japan thus identified themselves with the War of Independence of the Republic of Indonesia even though they were far away from home, and, accordingly, the former *Nantoku* students played a central role in this movement. And it was probably because of such activities which they conducted while in Japan that, when they finally returned home, there were scarcely any adverse views expressed against *Nantoku* students as having been "offspring" of the Japanese military administration.

CONCLUSION

Though begun with fanfare, the *Nantoku* program, which was the Japanese government's major cultural policy in the South, was immediately abandoned at the end of the war. The defeat was perhaps an opportune excuse to drop the program. The foreign students were, so to speak, deprived of the ladder when they went up to the roof. In that sense, wartime Japan's cultural policy was a flat failure.

When the policy was put into effect, the Japanese expected the students to absorb the "Japanese spirit" and to be earnest collaborators in establishing the "Greater East Asian Co-Prosperity Sphere." From the very beginning the program was envisioned as a part of Japan's overall cultural policy to have the Southern peoples develop an attitude of reliance on Japan. But Japan failed in this direction also. So we may conclude that the *Nantoku* program was a wartime cultural policy that failed to achieve its objectives in both concept and substance.

Then what meaning did it have for the Indonesian men who spent their youthful years in wartime Japan? As mentioned before, they made a resourceful self-adjustment to the sudden turn of events that came upon them with the end of the war. When all the financial help was discontinued and they were thrown out "naked into the field," most of them still managed to secure some means of sustaining themselves. As many as 17 Indonesian students (15 from Java, 2 from Sumatra) formally graduated from Japanese universities, with some even finishing the graduate course.

Furthermore, although they were all still at an extremely tender age when they might have been easily influenced by ideologically biased education, apparently none of them was affected by fanatic "Japanism." On the contrary, they were seemingly able to deal quite nimbly with the attempt to impose on them a set of Japanese values, and they seemed to be able to make rational comparisons with the European way of thought which they had acquired under Dutch colonial rule.

It is also possible to say that in Japan the *Nantoku* students had the opportunity to share and consolidate the feeling of being Indonesian. In their home country, the inhabitants were divided among three different jurisdictions under the Japanese Army and Navy, and there were various restrictions against the expression of nationalistic feelings. But being in Japan, these young men were unwittingly able to share the same arena and the same sentiments of being of the same nationality. In this connection, it should be noted that three of the Sumatran students (19 percent of the total) and eight of those from the Navy-occupied areas (38 percent) had received secondary education in major cities of Java, coming in direct contact with the prevalent nationalistic spirit of the late 1930s and the early 1940s.

Moreover, the sight of their fellow students from Burma and the

Philippines elated and excited over "independence," though nominal, must have inspired the Indonesian youth to such a degree that *Merdeka* became their immediate desire. In short, in Japan, they developed great momentum for strengthening their national consciousness and for identifying themselves with the "Republic of Indonesia" and subsequently were even more encouraged by the War of Independence that their compatriots were fighting at home. It is because of these experiences which they had gone through in Japan that they were able to be accepted easily back into Indonesian society without political and psychological frictions.

Finally, the writer wishes to point out that when evaluating Japan's *Nantoku* program, two different approaches must be kept in mind: one is an examination of the *Nantoku* program as an integral part of Japan's wartime cultural policy, and the other is what the *Nantoku* program meant for the Asian students who were personally involved and who spent their youthful years in Japan during the war.

In this sense it would be short-sighted and biased to assess the program as a "bright legacy" giving excess evaluation to the role that the fortunate grantees played in building the new nation after the war of independence was finally won.[35] At the same time, it would also be too one-sided to focus too much on the official objective of fostering "cooperators" in Japan's war effort and to label those *Nantoku* students as an "appendix to invasion" or "an abortive flower of history" who took advantage of Japan's wartime cultural policy.[36]

Notes and References

1. In Java, for instance, a "Propaganda Corps" was first installed in the 16th Army of the Southern Forces, and later attached to the Military Administration Headquarters supposedly in order to play an important part in Japan's pacification program. By order of the military authorities in Tokyo, about 30 famous "cultural figures," writers, painters, musicians, etc. were recruited in this "Propaganda Corps" and sent to Indonesia. They were expected to disseminate Japanese ideas on the current war to the Indonesians through various kinds of media such as publications, radio or films. Nevertheless, for large scale systematic cultural activities such as education, the administrative staff assigned to the job was not adequately qualified. This may be exemplified by the fact that the man assigned to the post of the chief of the Cultural Education Unit, Planning Section of the military administration was a prewar

manager of the Jakarta branch of the Bank of Taiwan. It was as late as December 1943 when a Cultural–Education Bureau was established in the Interior Department. Monbushō (Education Ministry), *Gakusei 80-Nenshi* (80 Years of School Education System) (Tokyo: Monbushō, 1954) pp. 468–80.

2. An important exception is Aiko Kurasawa, "Mobilization and control: A study of social change in rural Java 1942–1945," Ph.D. dissertation, Cornell University, 1988, Part 2.

3. On *Nantoku* students from the Philippines and Malaya, see Grant K. Goodman, *An Experiment in Wartime Inter-cultural Relations: Philippine Students in Japan, 1943–1945* (Ithaca: Cornell University Southeast Asia Program, 1962) and Yoji Akashi, "Kōa-kunrenjo to Nanpō Tokubetsu Ryūgakusei" ("Rising Asia Training School and the Special Overseas Students from the Southern Regions") in *Indonesia*, Tokyo: Waseda University Press, 1979.

4. Concerning the general background of the establishment of ISI, see ISI (ed.), *Kokusai Gakuyūkai Gaikan* (Outline of the ISI) (Tokyo: ISI, 1988), pp. 4–5. It is stated here that the government established ISI consulting influential private citizens in December 1935 in consideration of the increasing number of students coming to Japan from Southeast Asia since 1933–4. The main objective of the ISI was described as "to increase international cultural exchanges among students and to give protection and guidance to foreign students in Japan thereby to further international goodwill."

5. Kikaikuin Kenkyūkai (A Study Group of the Planning Board), *Dai-Tōa Kensetsu no Kihon Yōryō* (Basic Essentials for Establishing Greater East Asia), Tokyo: Kyōdō Tsūshin, 1943, Chapter 3.

6. Ibid., p. 49.

7. Monbushō (Education Ministry), "Ryūnichi Gakusei Shidō Yōryōan" ("Outline of Guidance for Foreign Students in Japan") November 28, 1941.

8. Gaimushō (Foreign Ministry), "Ryūgakusei Kyōgikai Setchi ni kansuru Monbushō ni taisuru Iken" ("Our Views about the Education Ministry's Proposal Concerning a Foreign Student Council") August 23, 1942.

9. Kokusai Gakuyūkai (ISI), "Dai Hachikai Rijikai Hōkoku Jikō" ("Issues reported at the 8th Directors' Meeting") April 1943. The same directive of the Greater East Asia Ministry concerning "travel expenditure, predeparture allowance and tuition fee" explains that for students coming from Area A (occupied areas) payment would be made by the Army and the Navy, and for those from Area B it would be made by the Greater East Asia Ministry – travel expenditure and predeparture allowance 250 yen per student, and tuition fee 100 yen per month

10. Kanazawa Hitoshi, *Omoidasu mama ni* (My Memories of the Past) (Tokyo: ISI, 1973), p. 58.

11. Jawa Shinbun (ed.), *Jawa Nenkan: Shōwa 19nen* (The Java Yearbook, 1943) (Jakarta: Jawa Shinbunsha, 1944), pp. 228–9.

12. Based upon my interviews with several former *Nantoku* students on the occasion of a symposium to commemorate the 40th anniversary of *Nantoku* program, Tokyo, November 1983.

13. Interview with Sam Soehaedi in Tokyo, November 1, 1983.
14. Students from Indo-China are not included here. Ten Vietnamese students came to Japan in February 1943, four months earlier than the *Nantoku*, based on the special Invitation Program which was embodied in the Cultural Agreement between Japan and Indo-China.
15. Kanazawa, *Omoidasu mama ni*, p. 84.
16. Kanazawa, *Omoidasu mama ni*, p. 62.
17. Some examples of "cultural conflict" between the Japanese side and Philippine students are known from the following memoirs: Toshio Suwa, "Nanpō Tokubetsu Ryūgakusei ni-kansuru Ki" ("A Note concerning *Nantoku*"), unpublished, 1983; Kadono Hiroko, *Tōnan Ajia no Otōtotachi* (My Younger Brothers from Southeast Asia) (Tokyo: Sankōsha, 1983).
18. *Jawa Shinbun*, September 12, 1943.
19. *Jawa Shinbun*, January 18, 1944.
20. The first year *Nantoku* students were admitted to the following schools:

	students
Hiroshima Higher Normal School	20
Miyazaki Agricultural College	10
Kurume Technical College	18
Kumamoto Medical College	8
The First Higher School	1
Tokyo Higher School	1
Azabu Middle School	3
Middle School Attached to Tokyo Teachers College	2
Police Training Course	11
Police Training School of Kanagawa Prefecture	11
Nishigahara Agricultural Research Center	5
Tokyo Fishery Laboratory	2
Omiya Husbandry Laboratory	2
Institute of Physics and Chemistry	2
Institute of Welfare Science	4
Total	100

Source: ISI, *The Business Report of 1944*.

21. Interview with Mr. Abdul Razak, Tokyo, November 1, 1983. However, some of the students in the western part of Japan who observed the increasing number of enemy planes in the sky sensed the deterioration of the Japanese military situation. P. Pane who was in Yamaguchi is one of them. He also recalls that the dormitory director told him at the time the atomic bomb was dropped at Hiroshima, "A tremendous bomb was dropped and the whole city is nearly devastated. But Japan will never lose. A similar bomb was recently produced in Japan also." Interview with Mr. Pelik Pane, in Tokyo, January 28, 1989.
22. Egami Yoshio, "Nanpō Tokubetsu Ryūgakusei no Rainichi" ("*Nantoku* students' visit to Japan") in *ISI Kaihō*, no.46, 1986, p. 23.
23. Kanazawa, *Omoidasu mama ni*, p. 98.
24. One of them is Yoga Sugama, a student in the second group from Java,

who became an influential army general under the Suharto regime.

25. According to Prof. Grant K. Goodman, who was in Japan as a SCAP officer, some of the Indonesian students with language skills profited financially in postwar Japanese society taking advantage of their access to the Post Exchange of the U.S. Forces. Prof. Goodman's letter to the writer is dated November 7, 1989.

26. Hassan Shadily (Sadiri), "A Memoir," in ISI's *Collections of Memoirs in Commemoration of 50th Anniversary of ISI*, 1986, p. 23. In the early 1950s Shadily majored in sociology at Cornell University and later became a co-author with John Echols of *An Indonesian English Dictionary* (Ithaca: Cornell University Press, 1961).

27. Sutan Sjahrir (trans. by C. Wolf, Jr.), *Out of Exile* (New York: The John Day Company, 1949), p. 195.

28. Hayashi Risuke and Arifin Bey, *Ajia ga Nippon ni Chūkoku-suru* (Asia advised Japan) (Tokyo: Shūei Shobō, 1982), pp. 38–9.

29. Leocadio de Asis, *Nanpō Tokubetsu Ryūgakusei Tokyo-Nikki* (Tokyo Dairy of a *Nantoku*) (Tokyo: Shūei Shobō 1982), p. 100.

30. Ibid., pp. 115–16.

31. *Jawa Shinbun*, September 22, 1944.

32. *Asahi Shinbun*, November 5, 1945.

33. M. Imron and Sori Harahap, "Indonesia's Japan Alumni in Indonesia's History," in *Second Conference ASCOJA* (ASEAN Council of Japan Alumni), 1978, p. 39.

34. Ibid., p. 39.

35. Ōta Kōki, "Nanpō Gunsei no Tokushitsu to Tenkai" ("Characteristics of the Japanese Military Administration and its Development") in Miyake Masaki (ed.), *Dainiji Sekai-Taisen to Gunbu Dokusai* (World War 2 and Military Dictatorship) (Tokyo: Daiichi Hoki, 1983), pp. 70–1.

36. Tanaka Hiroshi, "Ajia Ryūgakusei to Nippon" ("Asian foreign students and Japan") in Takigawa Tsutomu (ed.), *Shin Tōnan-Ajia Handobukku* (New Edition Handbook of Southeast Asia) (Tokyo: Kodansha, 1988), p. 423.

Appendix

Names of the *Nantoku* from Indonesia (Based on the *Nantoku* files of 1943 and 1944 of the International Students Institute)

I. Java

Name	Date of birth	Hometown
Soelaeman Affandi	August 14, 1925	Priangan (West Java)
Mochammad Tarmidi	March 24, 1925	Jakarta
Sam Soehaedi	April 8, 1923	Priangan (West Java)
Raden Fatwan	February 5, 1922	Kedus (Central Java)
R. Joesoef Odang	August 20, 1924	Bogor (West Java)
Raden Sidharto	June 10, 1923	Priangan (West Java)
Soedio	November 15, 1922	Kedivi (East Java)
Mohamad Saroedji	December 11, 1923	Madura (East Java)
Raden Soedjarwoko Danoesastro	September 17, 1922	Malang (East Java)
Djoko Soejoto	December 25, 1923	Malang (East Java)
Tjoetjoe	January 5, 1923	Banyumas (Central Java)
Soetama	September 7, 1925	Cirebon (West Java)
Yoga Soegama	May 12, 1925	Semarang (Central Java)
Adnan Koesoemaatmadja	April 17, 1923	Bogor (West Java)
Soekristo	June 22, 1924	Bodjonegoro (East Java)
Raden Moeskarna Sastranegara	October 20, 1922	Banten (West Java)
Joewono	September 24, 1923	Besuki (East Java)
Mohamad Soedjiman	May 2, 1923	Kedus (Central Java)
Raden Oetojo Soekaton	June 21, 1924	Malang (East Java)
Soepadi	February 10, 1924	Pati (East Java)
Raden Mas Soehardji	not given	not given
Sandjojo Notosoeparto	May 16, 1929	not given
Raden Mas Koestidjo	July 4, 1923	Yogyakarta (Central Java)
Raden Mas Soekisman	December 25, 1926	not given
Raden Moehamad Hasan Rahaja	June 1, 1924	Jakarta
Mas Moehamad Sjarif Padmadisastra	June 1919	Jakarta
Soeroso Resowidjojo	March 30,1924	Jakarta
Raden Machmoed Nataatmadja	September 20,1923	Priangan (West Java)

I. Java continued

Name	Date of birth	Hometown
Raden Moehamad Roewija Padmoja	April 24, 1923	Pati (East Java)
Koesnaeni Sastoras	March 14, 1924	Semarang (Central Java)
Raden Moelijona Boentaran	January 1, 1925	Semarang (Central Java)
Moehadi Haradjapoerawira	December 22, 1922	Madiun (East Java)
Mas Soedjono Mertodipoetoro	October 21, 1924	Semarang
Raden Soehasim	May 1, 1923	Kedine (East Java)
Soegija	April 15, 1922	Surabaya (East Java)
Raden Oemarmoja Stamboel	December 25, 1925	Malang (East Java)
Raden Oetoro Soekaton	September 29, 1922	Malang (East Java)
Soerodja Ranoediredja	September 17, 1923	Malang (East Java)
Roesjiadi	November 20, 1920	Madura (East Java)
Hasan Sadiri Koesmonegoro	May 19, 1922	Madura (East Java)
Raden Poespoharsono Djajadiningrat	October 7, 1920	Yogyakarta
Raden Mas Soeprastowo Kertapati	February 3, 1922	Banyamas (Central Java)
Raden Mas Soedarmo Martonagoro	June 26, 1922	Jakarta
Raden Mas Oesadarto Koesoemo Oetojo	January 3, 1923	Jakarta

II. Sumatra

Name	Date of birth	Hometown
Sjarif Adil Sagala	July 4, 1925	Riau
Achmad Sjorfai	September 14, 1924	Palembang
Saäri	June 23, 1923	Lampung
Mohamad Roesli Arif	November 1, 1923	Padang
Tengkoe Bahrin Yahya	April 24, 1925	Lampung
Tengkoe Moehammad Daoedsjah	November 14, 1924	Aceh

II. Sumatra continued

Name	Date of birth	Hometown
Dailama	November 7, 1923	Bangka
Arifin Bey	March 5, 1925	Padang-Panjang
Oemar Toesin	June 9, 1923	Palembang
Oemar Hassan Asjari	January 21, 1925	Palembang
Mohammad Zubil Asri	May 5, 1926	Palembang
Sjafuan Gatam	August 26, 1923	Bengkulu
Mohammad Jusuf	July 9, 1926	Kotoraja
Haris Nasution	May 22, 1923	Tapasuli
Noerman Noer	May 10, 1926	Batusangkal

III. Navy-Occupied Areas

Name	Date of birth	Hometown
Soejatim	November 22, 1919	Makassar
Siradjoeddin Baso	December 2, 1920	Bongtaing
Zainal Alam	August 3, 1923	Makassar
Andi Mamoen	October 10, 1920	Luwuk
Abdoerrachman Pulukadang	March 27, 1920	Menado
Jan Maurits Tanos	November 11, 1922	Cicibukan
Kandou Alexander Jan August Lamanauw	November 23, 1923	Menado
Roeland Alexander Pandelaki	May 23, 1924	Menado
Peter H. Saerang	August 2, 1923	Menado
Willem Alexander Frederik Josef Tumbelaka	April 24, 1921	Jakarta
Laurens Louise Manus	December 13, 1920	Makassar
Basroeni Hasboellah	December 28, 1925	Banjarmasin
Pelik Pane	February 16, 1924	Banjarmasin
Mas Ripaie	November 30, 1925	Banjarmasin
Moehamad Hasan	May 5, 1925	Banjarmasin
Kandjoen Prawiradiredja	May 20, 1923	Pontianak
Tadjoeddin	May 9, 1924	Pontianak
I. Abdoelmoeis	August 27, 1922	Samarinda
Darmawisata	March 9, 1925	Denpasar
I. Made Kepoetran	August 6, 1923	Buleleng
Ismael Aboekasim	December 25, 1923	Ambon

2 Films as Propaganda Media on Java under the Japanese, 1942–45

Aiko Kurasawa

One major impact of the Japanese occupation on the Javanese people was the introduction and development of new media for political propaganda. In order to carry out their policies smoothly in occupied Java, the Japanese military government paid great attention to how to "grasp people's minds" (*minshin ha'aku*) and how to "propagandize and tame them" (*senbu kōsaku*). They considered it indispensable for their war effort to mobilize the whole society (total mobilization) and to change the people's mentality completely. Believing that Indonesians had to be completely molded into a Japanese pattern of behavior and thinking, they aimed their propaganda at indoctrinating the Indonesian people so that they could become dependable partners in the Greater East Asia Co-Prosperity Sphere.

To put their propaganda schemes into operation the Japanese employed various media, such as newspapers, pamphlets, books, posters, photographs, radio broadcasting, exhibitions, speech-making, drama, traditional arts performances, paper picture shows (*kamishibai*), music, and movies. A striking characteristic of wartime Japanese propaganda was its use of media that would mainly appeal to a person's "auditory and visual" senses. Especially promoted were movies, performing arts, *kamishibai*, and music. The Japanese considered such media as the most effective means for influencing the uneducated and illiterate rural people who constituted the greater part of the Javanese population. The Japanese were aware that written media such as newspapers, books, magazines, and pamphlets might have some limited effect with regard to educated urban dwellers but were totally useless in the rural society.

BASIC FRAMEWORK OF JAPANESE PROPAGANDA
POLICY

Sendenbu (Propaganda Department)

It can be said that propaganda was, from the very beginning of the
occupation, one of the most vital tasks of the military government. Its
importance was such that, in order to manage propaganda affairs, an
independent department, *Sendenbu* was set up within the military
government (*Gunseikanbu*). Established in August 1942 it was in
charge of propaganda and information concerning civil administration, and was a separate organ from the Information Section of the
16th Army which was in charge of propaganda and information
concerning military operations.[1] In other words, *Sendenbu* activities
were directed towards the civilian population of Java, including
Indonesian, Eurasian, Asian minorities, and Japanese, while the
Information Section of the 16th Army carried out propaganda
vis-à-vis Japanese soldiers and Allied prisoners-of-war, and also,
through overseas broadcasts, *vis-à-vis* civilians in countries opposed
to Japan.

Although *Sendenbu* activities were confined to civilian affairs in
Indonesia, Japanese authorities never trusted control of this important department to civilian hands. It was always headed by an army
officer, first Colonel Machida Keiji (August 1942–October 1943),
then Major Adachi Hisayoshi (October 1943–March 1945), and lastly
Colonel Takahashi Kōryō (May–August 1945).[2] And of the three
sections of the department, namely (1) the Administration Section;
(2) the News and Press Section; and (3) the Propaganda Section, only
(3) was headed by a civilian official, while military officers with the
rank of lieutenant or second lieutenant headed the other two.[3]

The *Sendenbu* acted not only as an administrative office, but it also
directly executed propaganda operations. As the structure of military
administration became more complicated, however, several specialized bureaus in charge of different propaganda fields were set up as
extra-departmental bodies under the *Sendenbu*, and the execution of
propaganda operations was entrusted to them. Table 2.1 shows the
names and the operational fields of those organizations.

In addition to these, an organization named *Keimin Bunka Shidōsho*
or *Poesat Keboedajaan* (Popular Education and Cultural Direction
Center) was set up in April 1943 as an auxiliary organization of the
Sendenbu. Its main tasks were: (1) to promote traditional Indonesian

Table 2.1   Propaganda organizations and their operational field

Name of organization	Date of establishment	Function
Jawa Shinbunkai (Java Newspaper Corporation)	December 1942	publishing newspapers (management was entrusted to *Asahi Shinbun*)
Dōmei News Agency	August 1942	reporting
Jawa Hōsō Kanrikyoku (Java Broadcasting Control Bureau)	October 1942	domestic broadcasting (management was given to N.H.K., Japan Broadcasting Corporation)
Jawa Engeki Kyōkai (Java Theatrical Play Association)	unknown	presenting theatrical plays
Nippon Eigasha or Nichi'ei (Japan Motion Picture Company)	April 1943	producing movies
Eiga Haikyūsha or Eihai (Motion Picture Distributing Company)	April 1943	distributing movies

arts; (2) to introduce and disseminate Japanese culture; and (3) to educate and train Indonesian artists. Under the director of the *Sendenbu*, the Center consisted of five sections, namely: administration, literature, music, fine arts, performance arts (theatrical plays, dance, and film). In each section, under an Indonesian chief, Indonesian specialists (writers, poets, musical composers, painters, sculptors, scenario writers, and movie directors etc.) worked as full-time staff, and the *Sendenbu* sent Japanese instructors to train them.[4] Among the Japanese instructors were Takeda Rinzō (for literature), Iida Nobuo (for music), Kono Takashi, Ono Saseo and Yamamoto Tadashi (for fine arts), and Yasuda Kiyō and Kurata Fumihito (for performance arts).[5]

After establishment of those specialized organizations and bureaus, the *Sendenbu* itself no longer executed direct propaganda activities. It only produced propaganda plans and materials, and distributed them to the relevant working units.[6] Nevertheless, it continued to exercise great influence over the subsidiary organizations, playing the role of a sort of general headquarters for supervising and coordinating various fields of propaganda operations.

Local Propaganda Organizations

The main concern of the military government was how to expand their propaganda network to every nook and cranny of Javanese urban and rural life. From the very early stages of the occupation Japanese propaganda staff were sent out to the principal cities on Java (Jakarta, Bandung, Yogyakarta, Semarang, and Surabaya) to carry out propaganda activities, and later, a more elaborate and well-organized local body, called the District Operation Unit (*Chihō Kōsakutai*), was established in the above-named cities, with the addition of Malang.[7]

In addition to these District Operation Units, which were under the direct control of the *Sendenbu*, each residency office had its own propaganda and information section. At least one member of the staff in this section was a Japanese, sent from Jakarta exclusively to perform this function. At the lower administrative levels, such as the regency and sub-district, there were also Indonesian officials in charge of propaganda. In many cases, however, these officials were not working exclusively on propaganda, but concurrently carried on other functions as local government employees. These local government propaganda activities were under the control of the director of the Department of General Affairs (*Sōmubu*) of the military government in Jakarta, and had no institutional relation with the *Sendenbu*. Nor did the *Sendenbu* District Operation Units deliver the orders from their Jakarta headquarters to residency offices. Those two local propaganda networks existed separately, although they often cooperated with each other in their actual operations.[8]

Profile of the Propagandist

In recruiting both the central and local propaganda staff, the Japanese military government was very careful to choose talented persons. As mentioned above, the very top positions in the central office were usually occupied by military officers. And the highest position held by a civilian was the chief of the Propaganda Section (*Sendenka-chō*), who was actually the top man in charge of daily propaganda activities. This post was assigned to an experienced and talented Japanese official named Shimizu Hitoshi. A professional propagandist (*senden-kan*) who had entered government service by examination, he started his career as a propagandist in China in the 1930s. In Peking he was engaged in programs for indoctrinating the Chinese people through a Japanese-guided mass organization, called *Shin-minkai* (Association of New Citizens). After working in China he returned to Japan in 1940 and continued to work in a similar field as a leading staff member of the Imperial Rule Assistance Association (*Taisei Yokusankai*), a government-guided mass organization which later became the model for the *Jawa Hōkōkai* (Java Service Association). He later left this organization to join a newly established Cabinet Information Bureau (*Naikaku Jōhōkyoku*) until recruited by the 16th Army as an attached civilian in charge of propaganda.[9]

Under Shimizu many other talented Japanese worked as *Sendenbu* officials. They can be divided into two categories: first, those who were, like Shimizu, propaganda experts and who were mostly engaged in planning the programs. Second were the specialists in a particular field of the arts, such as writers, essayists, musicians, painters, caricaturists, and designers who were generally called *bunka-jin* (men of culture) in Japanese society. These individuals were mostly engaged in composing propaganda materials and carrying out the actual propaganda operations, together with their Indonesian counterparts. Quite a few first-class and well-known Japanese *bunka-jin* had been sent to Java,[10] which indicates how keenly the Japanese authorities were aware of the importance of propaganda in the occupied area. Many of these *bunkajin* joined the propaganda team at the personal request of Colonel Machida Keiji. Machida, though he was a professional military man, was a man deeply interested in literature and seemed to have had a very wide range of contacts with these *bunkajin*. There were some others who, though not personally acquainted with Machida, were urged to join by their colleagues who had responded to Machida's request. It is said that those *bunkajin* responded rather positively because they thought that they would be able to work more freely overseas than in Japan where tighter control was exerted over creative activities.

The Indonesian staff of the *Sendenbu* can also be divided into the above-mentioned two categories. The first group of Indonesians were recruited on the basis of such attributes as their prewar career, political orientation, position in traditional society, charismatic and stirring personalities, and ability in speech-making. As for their previous occupation, school teachers were particularly preferred. And those who had some experience in the anti-Dutch movement were warmly welcomed. Mr Muhammad Yamin, the *sanyo* (advisor) for the *Sendenbu*, was a typical example: he had been active in the anti-Dutch nationalist movement as a member of *Indonesia Muda* (Young Indonesia) and *Partindo* (Indonesia Party), and, at the same time, had worked as a school teacher.[11] Among the other staff of the *Sendenbu* was Sitti Noerdjannah, a woman who had taught in an Islamic School and had been active in Islamic movements.[12] Chairul Saleh and Sukarni, radical youths who later played important roles in the Indonesian independence struggle, were also *Sendenbu* officials. Though still young and inexperienced at that time, their potential character as agitators and their strong fighting spirit must have attracted Japanese attention. Besides those generalists there were also Indonesian writers and artists such as Raden Mas Soeroso (painter) and Iton Lasmana (designer in charge of advertisements), working for the *Sendenbu*. Many other well-known writers, musicians, and painters worked for the *Keimin Bunka Shidōsho*, among them Sanusi Pane (writer), Armijn Pane (writer), Utojo (musician), Simanjuntak (musician), Raden Koesbini (musician), Raden Agoes Djajasasoemita (painter), and Djauhar Arifin Soetomo (essayist and drama writer).[13]

The Yogyakarta Principality can be taken as an example of propaganda at the local level. The personnel composition of the District Operation Unit was more or less the same as that of the central office in Jakarta. It was headed by a civilian Japanese and under him were many propagandists, both Japanese and Indonesian. The Japanese staff were usually responsible for planning and supervising, while Indonesians mostly worked on carrying out the propaganda operations. There were nine full-time Indonesian staff members in the Yogyakarta Unit, i.e., two *kamishibai* (paper picture show) operators, four *manzai* (comic stage dialogue) performers, and three persons in charge of censorship. Publications or public speeches had to be censored by the *Sendenbu*, and there were full-time staff for that.

Two of the Indonesian staff were former school teachers: Besut Hadiwardoyo, who had been recruited as a *kamishibai* operator, had lost his job as a teacher when his school was closed down at the beginning of the Japanese occupation, and had then applied for this new job in propaganda. Prior to being accepted, he was taken, together with other applicants, to the market, where he was ordered to make a speech in Javanese on the spot. Apparently this was a test, and he, together with a tailor named Zainuddin, passed it. As a result he was given a full-time post in the Yogyakarta Operation Unit. According to Besut, one of the most important criteria applied in selecting the candidates was their speech-making skill.[14] Siswosu-marto was also a former school teacher. Towards the end of the Dutch period he lost his job because of his political activity in *Partindo*, and he was unemployed when the Japanese arrived. Seeing a recruiting advertisement he applied for the propaganda office and was accepted after taking a language examination in Japanese, Dutch and Indonesian.[15]

Besides those full-time staff members the local propaganda unit usually employed a large number of salaried informal and part-time cooperators who would help occasionally with particular requests. Generally speaking, local political leaders, religious leaders, singers, musicians, actors, *dalang* (performers of *wayang kulit* or shadow puppet plays), dancers, and clowns, etc., were often mobilized for propaganda operations. Japanese propaganda authorities were adept at taking advantage of these entertainers' fame and talent in order to attract popular interest. Among such cooperators in Yogyakarta were Begel Tombong (clown), Kadaria (actress of the *ketoprak*, traditional popular opera in Central and East Java), Bagio (clown and actor of *ketoprak*), and Mangun Ndoro (*dalang* or performer of shadow play).[16]

Furthermore, the unit enlisted help from many other ordinary citizens and villagers to back up the propaganda operations of the entertainers.[17] For example, in Gunung Kidul Regency in Yogya-karta, five local assistants, chosen from each district (*gun*) and called *pemimpin tonarigumi* (neighborhood association leaders), were offi-cially appointed to help propaganda activities by the Propaganda Section of the *Yogyakarta Kōchi Jimukyoku* (Principality Office) and were given a monthly allowance.[18] The Japanese seemed to have secured the cooperation of these Indonesians rather easily, but, in fact, the performers did so mainly because only by cooperating with the Japanese were they allowed to perform at all. Others cooperated because Japanese propaganda provided a modicum of entertainment in an otherwise dreary environment.

At such grass-roots levels the operations of the *Sendenbu* network and of the local government were often combined, with no clear distinction between them. These five cooperators continued their own occupations even after their appointment, and, whenever there was any direction from Yogyakarta, whether from the *Sendenbu* unit or the principality government, they carried it out. In choosing the cooperators the important criteria were their popularity, skill, and reputation in the society. Out of the five cooperators in Yogyakarta, one was an Islamic teacher, one an official in the sanitary section of the regency office, and one a dairy farmer.[19]

Besides these paid cooperators, there were also unpaid volunteers. In the Yogyakarta regency one of these volunteers was a sub-district (*son*) agricultural official who was in charge of promoting cotton planting (*mandor kapas*). Because he himself was an accomplished traditional dance performer and had close personal relations with many other artists and entertainers, he often arranged the Yogyakarta propaganda performances in his area.[20]

Lastly, mention should be made of Japanese volunteers who engaged in grass-roots level propaganda. One example is the 33 volunteer propagandists in Cirebon residency, who were chosen by the Resident (*shūchōkan*) from among Japanese civilians. Each of them was assigned to one sub-district (*son*), and, actually living in the area, they were assigned to giving information and guidance to the local inhabitants on a daily basis.[21]

Scheme and Media of Propaganda

The *Gunseikan*, the head of the military government, was responsible for deciding on the basic propaganda program for each fiscal year, in accordance with the general plan drawn up by the Southern Area Army (*Nanpō Sōgun*) Headquarters. Then, on receiving the order from the *Gunseikan*, the *Sendenbu* director made out the operative plan in consultation with the section chiefs.[22] All the concerned organizations and the District Operations Unit were then informed of this plan. At each stage of the occupation the main propaganda themes were changed to accord with the shift in the military administration's basic policies.

The most usual method of putting the propaganda schemes into operation was to send out a team of propagandists, consisting of movie projectionists, musicians, *kamishibai* operators, and drama players, to travel from village to village, performing in each. Before the performances began, there was usually a speech from either a *Sendenbu* official or a prominent local leader, generally before a large audience, because free admission to dramas and movies attracted thousands of spectators.

The government's political messages were also usually woven in a subtle way into the entertainment following the speech, but, however strong their political flavor, those performances were welcomed enthusiastically by the villagers, who were always eager for amusement because of its scarcity. Of all the propaganda media, however, movies seem to have had the biggest impact on rural society, both in terms of scale (quantity) and content, so in the following sections major attention will be paid to describing these films.

MOVIE PROPAGANDA

One of the most important wartime propaganda media was the movie, which prior to World War 2 had never been used as a tool of political indoctrination in Indonesia. The policies concerning production, distribution, and screening of movies in occupied Java were copies of those used in wartime Japan, which had gradually been formulated through the 1930s.

Movie Policy in Japan

As the war against China gradually escalated and the possibility increased for the outbreak of a world war, key Japanese officials in cultural affairs, aware of the enormous importance and effectiveness of movies as propaganda media, started to exercise a strong grip over the Japanese film industry. After a period of sporadic and fragmentary interference, the government finally established a legal basis for controlling the industry by issuing in October 1939 the "Motion Picture Law" (*Eiga Hō*),[23] which is said to have taken the German system as its model.[24]

One of the most important policies expressed in this law was the extension of firm government control over existing film companies. The law prescribed that any movie production and distribution company had to obtain government permission both to start and to continue its business. By this regulation the government could impose tremendous pressure on movie companies by deliberately withholding permission. The authorities thought that the fewer the companies, the easier they would be to control, and their ultimate intention was to integrate all movie businesses into one single channel. The first step had already been taken in this direction as early as 1935, when the Greater Japan Movie Association (*Dai Nippon Eiga Kyōkai*) was organized as a body to guide and manipulate the movie industry.[25] Furthermore, starting in October 1940 film production and distribution began to be supervised by the National Culture Council of the Imperial Rule Assistance Association (*Taisei Yokusankai*), as previously mentioned, a government-sponsored mass organization.[26] Finally government control over the movie industry reached its peak in early 1942 with the formation of a monopoly film distributor, *Eiga Haikyūsha* or *Eihai* (Japan Motion Picture Distributing Company) which amalgamated all existing film distributors under government guidance.[27] Later, in Java, too, this *Eihai* was to be in charge of movie distribution.

Another important issue prescribed in the Motion Picture Law of 1939 was regulation of the content of movies by preproduction censorship of the scripts. As the Japanese ultranationalistic ideology based on emperor worship was gradually enunciated in a clearer form, government authorities began to develop a concrete idea regarding the "desirable" themes and expressions for wartime movies. These they announced from time to time in the form of "notices" from the Ministry of Home Affairs.[28] Strict censorship was applied in accordance with the principles expressed in these directives.

The Motion Picture Law of 1939 also prescribed compulsory projection of news films and so-called "culture films" [*bunka eiga*] together with entertainment/feature films. Promotion of news and culture films was one of the most conspicuous characteristics of wartime Japanese movie policy. The government considered that such movies were more direct in transmitting government messages to the people and more effective as a means of propaganda. The term, "culture film" or *bunka eiga*, is said to have been a direct translation from the German *kultur film* which was promoted under the Hitler regime.[29] This term was originally applied to nonfiction educational films giving scientific and cultural information to the people. But the wartime culture films were, of course, politically oriented and usually expressed government intentions and desires. News films were as important as culture films, and their production was later put under strict government control. In April 1940 all existing news film makers were amalgamated into a single company named *Nippon Nyūsu Eigasha* (Japan News Film Company), which began to edit a weekly newsreel under the title of "*Nippon Nyūsu*" ("Japan News"). It appeared throughout the war up to December 1945, a total of 254 newsreels.[30] Quite a few items on occupied Southeast Asia were reported in these news films.[31]

In this way the government legally acquired strong control over the film industry. All this positive interference shows how keenly the Japanese authorities were aware of the importance and effectiveness of movies as a part of the operation of psychological warfare.

Movie Policy in Java

Basically the same policy was applied in occupied Java. From the very beginning the military government viewed enforcement of total control over the movie industry as an urgent task. As soon as the 16th Army took over in Java, the *Sendenbu* staff accompanying the military forces confiscated all existing movie companies, and then, in October 1942, they set up a provisional organization to carry out movie policy. This was called *Jawa Eiga Kōsha* (Java Motion Picture Corporation) and was headed by Oya Sōichi, a famous Japanese writer who had been employed as a member of the *Sendenbu* staff. Before coming to Java he was working for *Man'ei* or *Manshū Eigasha* (Manchuria Movie Production Company), which was set up under the auspices of the Japanese army and engaged in producing films based on Japanese policy.

This temporary measure was, however, soon revised on the basis of "*Nanpō Eiga Kōsaku Yōryō*" ("The Outline on Film Propaganda in Southern Areas") issued in September 1942 by the Tokyo government. This "outline" was aimed at formulating a unified movie policy for all occupied areas in Southeast Asia. It was decided that management of the movie industry in occupied areas should be entrusted to two Japanese corporations, namely *Nichi'ei* (Japan Motion Picture Company) and *Eihai* (Japan Motion Picture Distributing Company). *Nichi'ei* was a film production company, while *Eihai* was the monopoly film distribution company set up in early 1942 under the sponsorship of the government (see above). Both had head offices in Tokyo. Branches were set up in Java, and thus the movie industry of Java was incorporated into a larger network encompassing the whole area of the Greater East Asia Co-Prosperity Sphere with Tokyo as its center.[32] Upon establishment of the branches of *Nichi'ei* and *Eihai*, the *Jawa Eiga Kōsha* was dissolved.

Movies Shown in Java

Prior to the war American films had the biggest share of the Javanese movie market constituting about 65 percent of the total movies in 1939. Chinese (12 percent), French (4.8 percent), German (4.5

percent), English (3.4 percent), and Dutch (3.1 percent) films followed in that order. On the other hand, very few Japanese films had been imported to Java (0.2 percent), and domestic movies had made up a very limited share (2.9 percent).[33] However, the Japanese occupation brought a complete change to the movie market in Java. Showing films from "enemy" countries was strictly prohibited except for a short period until April 1, 1943.[34] To replace them a great number of Japanese movies began to be imported. It was officially decided to import 52 items annually. Besides these, it was decided to import 32 Chinese films and 6 from the Axis countries.[35] It is doubtful, however, that those Chinese and Axis movies were ever actually brought in. On the other hand, domestic movie production in Java was also strongly encouraged, so that movies seen in Java during the occupation were mostly either imported Japanese films or domestic ones produced in Java.

Japanese Movies
The Japanese films were carefully chosen and only those considered particularly useful as propaganda were imported. These were the movies which clearly enunciated desirable moral teaching and political indoctrination which the government intended to transmit to the Javanese population. As mentioned earlier, the Japanese government announced their official view concerning the content of movies in the form of "notices."

The first clear-cut directive was expressed in July 1938 by the Ministry of Home Affairs at a meeting in Tokyo with the representatives of scenario writers. This read as follows:

1. Western-influenced individualistic ideas should be eliminated.
2. Japanese spirit, especially the virtue of the family system should be exalted, and the spirit of self-sacrifice for the benefit of nation and society should be encouraged.
3. Movies should take a positive role in educating the masses in order to discourage Westernization of young people, especially of young women.
4. Frivolous and flippant behavior and utterances should be swept off the screen, and efforts should be made to strengthen respect for elders.[36]

Then in 1940 additional directions were given by the Ministry of Home Affairs. These read as follows:

1. What is desired is entertainment through a sound screenplay with a positive theme.
2. Appearance of comedians and comic dialogists in movies is not particularly restricted at this stage, but it might be limited if there are excesses.
3. The following should be prohibited:
   - stories of a petit-bourgeois character
   - stories which describe the happiness of individual persons only
   - scenes of a woman smoking
   - café scenes (a place for entertainment serving hard liquor)
   - frivolous and flippant behavior.
4. It is recommended that films be produced introducing productive sectors of the society, such as rural life.
5. Preproduction script censorship should be strictly carried out and, if any problem is found, rewriting will be ordered.[37]

The films which clearly embodied those government intentions were called *kokusaku eiga* (national policy movies) and received special recommendations from the government. In the years 1942–45 this kind of movie formed a high percentage of the Japanese film market as is shown in Table 2.2:

Most of the Japanese movies introduced into Java must have belonged to these "national policy movies." The titles and brief outlines of some of the plots of the movies are listed in Appendix I. In terms of topic, the films can be divided into the following nine categories (numbers refer to the examples in Appendix I):

(a) those which emphasize friendship between Japan and Asian nations and the pedagogic role of Japan in this (3, 15, 16, 23, 49);
(b) those encouraging exaltation of patriotism and devotion to the nation (7, 9, 14, 15, 18, 19, 28, 29, 35, 36, 38, 57);
(c) those describing military operations and emphasizing the strength of Japanese military forces (1, 2, 10, 11, 12, 21, 24, 25, 26, 27, 32, 34, 46, 47, 58);
(d) those emphasizing the evil of Western nations (6, 13, 34);
(e) those emphasizing a moral based on Japanese values, such as self-sacrifice, motherly love, respect for elders, sincere friendship, modesty of women, diligence, and loyalty (3, 4, 5, 8, 9, 14, 17, 22);
(f) those emphasizing increases in production and other wartime campaigns (7, 20, 21);

(g) those for instruction and educational purposes (45, 48, 50, 53, 54, 55, 56);
(h) others (37, 39, 42, 51, 52);
(i) content unknown (30, 31, 33, 40, 41, 43, 44).

Table 2.2   Share of *kokusaku eiga* produced in Japan during World War 2

Year	Number of feature films (excluding samurai films) produced: A	Number of "national policy films" produced: B*	Percentage of B to A
1942	52	11	21
1943	40	14	35
1944	29	18	62
1945	15	9	60

Source: Eiga Kōsha "Nihon Eiga Sakuhin Mokuroku" ("List of Japanese feature-films") (Tokyo, 1945)
*The films defined as "national policy movie" here are those with the main theme on "war," "counter-espionage," "patriotism," "industry," and "development of new land."

All the 58 items listed in Appendix I seem to illustrate the general tendencies and character of wartime Japanese films. The themes included in the above categories accord with the analysis of the OSS (Office of Strategic Services), the American Intelligence Service during World War 2, which, after reviewing the content of 20 recent Japanese movies in March 1944, pointed to the following elements as providing their dominant themes:

- filial piety: roughly corresponding to the theme in category (e)
- faithful wife: roughly corresponding to the theme in category (e)
- patriotism: roughly corresponding to the theme in category (b)
- Japan's role in Greater East Asia: roughly corresponding to the theme in category (a)[38]

In Java some of those Japanese films were shown with Indonesian subtitles. Translation was made by the local *Eihai* staff (both Japanese and Indonesian) in Java who could understand both languages. In a society like that of wartime Java where the illiteracy rate was very high, however, sub titles did not have much significance. Therefore there was usually an interpreter standing beside the screen, and he explained what was being projected in whatever language was spoken in that area. Some other Japanese films, which were particularly made for the people in Southeast Asia, originally had narration in Indonesian when they were made in Tokyo.[39] In this case, too, an interpreter was often used because in Java most of the population spoke local languages such as Javanese and Sundanese and were not fluent in Indonesian. The rest of the movies were screened neither with subtitles nor voice-over, and in those cases an interpreter was really indispensable. Very few of those interpreters could, however, understand Japanese, and it was impossible for them to make word for word translation. Instead they were previously told the story or contents of the film and just explained the general meaning.

Movies Produced in Java
It was not until the closing years of Dutch rule that movie-making on Java began to be at all a money-making business. In 1941 there were only nine Chinese-owned movie production companies in Java (seven were in Jakarta, one each in Surabaya and Malang).[40] The number of locally made movies in the Dutch period was very small; the length of domestic film censored in 1939 was only 44,082 meters, which was only a 2.9 percent share of the film market.[41] Table 2.3 shows the number of film-making companies and films produced during 1936–41.

Table 2.3   Number of film-makers and films produced, 1936–41

Year	Films produced	Film-makers
1936	2	2
1937	3	2
1938	4	3
1939	4	2
1940	13	7
1941	32	10

Source: *Archipel*, No. 5 (1973), pp. 61–2

The Japanese military government, however, encouraged domestic movie production on a large scale. In September 1942 *Jawa Eiga Kōsha* started to produce movies at their studio in Jatinegara, which had been confiscated from the Dutch.[42] After *Nippon Eigasha* or *Nichi'ei* had been assigned to operate as a monopoly company in occupied Southeast Asia, it took over the film-making business in Java. An office to supervise all Southeast Asia was set up in Singapore, and a Jakarta branch was opened under it in April 1943. The Jakarta branch was later enlarged into the *Jakaruta Seisakujo* (Jakarta Producing Unit), one of the two units in Southeast Asia which engaged in film-making and supplying films, while six other branches simply operated as liaison offices and only carried out the shooting of news films.[43] The Japanese confiscated a Dutch movie producing company, Multifilm, and made use of it. This Dutch company was owned by a Dutchman named J. C. Mol. He founded Multifilm company in Haarlem, The Netherlands, in 1928. In 1939 he came to Indonesia to make a color movie about this country upon request of the passenger-line company, Rotterdamsche Lloyd. When World War 2 started in the fall of 1939, he was still there and unable to return to Europe. Then he founded Multifilm Batavia and produced several anti-Japanese propaganda films for the Dutch government-in-exile.[44] After the confiscation of Multifilm by the Japanese, he was forced to collaborate with the Japanese and kept working for *Nichi'ei* through the war period.[45]

The Indonesian staff of *Nichi'ei* was recruited from among former employees of prewar movie production companies, which had all been dissolved by the Japanese. All the key positions were, however, occupied by Japanese staff sent from Tokyo, including Nagano Shichirō (as head of *Nichi'ei* Java branch) and the movie director, Kurata Bunjin, who was known for his distinguished documentary film titled "*Yukiguni*" ("Snow Country").[46]

It is not clear how many films were produced altogether in Java during the Japanese occupation. According to Hirai Masao, a former staff member of *Nichi'ei* Jakarta branch, most of the films were destroyed and thrown away by the Japanese themselves at the time of their surrender (August 1945), and therefore only the remnants (for the titles and content, see Appendix II) were confiscated by the Allied forces.[47] Most of the confiscated films were later sent to the Netherlands, and stored at the Rijksinstituut voor Oorlogsdocumentatie in Amsterdam.[48] When a research team of R.V.O. catalogued these in 1962, there were at least 155 reels, many of which had been made in Java.[49] Those films were then dispersed, and as far as the writer could confirm, some of the reels that were once kept at the Film Museum in Amsterdam have now been transferred to the Film Archive Section of Rijks Voorlichting Dienst (National Information Service) in The Hague.[50]

The movies made in Java, although based on the same ideological and moral concepts as those made in Japan, were even more clearly "national policy movies." They were produced to fit more closely with the local situation and need, and usually had an even more explicit propagandistic and instructive character. Accordingly, they were less devoted to providing entertainment and amusement. Mr Jansen, a staff member of Stichting Film en Wetenschap (Dutch Foundation for Films and Science), who had the opportunity of watching the 155 reels of confiscated movies, has classified them into the following four categories:

(a) those which set up Japanese supreme military power against the defeated British and American Forces (23 items);
(b) those made after early 1943 which use the "religious concept" of *hakkō ichiu* (eight corners of the world under roof) to sanction the expansionist policy of the Japanese (54 items);
(c) those made after the end of 1943 which emphasize the role played by Indonesian society within the Great Asian Commonwealth, i.e., devolution (66 items);
(d) those made after November 1944 which appeal bluntly to Indonesian nationalism and instincts of self-defense, a sort of self-glorification of Indonesia (12 items).[51]

In Java, as in Japan, production of documentary, culture, and news films was particularly encouraged. It started in September 1942 as soon as *Jawa Eiga Kōsha* opened their studio in Jatinegara, and after April 1943 was continued by *Nichi'ei*. According to *Jawa Nenkan*, *Nichi'ei* in 1943 was supplying a new item of documentary or culture film every two weeks, which means 24 items annually.[52] If they maintained this pace of production, the number of films produced by the end of the occupation must have been large. The films were usually short (10–20 minutes), were narrated in Indonesian and had very clear-cut propaganda themes. (For the titles and content, see Appendix II.)

The news films were first issued monthly by *Jawa Eiga Kōsha* under the title of *Jawa Bahroe* (New Java) until the eighth issue in March 1943. Then *Nichi'ei* produced a new fortnightly series called *Berita Film di Jawa/Jawa Nūysu* (Java News). This continued up to issue No. 19 of the series which appeared in December 1943. Then, from the beginning of 1944 newsreels were made under a new name, *Nanpō Hōdō* (Southern News).[53] (For the main topics of the news films, see Appendix III.) These newsreels, which were edited in Java, covered not only domestic news, but also that coming from other occupied areas in Southeast Asia. All the newsreels were narrated in Indonesian. Besides, *Jawa Nyūsu* and *Nanpō Hōdō* also had Japanese narration spoken after the Indonesian. The news films shot outside Java by the reporters from each local *Nichi'ei* branch were sent to Jakarta and edited into one newsreel volume which was distributed to all these areas.

The news films were explicitly instructive in nature, and also had the following characteristics. Firstly, unlike ordinary newsreels, they were not much concerned about reporting social incidents which involved specific individuals, such as crimes, traffic accidents, and fires; rather, much more space was allocated to reporting events involving the total society, such as activities of social-political organizations, youth training, production increases, speeches by government and military leaders, victorious battles, etc. And in reporting this "news" the reporters' main concern was always to give moral and technical instruction as well as to transmit the government's messages.

Secondly, the news films were not only concerned about reporting "news," but often spent time on purely technical and moral teaching as did the culture films. They gave information on such techniques as fishing, cotton planting, cotton weaving, Japanese customs, ceramic manufacturing, and health maintenance.

Thirdly, the news films often spent considerable time on reporting the speeches of prominent Indonesian leaders. Most frequently appearing on the screen was, of course, Soekarno.

Fourthly, the Indonesian narration for the films was given in the peculiar wartime Japanese style, which sounds like a war cry.

Production of feature films, on the other hand, started much later; the first, *"Kemakmoeran"* ("Prosperity"), was screened in January 1944, and the second, *"Berdjoeang"* ("Fighting"), appeared in March of the same year.[54] The themes of these films were dictated by the *Sendenbu*, and, following this, the Japanese staff of *Nichi'ei* made a brief outline of the story, which was then submitted to the *Sendenbu* to be censored. Only after the story passed the censors, was the full scenario written in Indonesian.[55] The films were spoken in Indonesian, and the actors were recruited from among *pribumi* (native Indonesians).

The instructions conveyed through these motion pictures were not confined to the political and spiritual sphere but also included practical and technical teaching. This was especially evident in culture and news films. For example, films such as *"Pemakaran Tombak*

Bamboo" ("The Use of the Bamboo Spear"), and *"Indonesia Raya"* ("Great Indonesia") had the immediate and concrete purpose of teaching military skills and the national anthem respectively. There were also the movies giving lessons on agricultural techniques and handicraft skills such as weaving, plowing, planting paddy, and making rope. The movies on the *tonarigumi* were to illustrate the daily activities of the neighborhood association and to develop a correct understanding of its role and nature. *"Taiteki Kanshi"* ("Watching Out for the Enemy") instructed Indonesians how to be alert against the enemy. Such use of films as a means of technical instruction was an entirely new departure for both Japanese and Javanese, and originated in the wartime situation. They remind us of contemporary Japanese educational TV programs, which are used for school education as well as for social education. In fact these wartime films can be considered as the forerunner of contemporary audio-visual education.

The topics of culture films and news reports seen by the writer can be classified as in Table 2.4.

Table 2.4   Topics of the films[56]

Topics	News reports	Culture films
(a) concerning political developments and mass movements in Indonesia	16	6
(b) introducing Japanese military forces and the process of war	6	0
(c) concerning defense of the fatherland	11	9
(d) concerning economic affairs (production increase, labor, construction etc.)	10	11
(e) introducing events and life in Java	6	0
(f) concerning education	5	1
(g) encouraging civic action (saving, health, neighborhood association)	3	5
(h) concerning other Japanese occupied areas in Southeast Asia	6	0
(i) introducing Japan and news in Japan	5	0
Total	68	32

As far as these examples are concerned, the most frequent topic of the news films are those concerning political development and mass movements, and then follow those on defense and economic affairs.

In the case of culture films, defense and economic affairs are the most frequent topics. Most of the culture films concerning political developments and some of those concerning civic action overlap with news reports.

It is impressive that, despite the limited facilities, staff, and experience, quite a few movies were produced in wartime Java.[57] In comparison with the situation of the prewar movie industry considerable development occurred during the Japanese occupation not only in terms of the length of the films produced, but also in their quality. Some of the movies which the writer herself has seen were of reasonably high artistic quality.

As for the influence of Japanese film-making on the Indonesian staff, Usmar Ismail, a scenario writer who used to work for the *Keimin Bunka Shidōsho*, has written as follows:

The truly new climate, both in terms of content and process of film making, came at the time of the Japanese Occupation. At that time we first came to be aware of the function of film as a means of social communication. One more thing to be mentioned is protection of language and as its result . . . it came to be clear that films began to grow and come closer to the national consciousness.[58]

As for progress made in the studio's working techniques, Armijn Pane has written as follows:

Japanese film makers worked in a systematic way, both in preparation and film making itself. It is different from the working techniques in Chinese [film] companies [in the prewar period], which were restrained by the notion of keeping production costs low, and the Indonesian staff really learned a lot [from the Japanese] . . . Since performances were preceded by rehearsals of the dialogue, the way of speaking the language became very fluent: the language used [during the Japanese occupation] was no longer *bahasa Melayu-Tionghoa* [Sino-Malay dialect] or that of the newspapers, but a more correct form . . .[59]

After the Japanese surrender *Nichi'ei* was taken over by the government of the Republic of Indonesia, and its facilities were put under the control of the Directorate of Movies and Communication of the Department of Information, headed by R. M. Sutarto. When the

Republican government moved to Yogyakarta, they could take only a part of those facilities, but with them they produced several documentary films during the Revolution.[60]

Movie Distribution in Javanese Society

Movie distribution and screening was under the management of *Eihai*. Its Jakarta branch (*Jawa Eihai*) was set up in April 1943, a year after the Japanese occupied Java, with Mitsuhashi Tessei, former head of the management section, Tōhō Movie Production Company, as its president. Having close relations with the *Sendenbu*, *Jawa Eihai* formulated and carried out the general program of using movies for propaganda purposes: it engaged in selecting the movies to be distributed, allocating them to the local theaters, managing all the confiscated movie theaters, carrying out open-air movie screenings, etc.[61]

The movies, carefully selected and produced, were then distributed to the movie theaters all over Java. According to *Jawa Nenkan*, 117 theaters operated as ordinary commercial theaters in April 1943 when *Eihai* was set up.[62] Chinese capital supported 95 percent of those theaters, but after the Japanese came, all of them were put under Japanese control; the theaters were then divided into four ranks and the admission fee for each of them was regulated by *Eihai* as shown in Table 2.5.

Table 2.5   Admission fee to movie theaters[63]

Rank of theater	1st class seat	2nd class seat	3rd class seat	4th class seat
1st	80 cents	40 cents	30 cents	–
2nd	60 "	40 "	20 "	–
3rd	50 "	30 "	20 "	10 cents
4th	40 "	25 "	15 "	10 "

The difference between the most expensive ticket (80 cents) and the cheapest one (10 cents) was much smaller than in Dutch days, when the fee had ranged from 6 cents (equivalent to 13 cents under Japanese rule) to 2 guilders (equivalent to 4 yen 40 cents under Japanese rule).[64] *Jawa Eihai* also decreed that 50 percent of all the seats in theaters of every rank should be in the cheapest class, so that many poor Indonesian *pribumi* could have easy access to the movies, while in the Dutch period the share assigned to this class had been only 5–10 percent.[65] The cheapest admission fee under Japanese rule, 10 cents, was equivalent to the official price for one kilogram of husked rice (*beras*) as of April 1944.[66]

Besides those ordinary commercial theaters, there were also several specialized theaters with specified purposes, as follows:

(a) those directly owned by *Jawa Eihai* and operated for propaganda purposes only: 35 theaters (23 in West Java, 3 in Central Java, and 9 in East Java);[67]

(b) those open to Japanese only: 6 theaters (Tokyo Theater in Jakarta, Ginza Theater in Bandung, Nippon Theater in Semarang, Tōa Theater in Yogyakarta, Nippon Theater in Surabaya and Kyōei Theater in Malang);

(c) a theater for news and short culture films only (free admission): one theater in Semarang (Semarang Hōdō *Gekijo*);

(d) a theater for school children for educational purposes (free admission): one theater in Jakarta (Ya'eshio *Gekijō*).[68]

All the measures *Jawa Eihai* took in managing the movie theaters indicate how eager the Japanese authorities were to encourage the masses, especially the poorer people, to watch movies. However, the problem was that locational distribution of the movie theaters was very uneven, with an extreme concentration in large cities. Since most of the theaters continued to operate under Japanese rule, this distribution was to a large extent still applicable to this later period. In terms of ratio *vis-à-vis* the population (which totaled about 50 million as of 1943), the number of theaters in Java was small, i.e., one theater per 400,000 persons.[69] The number of theaters per one million persons varied widely among the residencies, ranging from 0.5 in Bojonegoro to 8.2 in Surabaya. There were a relatively large number of theaters in such residencies as Surabaya, Besuki, Malang, and Jakarta, while Bojonegoro, Cirebon, Madiun, and Pekalongan had very few. It is said that the 129 theaters were all located in urban areas; according to research made by *Nichi'ei* in early 1942, 52 of them were concentrated in the following 7 large cities: Jakarta (13), Surabaya (12), Semarang (7), Bandung (7), Malang (6), Surakarta (4), and Yogyakarta (3).[70]

The remaining theaters were apparently dispersed among middle and small towns all over Java, but it seems that there were none in rural areas, where the bulk of the Javanese population lived. It was because of that that the government got the idea of promoting the "traveling theater" or "mobile cinema" to fill the lack of commercial theaters.

Mobile Cinema

The idea of the mobile cinema itself was not new for either Indonesians or Japanese. In prewar Indonesia private companies had sometimes used it for advertising their products.[71] However, the attempt during the Japanese occupation to use the mobile cinema on a large scale for political indoctrination was totally new to Indonesian society. This was first begun in August 1942, and with the establishment of *Jawa Eihai* was further developed.[72] By that time the Japanese had had enough experience in using mobile cinemas in Japan, and this was applied to Java.[73] The *Eihai* central office sent 48 movie projection experts, together with the necessary facilities, to promote traveling theaters in occupied Southeast Asia.[74] Six of these experts were sent to Java.[75] By December 1943 five operational bases for the mobile cinema had been established in Jakarta, Semarang, Surabaya, Yogyakarta, and Malang, with 15 projecting teams, some headed by Japanese, and others by Indonesians.[76] These teams traveled from one village to another, carrying a movie projector, generator, and films (16mm) in a truck. Each team consisted of a member of *Jawa Eihai* (usually the projecting engineer), a local *Sendenbu* official, an interpreter, and a truck driver, etc. According to *Jawa Nenkan* during the five months between July and November 1943 a traveling team screened the film, *"Hawaii Marei Oki Kaisen"* ("The War at Sea from Hawaii to Malaya"), at more than 220 places.[77] At several important locations Soekarno was present at the performance.[78]

Tours were also often arranged for particular occasions and ceremonial events. For example at *Kō-A Sai* (Anniversary of the Outbreak of the Greater East Asian War) in December 1943, there were open-air movie screenings at eight places in Jakarta before a total of 53,000 spectators, at eight places in the Jakarta residency before a total of 104,000 spectators, and at eight places in the Bogor residency before a total of 96,000 spectators.[79]

Usually only one or two villages were chosen from each *son* (sub-district) or *gun* (district) as the screening sites, and the people of the neighboring villages were invited. The movies were shown in the open air at an empty expanse of ground (*lapangan*) near the *Balai Desa* (village office), and were open to anyone free of charge. Inhabitants of all the neighboring villages had previously been notified through village officials and *tonarigumi* heads.

Unlike other mass meetings the authorities had little trouble in attracting people in the rural areas to the movie shows.[80] Most of the writer's informants stated that they had seen movies at least once during the Japanese occupation, and this had been usually their first experience of watching movies.

The movie tours were sometimes aimed at a particular audience such as *rōmusha* (forced laborers), factory laborers, and school children. For example, it was reported that between December 16 and 30, 1943, mobile cinemas performed at 13 places in Banten residency to entertain a total of 126,000 *rōmusha*, who were engaged in airfield construction, mining, and other essential work.[81] Films were also shown in the same month for 3,000 *rōmusha* waiting in Jakarta for shipping to take them to Sumatra and Borneo.[82]

JAPANESE PERCEPTION OF PROPAGANDA

In determining the most effective propaganda means the cultural and language background of the society was very important. The Japanese propagandists were aware that in Java literacy was still very low, and for this reason, as I have noted, they emphasized "auditory and visual" media such as movies, in particular, performing arts, *kamishibai*, music, and posters.

The language to be used as the medium for propaganda was another important consideration. The Japanese were confronted with the heterogeneity and complexity of language in Javanese society. They banned Dutch as an "enemy" language, and despite their desire to employ Japanese as a *lingua franca* for the Greater East Asia Co-Prosperity Sphere, the military authorities were aware that the Japanese language was still far from being a practical medium for communication. It was therefore inevitable that they should make use of *bahasa Indonesia* (Indonesian). Indonesian became the standard language of all propaganda materials created in Java. Local films were made with Indonesian speech and narration, and so were the plays and radio broadcasts. And in the case of Japanese films, Indonesian subtitles were added.

The Japanese soon found, however, that the people on Java did not necessarily have a good command of the Indonesian language. Although since the early twentieth century the Dutch colonial government had used Indonesian as the second official language after

Dutch and it had been employed in the lower levels of the administration, its use in daily life was very limited. In cities and in the coastal areas it was widely employed for interethnic communication, but most rural people in the interior had a very limited command of the language. Javanese and Sundanese were their daily media of communication.

Therefore in carrying out their propaganda activities, the Japanese had to have their messages retranslated from Indonesian into local languages. During propaganda tours in the rural areas, local members of the propaganda agency had to translate the speeches from Indonesian and summarize the content of the movies and plays in Javanese or Sundanese.[83] Since very few Japanese had command of these local languages, they were, thus, gradually deprived of supervision and control over the content of their propaganda.

Japanese propaganda authorities seem to have been aware of this complex language situation and therefore became even more convinced of the necessity of stressing visual appeals in their propaganda activities. They strengthened their dependence on movies, theatrical plays, and *kamishibai*, which could be understood with minimum use of language. And more straightforward and simple expressions were used in creating these propaganda materials.

The entertainment or art content of these materials was of only secondary importance. Yet Japanese propaganda leaders did not totally neglect this aspect, believing that crude propaganda would bring a negative reaction and that the higher the artistic quality, the larger would be the propaganda effect. The Japanese concern was, therefore, how to increase the propaganda effect without impairing its entertainment value or art aspects. Bringing first-class scenario writers, movie directors, musicians, and artists on to the *Sendenbu* staff indicates that the Japanese were truly anxious to maintain a high artistic quality in their propaganda. There were repeated discussions by experts to find out how to harmonize a propaganda purpose with artistic quality.[84] The quality and form of propaganda activity ranged from high culture with less propaganda flavor to a simple transmission of government information. Generally speaking the propaganda materials produced in Java tended to be more tightly and directly geared to propaganda purposes and less oriented to entertainment than those imported from Japan. Yet, some of the movies and posters made in Java were fairly sophisticated in spite of their strong propaganda flavor. Especially impressive to the writer was the effective use of music in the movies and the refined color-combination in posters.

What were the main themes of Japanese propaganda? It seems that there was both a long-term indoctrination plan and a short-term immediate propaganda target. During the three and a half years of Japanese occupation propaganda activities oscillated between those two poles. Perhaps the ultimate goal of Japanese propaganda was to mobilize the whole of Indonesian society for Japan's war effort. To achieve that purpose they may have believed it necessary to transform the mentality of the Indonesian people into that of Japanese and to assimilate Indonesian society with that of Japan as had been attempted in Taiwan and Korea. Seen in this perspective, then, there had to be mental indoctrination encouraging particular Japanese virtues and morals, such as piety, modesty, motherly love, and diligence. Thus the government tried to present an image of the ideal man and woman in wartime displaying these virtues. Also the ideological teaching on the aim of the Greater East Asia Co-Prosperity Sphere had to permeate the society and be accepted by it.

In actual propaganda activities, however, more emphasis was put on practical themes with a concrete goal, partly perhaps because Indonesians showed aversion to "Japanization" and to being merged into what was called Greater East Asian culture. Indonesians did not easily accept Japanese advocacy of a "common race and common ancestor" and of cultural affinity between Japan and Indonesia. As the war situation became critical for the Japanese and as there was urgent need to acquire more positive cooperation from Indonesians, the Japanese had to make certain concessions so as not to provoke unnecessary friction with Indonesians. The Japanese authorities, realizing this, gradually switched their policy, and their propaganda target had to be adjusted to more immediate social-economic needs. It is perhaps because of this that, compared with that in Japan, the propaganda in Java had a more practical orientation, and ideological indoctrination and moral instruction were only of secondary importance.

Such a disparity is seen in the changes made in the annual propaganda theme. According to Adachi, the former *Sendenbu* director, the main propaganda themes adopted for each fiscal year were as follows:

1942: The purpose of the Greater East Asia War
      The idea of the Greater East Asia Co-Prosperity Sphere
      – "Asia is One"
      – 3-A Movement [A movement engineered by the *Sendenbu* with the slogan: "Japan: the Light of Asia, Protector of Asia and the Leader of Asia"];

1943: The idea of the Greater East Asia Co-prosperity Sphere
     – promotion of increased food production
     – paddy delivery
     – recruitment of *rōmusha* [from the latter half of the year]
     – concentrating all power of inhabitants and promoting friendship among them
     – strengthening war power
     – defense of Java
1944: Driving home the intentions of the Military Administration
     – reliance of inhabitants upon Japan
     – Greater East Asia Conference
     – promotion of increased food production
     – sparing and saving
     – recruitment of *rōmusha*
     – entertainment for Japanese and inhabitants [from the latter half of the year]
1945: Defense of fatherland
     – security from spies; *"Awas, Mata-mata Moesoeh"* ["Be careful of Enemy Spies"]
     – entertainment for Japanese and local inhabitants
     – promotion of the fighting spirit of the Japanese[85]

Such propaganda themes clearly reflected the basic principles and urgent needs of the military government at each specific time.

During the first year the themes were more ideologically oriented; the government's concern was with informing people of Japanese intentions in waging war and occupying Indonesia, together with emphasizing the evil of the West. The target of the propaganda activity at that stage was to induce the local population to discard anti-Japanese feelings and persuade them into joining in the construction of a new order. Such ideological instruction was, of course, the basis of Japanese propaganda, and it continued, with some variations, to be advocated throughout the occupation period.

After the second year, however, more practical and materialistic themes were added to this ideological one, as economic exploitation came to be the most urgent need of the military government, as the war situation became more and more adverse to the Japanese, and as the probability of an Allied counterattack on Java became a reality. In 1944 "sparing and saving" was added, and in 1945 "security from spies," showed the deterioration of the situation. Most of the individual topics can be divided into two major categories: "defense" and "economy." In other words Japanese propaganda was mainly directed at arousing the fighting and working spirit of the Javanese people, which was indispensable for continuing the war. However, in promoting those propaganda aims, the Japanese were careful not to relate them to benefits for Japan, emphasizing rather that they were all for the safety and prosperity of Indonesia. This tendency was further strengthened after the promise of Indonesian Independence in September 1944.

Another notable change was the growing emphasis on entertainment after the latter half of 1944. This indicates the widespread psychological strain under which both Japanese and Indonesians were suffering at that time and the need to alleviate this. Shortage of foodstuffs, clothing materials, and almost all other important commodities, incessant appeals for devotion to the nation and for the sacrifice of individual happiness and pleasure, strong pressure to cooperate with the government, fear of *Kempeitai* (Japanese military police) brutality, possible suspicion of espionage – all those difficulties compelled people to live in a high state of tension. Japanese government authorities recognized that life was becoming too austere to provide meaningful incentives for the people to work, and that such austerity might lead them into anti-Japanese and anti-war sentiments. To mitigate the social tension the *Sendenbu* authorities considered it important to provide more entertainment. There was also an idea among Japanese propaganda leaders that entertainment could be a good incentive to increase production and strengthen national defense.[86] In line with this, more entertainment with fewer crude propaganda elements began to be encouraged. This does not necessarily mean the total elimination of propaganda, but simply that the emphasis was now on raising morale through entertainment. This same change in policy was introduced in Japan at about the same stage of the war.[87]

EFFECT OF JAPANESE PROPAGANDA

What was the people's reaction to these propaganda activities and to what extent were they effective for the Japanese in attaining their goals? First of all, it is a question as to how far the Indonesian population understood the theme and content of the propaganda. In spite of all the authorities' efforts to cope with the language problems, it is still doubtful whether the audiences really grasped the ideas and intentions of the propaganda directors, and even if they did understand the story, whether they accepted the Japanese value concepts presented here. Though the moral teaching emphasized through these media was more or less universal, the way these moral concepts were expressed was peculiarly Japanese, because in those days any Japanese value concept was closely linked with the basic ideology of self-sacrifice for the sake of the Emperor who was equivalent to the nation. Did the Indonesians then accept those propaganda activities solely as entertainment? With reference to Japanese broadcasting, for example, a Javanese informant noted:

> When the Japanese broadcast music in Java, many people would listen, but when propaganda commenced, some walked away, saying: *"Nihon-Bohong"* [Nippon-Lies].[88]

In considering the effects of Japanese propaganda, a distinction should be made between the reaction of urban intellectuals and that of the uneducated masses. For the former, who were generally more exposed to other kinds of amusement, propaganda-laden movies and theatrical performances were not as exciting as they were for the mass of the population, who were living in a monotonous environment and were eager for stimulation. In terms of artistic quality and entertainment value, the performances might not have met urban standards but might have been sophisticated enough for rural audiences. With regard to the effect of the propaganda messages, educated people were generally better-informed on world affairs and had a wider range of knowledge, which would have given them the basis for a more rational and accurate judgement of the propaganda message. The uneducated people, on the other hand, who were less exposed to information, tended to accept the propaganda at its face value.

Thus, as a whole, Japanese-style propaganda seems to have been more effective among the uneducated mass of the population, especially those living in rural areas isolated from other information sources. In the villages the performances staged by traveling propaganda teams seem to have attracted large numbers of spectators. Of course, a large audience does not necessarily mean favorable acceptance of the propaganda message. The spectators were usually attracted by the entertainment with only a slight awareness that they were going to be "indoctrinated."

In its impact Japanese indoctrination may have been strongest among the younger generation, both urban and rural. A Dutch intelligence report, in spite of its basically negative evaluation of the effect of Japanese propaganda, has given a rather different insight with regard to young people. It reported as follows:

There will also be a certain number of people, especially amongst the youths, who will have taken in the Japanese propaganda, and therefore co-operate fully with the Japanese, either because they believe in the Japanese promise for Independence, or because they admire Japan and its Greater East Asian principles or because they hope for material benefit.[89]

It is true to some extent that the Japanese propaganda authorities regarded the younger generation as the most important target of their indoctrination. And in applying propaganda techniques consideration was given to appealing to this group. Also, the younger generation had more opportunity to be exposed to Japanese propaganda, because the movies, plays, and *kamishibai* were often performed at schools and local meetings of *Seinendan* (Youth Corps), *Barisan Pelopor* (Vanguard Corps), and *Keibōdan* (Vigilance Corps), most of whose members were youths.

However, for the Javanese people in general, Japanese propaganda seems to have been less effective in educating and molding them in the direction desired by the military authorities, although some of the army movies might have been useful in impressing Indonesians with the strength of Japan. Yet the propaganda was more significant in the sense that it provided most rural people with accessibility to modern entertainment media such as movies. Those media enlarged their mental environment and surroundings and brought the people into contact with the larger society. Through the screen, they first saw the faces of their national leaders and the great capital city of their "nation," and thus came to be more familiar with the events going on outside their immediate society. This increase in the volume of information they received was one undoubtedly lasting effect of Japanese propaganda efforts.

Notes and References

1. Towards the end of the war, in April 1945, however, these two separate offices were amalgamated into a single new office which carried out both military and civil propaganda.
2. Adachi, Ōhashi, Yoshikawa and Tsuda, "Replies of questionnaire concerning *Sendenbu*" (A report in English submitted by former *Sendenbu* Director and officials to the Allied Forces after the capitulation of the Japanese Army.) April 14, 1947 Jakarta. This document is now located in the Archives of the Dutch Ministry of Defence in The Hague under the file number GG21-1947 *Japan's Marine Archief, deel I*.
3. After the amalgamation of the former Information Section of the 16th Army and the *Sendenbu* in May 1945, military control of propaganda activity was further strengthened, and five sections of this new office were headed by military officers. See Adachi *et al.*, "Replies of questionnaire concerning *Sendenbu*."
4. Jawa Gunseikanbu, *Jawa Nenkan*, 1944 (Jakarta, 1944), pp. 167–8, and *Djawa Baroe*, no. 8, April 1, 1943, pp. 8–10.
5. Those people were all civilians (*gunzoku*) attached to the *Sendenbu*.
6. Adachi *et al.*, "Replies of questionnaire concerning *Sendenbu*."
7. It was not clear when these local units were officially established. *Sendenbu* Director, Colonel Adachi, reported that it was after February 1944 and stated that the Jakarta unit was set up in August 1944 and the Malang branch in October 1944. But mention had already been made of the activities of Bandung, Semarang, Yogyakarta and Surabaya units in "*Sendenbu* Monthly Report" No. 22, December 1943 (translated into English as "Captured Enemy Publication No. 211" by Allied Intelligence Office and now found at the Public Record Office in London under the file No. W.O.208/2483); while *Asia Raya* (daily newspaper published in Jakarta) reported establishment of all of those units in its May 16, 1944 issue.
8. Adachi *et al.*, "Replies of questionnaire concerning *Sendenbu*."
9. Interview with Shimizu (Tokyo), February 1980.
10. Among them were Ōya Sōichi (writer), Ono Saseo (caricaturist), Yokoyama Ryūichi (caricaturist), Minami Seizen (painter), Iida Nobuo (music composer), Ōki Atsuo (poet), Takeda Rintarō (writer), Kurata Bunjin (movie director), and Hinatsu Eitarō (movie director). It is said that Hinatsu, a Korean by origin, stayed in Indonesia even after the Japanese surrender and contributed to film-making and drama directing under the Indonesian name, Dr Huyung. In 1948 he set up the Cine Drama Instituut in Yogyakarta. Misbach Jusa Biran, trans by Matsuno Akihisa, "Indonesia Eiga Shōshi" ("Short History of Indonesian Films") in Satō Tadao, Shirai Yoshio, Shimizu Akira and Donald Richie, *Eiga ga Ōsama no Kuni* (The Land Where Films are Treated as King) (Tokyo: Hanashi no Tokushū, 1982), p. 210, fn. 10, and Salim Said, *Profil Dunia Film Indonesia* (The Profile of the Film World in Indonesia) (Jakarta: Grafiti Pers, 1982), p. 39.
11. Jawa Gunseikanbu, *Orang Indonesia Jang Terkemoeka di Djawa*

(Prominent Indonesians in Java) (Jakarta: 1944), p. 472. Hereafter, this will be referred to as *Terkemoeka.*
12. Ibid., p. 476.
13. *Jawa Nenkan*, p. 168, and *Terkemoeka*, p. 427.
14. Interview with Besut Hadiwardoyo (Yogyakarta), November 9, 1980. After January 1945 he was active in radio broadcasting, and even at the time of the writer's interview he was a wellknown radio entertainer in Yogyakarta. This shows that he is an extraordinarily talented speaker, and the Japanese propaganda officials in Yogyakarta did not fail to discover this talent.
15. Interview with Siswosumarto (Yogyakarta), November 12, 1980.
16. Ibid.
17. According to Shimizu Hitoshi, the *Sendenbu* tried to have at least one informal cooperator in every 20–30 households both in urban and rural society. (Interview with Shimizu, Feb., 1980.
18. This unique position apparently was the creation of Selosoemardjan (high official at Yogyakarta Principality) who was in charge of expanding *tonarigumi* in Yogyakarta. The post was higher than *azachō* (the head of a hamlet) and there was only one in each *gun* (district).
19. Interview with Pawirosumarta, one of those former *pemimpin tonari- gumi* at Playen, Gunung Kidul, October 22, 1980.
20. Interview with this *mandor kapas*, Suko (Karangmojo, Gunung Kidul), November 1, 1980.
21. *Jawa Shinbun*, November 5, 1944.
22. Adachi *et al.*, "Replies of questionnaire concerning *Sendenbu.*"
23. Tanaka Junichirō, *Nihon Eiga Hattatsushi* Vol. III (Historical Development of Japanese Movies) (Tokyo: Chūō Kōron, 1976), pp. 14–15.
24. Lisa Pontecorvo *et al.*, "The Far East and World War II" (unpublished broadcast note of a BBC TV program), 1973, pp. 3–4.
25. Tanaka Junichirō, *Nihon Eiga Hattatsushi* III, p. 151. This association was set up under the auspices of the Ministries of Home Affairs and of Education.
26. Office of Strategic Services (O.S.S.), Research and Analysis Branch, "Japanese Films; a Phase of Psychological Warfare" (R & A 1307), unpublished report (Washington D.C., March 30, 1944), p. 20.
27. Tanaka Junichirō, *Nihon Eiga Hattatsushi*, III, pp. 83–5. It is said that this amalgamation was done under the strong leadership of the Cabinet Information Bureau (*Naikaku Jōhōkyoku*) and the Greater Japan Movie Association.
28. The first notice was issued soon after the outbreak of Sino-Japanese hostilities in July 1937, then further notices were given in July 1938 and 1940. For details, see Chiba Nobuo, *Sekai no Eiga Sakka No. 31: Nihon Eigashi* (Film Directors of the World No. 31: History of Japanese Film) (Tokyo: Kinema Junpōsha, 1976), pp. 78, 83. Hereafter, it will be referred to as *Nihon Eigashi.*
29. Ibid., p. 95.
30. Those films are now available at NHK (Japan Broadcasting Corporation) Service Center in Tokyo. The list and the brief contents of the news were

68   *Films as Propaganda Media on Java*

published by this Center in 1980 under the title of *Nippon Nyūsu de Tsuzuru Gekidō no Kiroku: Nippon Nyūsu Senchūhen, Shōwa 15–20* (Record of Upheaval Seen in the Nippon Nyūsu: Nippon Nyūsu During the War 1940–45). Mainichi Newspaper Company also published a book in 1977, illustrating some of the important scenes (pictures) from those newsreels. It is titled *Nihon Nyūsu Eigashi: Kaisen Zenya Kara Shūsen Chokugo Made* (The History of Japanese Newsfilms: from the Eve of Outbreak of War to the Immediate Post-war Days).

31. During three and half years of the Japanese occupation, Java appeared in this series of *Nippon Nyūsu* 18 times (6 times in 1942, 7 times in 1943, 4 times in 1944, and once in 1945).
32. Tanaka Junichirō, *Nihon Eiga Hattatsushi*, III, p. 116.
33. "Films censored in 1939" in Netherlands East Indies, Het Centraal Kantoor voor de Statistiek van het Department van Economische Zaken, *Indisch Verslag 1940* (Batavia: Landsdrukkerij, 1940), p. 130. According to this, the total length of film censored in 1939 was 1,526,708 meters of which only 44,082 meters was domestic film.
34. "Zadankai: Nippon Eiga no Nanpō Kōsaku o Kataru" ("Discussion: Talking about Japanese Film Propaganda in the Southern Areas"), *Nippon Eiga* (July 1943), p. 30.
35. Tanaka Junichirō, *Nihon Eiga Hattatsushi*, III, pp. 116–17.
36. *Nihon Eigashi*, p. 83.
37. Ibid., p. 83.
38. O.S.S., "Japanese Films: A Phase of Psychological Warfare," p. 18.
39. Those films had several versions with the narration in different languages, such as Burmese, Vietnamese, and Tagalog.
40. Nichi'ei Bunka Eigabu (Culture Film Section, Nichi'ei), "Ran'in no Eigakai to Nippon Eiga no Hankyō" ("Movie Industry in N.E.I. and Response to Japanese Films"), *Eiga Junpō*, April 1, 1942, p. 23.
41. *Indisch Verslag 1940*, p. 130.
42. *Djawa Baroe*, No. 13, July 1, 1943, pp. 24–5.
43. *Jawa Nenkan*, p. 170, and interview with Hirai Masao, former staff of *Nichi'ei* Jakarta branch (Kyoto), March 3, 1980. Another movie-producing unit in Southeast Asia was set up in Manila. Among the other six ordinary branches were those in Medan and Makassar.
44. Bert Hogenkamp, *De Nederlandse documentaire film 1920–1940*, (Amsterdam: Van Gennep, 1989). The writer acquired this information from Prof. Dr W. C. Ultee, Prof. of Sociology, Catholic University of Nijmegen.
45. Takaba Takashi, "Jawa Kōryaku to Bunka Butai" ("Military Invasion of Java and the Culture Unit") (Nippon Nyūsu Kiroku Iinkai), *Nyūsu Kamera no mita Gekidō no Shōwa*, (*Shōwa* Era seen through News Camera) (Nihon Hōsō Kyōkai 1979) p. 92. Takaba was working as a cameraman at *Nichiei* Jakarta branch.
46. Tanaka Junichirō, *Nihon Eiga Hattatsushi*, III, p. 116. According to Hirai (interview, March 3, 1980) the official status of the Japanese members of the staff was as "military civilians" under supervision of the Japanese Cabinet Information Bureau.
47. Interview with Hirai, March 3, 1980.

48. Interviews October, 1979 and June, 1986 with Mr Jansen, a staff member of Stichting Film en Wetenschap (Dutch Foundation for Films and Science) in Utrecht, who once carried out research on those films.
49. According to Mr Jansen, those 155 reels seem to cover the most important part of all confiscated Japanese films. 155 reels do not mean 155 items, for usually one item consisted of 2–4 reels. Interview with Jansen (Utrecht), October, 1979 and June, 1986.
50. The audio-visual section of the Dutch Information Service just started cataloguing these films when the writer visited in June 1986, and they were still being catalogued in June 1989 when she visited again. As of June 1989, 24 news reels, 22 culture films and one feature film had already been catalogued and the writer was given the opportunity to look at them.
51. Jansen's unpublished manuscript on Japanese propaganda films in Indonesia.
52. *Jawa Nenkan*, p. 170.
53. Ibid., pp. 169–70.
54. Ibid., p. 170.
55. Interview with Hirai, March 3, 1980.
56. Compiled by the writer through content analysis of 19 newsreels including 68 reports and 32 culture films which the writer has either seen herself or knows about. For details on the 68 news reports, see the items with * in Appendix III. For the titles of the 32 culture films consulted here, see the first 32 items in Appendix II.
57. Besides the films listed in Appendix II, there was also a film intended to be shown to the people in enemy countries, particularly Australians. It was produced by the intelligence agency of the 16th Army, but the facilities of *Nichi'ei* were used. It was titled *Calling Australia* and describes how POWs in Java were well treated. The director of this film was Hinatsu Eitarō, a Korean. For more detail, see Utsumi Aiko and Murai Yoshinori *Sineasuto Fuyung no Shōwa* (*Shōwa* Era of a Cineast Fuyung) (Tokyo: Gaifūsha, 1987).
58. Usmar Ismail, "Sari Soal dalam Film-film Indonesia" ("Basic Questions in Indonesian films"), *Star News*, vol. III, no. 5, September 25, 1954, p. 30. Cited in Salim Said, *Profil Dunia Film Indonesia*, p. 34.
59. Armijn Pané, "Produksi film Cerita di Indonesia" ("Production of Feature Film in Indonesia"), *Indonesia*, vol. IV, nos. 1–2 (January–February, 1953), p. 52, cited in Salim Said, *Profil Dunia Film Indonesia*, pp. 34–5.
60. "Indonesia Eiga Shōshi," p. 210 fn. 12. But it is said that there was no production of films except newsreels between August 1945 and 1947. *Profil Dunia Film Indonesia*, p. 37.
61. Interview with Kudō Ki'ichi, a former official of *Jawa Eihai* (Osaka), February, 1980.
62. *Jawa Nenkan*, p. 171.
63. Ibid., p. 170.
64. Ibid., p. 170. The information about the admission fee in the Dutch period was also confirmed by "Ran'in no Eigakai to Nippon Eiga no Hankyō," p. 23.

65. *Jawa Nenkan*, p. 170.
66. Jawa Gunseikanbu, *Kanpō*, No. 16, Jakarta, April 1943 (official gazette of Japanese military administration in Java, reprinted by Ryūkei Shosha).
67. The figure for West Java is printed in *Jawa Nenkan* as 32, but this seems to be a misprint for the correct number of 23.
68. *Jawa Nenkan*, pp. 171–2.
69. This is clear if these figures are compared with the case of Japan, where there were 2,350 movie theaters in those days (Tanaka Junichirō, *Nihon Eiga Hattatsushi* III, p. 83), and their ratio to the population (about 76 million) was one theater for about 32,000 persons.
70. "Ran'in no Eigakai to Nihon Eiga no Hankyō," p. 23. In *Nihon Eiga Hattatsushi* III, Tanaka Junichirō gives different figures as follows (p. 121): Jakarta, 20; Surabaya, 24; Semarang, 9; Bandung, 11.
71. "Ran'in no Eigakai to Nihon Eiga no Hankyō" pp. 23–24. For example, a Japanese eye medicine company carried out an open-air movie performance in 1940 at 40 different places in Java. At that time the movies screened were not direct commercial advertisements but Japanese culture films and animation films. Prior to the projection Japanese and Javanese music was played over a gramophone to attract a large audience. It is said that each time there were at least 1,500 in the audience.
72. *Jawa Nenkan*, p. 171.
73. In Japan these attempts had been made separately by various agencies, such as newspaper companies, movie production companies, and mass organizations since the early 1930s. For details, see Hoshino Jirokichi, "Idô Eiga no Shimei" ("The Mission of Travelling Theaters"), *Eiga Junpō*, September 21, 1942 and *Nihon Eigashi*, p. 98.
74. Tanaka Junichirō *Nihon Eiga Hattatsushi* III, p. 145, and interview with Kudō, Feb., 1980.
75. Interview with Kamino Eiji (Tokyo), July 21, 1986. He was one of the six experts sent to Java. They arrived in Java in mid-1943, and it was only after that that systematic performances of the mobile cinema started.
76. *Jawa Nenkan*, p. 171. *Jawa Eihai* further had a plan to expand the operation of traveling theaters by setting up one team in each residency and principality, but apparently the plan was not realized.
77. *Jawa Nenkan*, p. 171.
78. Interview with Kamino, July 21, 1986.
79. "*Sendenbu* Monthly Report," no. 22, December 1943.
80. Interview with Kamino, July 21, 1986.
81. "Sendenbu Monthly Report," no. 22, December 1943.
82. Ibid.
83. Interview with Kamino, July 21, 1986. This was done not only by the mobile cinema, but at the ordinary commercial theaters too.
84. For example, see an article titled "Kemadjoean Dalam Doenia Seni Sandiwara" ("Development in the World of Theatrical Play as Art"), in *Djawa Baroe*, No. 14, July 15, 1945.
85. Adachi *et al.*, "Replies of questionnaire concerning *Sendenbu*" (English in the original text slightly changed to make it clearer.).

86. *Nippon Nyūsu Eigashi*, p. 433. In *"Nippon Nyūsu"*, no. 222 (August 31, 1944), a newsreel shown in Japan, an item on the mobile cinema in Java was included, and the commentator stated there that "laughter would stimulate greater production."
87. In 1944 the government directed N.H.K. to put more emphasis on entertainment in radio programs. Yamamoto Fumio (ed.) *Nihon Masu Komyunikeshon-shi* (History of Mass Communication in Japan), (Tokyo: Tōkai University Press, 1970), p. 208.
88. "NEFIS Interrogation Report" (series of interrogations of Indonesian *heiho*, *rōmusha*, and others who were captured outside Java prior to August 1945). Brisbane, 1943–45, H-archief at Navy Archives in The Hague, No. 248, August 1944.
89. "Propaganda in the Netherlands East Indies," Sektie Krijgsgeschiedenis Archive 059–22, p. 17.

Appendix I: Japanese Films Shown in Java

(1) *Marei Senki/Tjahaja Dai Nippon di Melaju* (Malayan War Record)
Type: War documentary on military operations in Malaya (narrated in Indonesian).
Produced: 1942, by the news section of the Japanese Army.
Note: This film is notable for its depiction of General Yamashita Tomoyuki demanding surrender from the defeated General Arthur E. Percival.

(2) *Hawai-Marei Oki Kaisen* (The War at Sea from Hawaii to Malaya)
Type: Feature film based on military operations in Malaya and Hawaii.
Produced: 1942.
Released in Java: 1943.
Story: About a young man who, after completing rigorous training at the Naval Aviation School, rendered distinguished service in the war. Many shots depict the intensive drill and physical exercise required of the Japanese military and emphasize the discipline and physical strength of the Japanese armed forces.
Note: The film was released in Japan on the first anniversary of the outbreak of war (December 1942), and earned 1,150,000 yen during its first eight days, while the cost for production and advertisement was only 920,000 yen. It was shown all over the occupied areas, drawing its largest audiences in French Indo-China and the Philippines, and its second largest audiences in Shanghai and Hong Kong among all the films shown in those areas during the Japanese occupation.[1] In Java it was shown at 220 places by mobile cinema teams between July and November 1943.[2]

(3) *Nishizumi Sensha-chō Den/Pahlawan Tank Nishizumi* (Tank Commander Nishizumi)
Type: Feature film (with Indonesian subtitles).
Produced: 1940.
Story: About a Japanese military officer who was a very humane person and showed sympathy towards an injured Chinese woman and baby, but was finally killed by a Chinese soldier. He is described as a man who died an ideal military man.

(4) *Otoko no Iki/Semangat Lelaki* (Spirit of Man)
Type: Feature film (with Indonesian subtitles).
Produced: July, 1943.
Released in Java: July 1, 1943.
Reviewed: *Djawa Baroe*, no. 12, June 15, 1943.
Story: About the family of a shipping agent in downtown Tokyo. Deals with such topics as the dilemma between duty and humaneness, and the confrontation between old ways of thinking and new ones.

(5) *On'na no Kyōshitsu/Soeka-doeka Peladjar-wanita* (Classroom of Female Students)
Type: Feature film (with Indonesian subtitles).

---

[1] *Nihon Eigashi*, pp. 125–6.
[2] *Jawa Nenkan*, p. 171.

Released in Java: August 1, 1943.
Story: About seven girls (six Japanese and one Chinese) studying at a women's medical college. Describes rivalries, hostilities, and friendship among the seven classmates.
(6) *Eikoku Kuzururu no Hi/Sa'at Inggeris Roentoeh* (The Day England Fell)
Type: Feature film (with Indonesian subtitles).
Produced: November 1942.
Released in Java: Mid-August 1943.
Reviewed: *Djawa Baroe*, no. 15, August 1, 1943.
Story: About a Japanese man, born and bred in Hong Kong, at the time of the Japanese invasion of Hong Kong. He is recruited by the Japanese Army and participates in military operations in Hong Kong, while his family is interned as prisoners of war. By describing the situation of this family from the immediate prewar days until the Japanese victory over the British in Hong Kong, the emphasis is put on racial discrimination and the brutality of the British toward Asians.
(7) *Tsubasa no Gaika/Kemenangan Sajap* (Victory of Wings)
Type: Feature film (with Indonesian subtitles).
Produced: 1942.
Released in Java: Mid-September 1943.
Reviewed: *Djawa Baroe*, no. 16, August 15, 1943.
Story: About a man and his stepbrother who lost their father long ago because of an airplane accident, and who, in obedience to their father's will, become pilots and devote themselves to developing a new fighter plane.
(8) *Hahakogusa/Panggilan Iboe* (A Mother's Calling)
Type: Feature film (with Indonesian subtitles).
Produced: June 1942.
Released in Java: *circa* October, 1943.
Reviewed: *Djawa Baroe*, no. 18, September 16, 1943.
Story: About a woman who sacrifices herself and marries a man with two small children. She brings them up with deep love. Emphasis is put on her self-sacrifice and strong love for her stepchildren.
(9) *Nankai no Hanataba* (Bouquet in the Southern Ocean)
Type: Feature film.
Produced: May, 1943.
Released in Java: Late 1943.
Story: Describes men working to develop an air route in the Southern Areas. Emphasis is put on friendship, responsibility, and self-sacrifice.
Note: Traveling teams put on performances of this film for *rōmusha* at thirteen places in Banten in December 1943, drawing audiences totaling 1,126,000.[3]
(10) *Shōgun to Sanbō to Hei* (General, General Staff, and Soldier)
Type: Feature film.
Produced: 1942.
Released in Java: Late 1943.

[3] "*Sendenbu* Monthly Report," no. 22.

Story: About troops operating in Northern China.
Note: On the second anniversary of the outbreak of war (December 1943) this film was shown at eight places in Jakarta by a traveling team and drew audiences totaling 104,000.[4]

(11) *Shingapōru Sōkōgeki/Serangan Singapore* (All-out Attack on Singapore)
Type: Feature film (with Indonesian subtitles).
Produced: April, 1943.
Released in Java: After November, 1943.
Reviewed: *Djawa Baroe*, no. 21, November 1, 1943
Story: Dramatization of Japanese attack on Singapore
Note: On the second anniversary of the outbreak of war (December 1943) this film was shown at eight places in Bogor and drew audiences totaling 96,000.[5]

(12) *Rikugun Kōkūsenki/Sajap Melipoeti Birma* (Wings over Burma)
Type: Documentary film on the Japanese attack on Burma in January 1942.
Produced: 1942.
Released in Java: after November, 1943.
Reviewed: *Djawa Baroe*, no. 22, November 15, 1943.

(13) *Ahen Sensō/Perang Tjandoe* (The Opium War)
Type: Feature film with Indonesian subtitles).
Produced: January, 1943.
Released in Java: After December, 1943.
Reviewed: *Djawa Baroe*, no. 24, December 15, 1943.
Story: About the Opium War in the nineteenth century between Britain and China. The emphasis is put on the evils of British imperialism which sought the benefit of Britain at the expense of the Chinese people. Chinese politician Lin Tse-hsu is described as an Asian hero. Indonesian version of this film was made in December 1943 and distributed all over Java.

(14) *Otoko/Djantan* (A Man)
Type: Feature film (with Indonesian subtitles).
Released in Java: After January, 1944.
Reviewed: *Djawa Baroe*, no. 2, January 15, 1944.
Story: Concerning a Japanese engineer who works in Manchuria to build a railway tunnel which is vital for the national interest of Japan. His heroic behavior at the time of a construction accident and the devotion of two women to him is described. Through the behavior of one of the women who lost his love to her rival, it is emphasized that service to nation is more important than personal love.

(15) *Bōrō no Kesshitai/Barisan Mati di Menara Pendjaga* (Suicide Troops of the Watch Tower)
Type: Feature film (with Indonesian subtitles).
Produced: April, 1943.
Released in Java: After February, 1944.
Reviewed: *Djawa Baroe*, no. 4, February 15, 1944.

[4] Ibid.
[5] Ibid.

Story: About Japanese and Korean policemen working together at the border area in northern Korea. Describes patriotic spirit through their fighting against bandits.

(16) *Tatakai no Machi/Kota Berdjoeang* (A Town of Fighting)
Type: Feature film (with Indonesian subtitles).
Produced: February, 1943.
Released in Java: After April, 1944.
Reviewed: *Djawa Baroe*, no. 7, April, 1944.
Story: Takes place in a Chinese town in 1941. Describes friendship between China and Japan through a Chinese actress and a Japanese young man studying Chinese literature. Also described is the disorder and evil of the Chinese army.

(17) *Shinsetsu/Saldjoe Soetji* (Sacred Snow)
Type: Feature film (with Indonesian subtitles).
Produced: October, 1942.
Released in Java: After May, 1944.
Reviewed: *Djawa Baroe*, no. 9, May 1, 1944.
Story: About a love triangle involving an elementary school teacher and two women. Emphasis is on his devotion to education and the modest and compliant attitudes of two rival women.

(18) *Kaigun/Angkatan Laoet* (Navy)
Type: Feature film (with Indonesian subtitles).
Produced: December, 1943.
Released in Java: After May, 1944.
Reviewed: *Djawa Baroe*, no. 10, May 15, 1944.
Story: Describing the life of a Japanese young man from his entrance into the Naval Academy (1934) until his death in the attack on Pearl Harbor (1941). Emphasis is put on the training at the Naval Academy and the strong patriotic spirit of a navy man.

(19) *Shusseimae 12 Jikan/12 Djam Seboeloem Berangkat ke Medan Perang* (12 Hours before Departure for the Front)
Type: Feature film (with Indonesian subtitles).
Released in Java: After August, 1944.
Reviewed: *Djawa Baroe*, no. 14, July 15, 1944.
Story: Describing the behavior of five medical students on the eve of their departure for the front. One was conducting his last medical operation, offering his own blood to the patient. One was meeting his younger sister and asked her to take care of their old mother. One was attending a musical concert at the Public Hall. One was arranging a meeting between his elder sister and her boyfriend and urging them to get married. One was sitting in Zen meditation.

(20) *Neppū* (Hot Wind)
Type: Feature film (with Indonesian subtitles).
Produced: 1943.
Released in Java: After August, 1944.
Reviewed: *Djawa Baroe*, no. 15, August 1, 1944.
Story: About a young engineer working for an iron foundry. He devotes himself to raising the working spirit of the laborers and to attaining increased steel production.

(21) *Fuchinkan Gekichin/Torpedo Tempaan Djiwa* (Sinking of the Unsinkable Warship)
Type: Feature film (with Indonesian subtitles).
Released in Java: September, 1944.
Reviewed: *Djawa Baroe*, no. 16, August 15, 1944.
Story: About two engineers working for a torpedo manufacturing factory. They succeed in increasing production by 100 percent, and with those torpedoes the Japanese navy succeeds in destroying the British warship, *"The Prince of Wales."*

(22) *Sugata Sanshirō* (Story of Sugata Sanshirō: the Founder of Judo)
Type: Feature film.
Produced: March, 1943.
Story: About the Japanese creator of judo in the Meiji period. Emphasis is put on self-discipline and rigourous training.
Note: The first work by the famous Japanese movie director, Kurosawa Akira.

(23) *Shina no Yoru* (China Nights)
Type: Feature film (love story).
Produced: 1940.
Released in Java: August, 1945.
Story: Describing the love between a Japanese sailor and a Chinese girl in Shanghai. The sailor protects the girl from molestation, and as a result of these adventures the Chinese girl abandons her hatred of the Japanese and becomes a supporter of Japanese Pan-Asianism.
Note: The film is unique because it has different endings depending on where it was shown, with different versions shown in different areas. The version shown in China ends with the symbolic wedding of China to Japan through the marriage of the hero and heroine, while in the version for Japanese audiences the hero is called to duty before their marriage is consummated. He leaves his bride, is wounded by her countrymen, and loses his life on the battle front. On learning the news, she commits suicide by drowning. The version for Southeast Asian audiences, however, does not end there, but goes further: the news of his death proves to be false, and although wounded in the battle with Communist guerrillas, he returns just as she is about to throw herself into the river and saves her. The film thus ends on the happy symbolic note of Japan rescuing China, saving China from communism, and the two living happily ever after. (For details, see "Japanese Films: A Phase of Psychological Warfare," p. 15 (Note 26, this chapter); also Anderson and Richie, *The Japanese Film: Art and Industry*, Rutland, Vermont and Tokyo: Charles E. Tuttle Co., 1959) pp. 154–5.)

(24) *Momotarō no Umiwashi* (Sea-eagle Momotarō)
Type: Animated film.
Released in Java: 1944.
Story: Taken from a traditional Japanese fairy tale, in which a hero called "Momotarō" fights against evil giants to save the villagers from their wicked behavior. Here the Allied Forces are compared to the giants and Japan to Momotarō.

(25) *Sora no Shinpei* (Divine Soldiers of the Sky)

Type: Documentary film on operations of Japanese parachute troops in Palembang.
Produced: 1942.
Released in Java: December, 1943.

(26) *Tōyō no Gaika* (Victory Song of the Orient)
Type: Documentary film on Japanese military operation in the Philippines.
Produced: 1942, by news section of the Japanese Army.
Released in Java: February, 1944.

(27) *Shanghai Rikusentai* (Marines in Shanghai)
Type: Feature film.
Produced: 1939.
Story: About Japanese Marines engaged in fighting to the death in Shanghai.

(28) *Dai Goretsu no Kyōfu* (Fifth Column Fear)
Type: Feature film.
Produced: 1942.
Story: Espionage.

(29) *Aikoku no Hana* (Flower of Patriotism)
Type: Feature film.
Produced: November, 1942.
Story: Romantic love story of a military nurse and her devotion to the nation.
Note: This film made a strong impression on the Javanese because of its theme song with the same title. The song became so popular that even forty years after the war, Indonesian informants would often sing it.

(30) *Hanayakanaru Gensō* (Brilliant Illusion)
Type: Musical film.
Produced: 1943.

(31) *Wakaki Hi no Yorokobi* (Joy in Younger Days)
Type: Feature film.
Produced: June 1943.

(32) *Aiki Minami e Tobu* (Flying South in His Plane)
Type: Feature film.
Produced: September, 1943, under supervision of the Army Aviation Corps Headquarters.
Story: Praise of Army Air Troops.

(33) *Kachidoki Ondo* (Song of Victory)
Type: Feature film.
Produced: January 1944.

(34) *Ano Hata o Ute* (Fire on That Flag!)
Type: Feature film.
Produced: February, 1944 (filming done in the Philippines, joined by Filipino actors).
Story: Dramatization of the fighting, emphasizing the brutality of the U.S. Army contrasted with the humanity of the Japanese Army. With a symbolic scene of the American flag taken down and the Japanese flag hoisted, the Japanese role as liberator is emphasized.

(35) *Suihei San* (Sailor)

Type: Feature film.
Produced: May, 1944.
Story: Propaganda for recruitment of sailors for the Navy.
(36) *Teki wa Ikuman Aritotemo* (How Many Thousands the Enemy Might Be)
Type: Feature film (comedy).
Produced: August, 1944.
Story: About recruitment of the Boys' Aviation Corps.
(37) *Kagirinaki Zenshin* (Endless Advance)
Type: Feature film.
Produced: 1937.
Story: About the antagonism and alienation in a capitalist society experienced by an employee in a Japanese company.
(38) *Kessen no Ōzora e* (Toward the Decisive Battle in the Sky)
Type: Feature film.
Produced: September, 1943.
Story: About trainees at the Aviation Corps Training School. Describes them as the hope of the future.
(39) *Himetaru Kakugo* (Hidden Resolve)
Type: Feature film.
Produced: November, 1943.
Story: About the austere life of the populace in the back streets of the Ginza, Tokyo.
(40) *Fuji ni Chikau* (Swear an Oath to Mount Fuji)
(41) *Kōjō no Tsuki* (The Moon over a Deserted Castle)
(42) *Enoken no Bakudanji* (Enoken, The Thunderstorm Man)
Type: Feature film (comedy).
Produced: 1941.
(43) *Saisho no Ippun* (The First Minute)
(44) *Chishima* (Kurile Islands)
(45) *Bōtaoshi* (Pulling down the Pole)
Type: Documentary film (with background music and no narration).
Content: Introducing physical exercise of Japanese school children.

The following are the films made in Japan mainly for the people in Japanese-occupied areas:

(46) *Gunkan Minami e Yuku* (A Warship Going South)
Type: Documentary film.
(47) *Ajia Raya* (Greater Asia)
Type: Documentary film (narrated in Indonesian).
Main theme: Political propaganda on Japan's role in Asia.
Content: Propaganda film introducing Japanese military achievements through severe fighting in China and other areas. Emphasizes that the Japanese Army does not act aggressively and that its purpose is to bring about the liberation of Greater East Asia. Includes a scene of Indonesians and Japanese having a big open-air party.
(48) *AIUEO no Uta* (Song of AIUEO)
Type: Culture film (with background music but no narration).
Main theme: Instruction in Japanese language.

Content: Film with the purpose of teaching the Japanese alphabet, "A-I-U-E-O," to children. With the AIUEO song as background music, fifty Japanese *kana* syllabary are shown (animation) one by one. There is also a scene of an elementary school, where pupils are studying Japanese.

(49) *Kepada Saudara-Saudara di Negeri Selatan/Nanpō no Tomo e* (To Our Fellows in the Southern Nations)
Type: Documentary film (narrated in Indonesian).
Content: Introduces the life of Southeast Asian students studying in Japan.

(50) *Min'na Genki Da* (Everybody is Healthy).
Type: Documentary film (with background music and no narration).
Content: Introducing the school life of Japanese elementary school children.

(51) *Aikoku no Hana* (The Flower of Patriotism)
Type: Documentary film (narrated in Indonesian with the song of *Aikoku no Hana* as the background music).
Content: Introducing scenery and life in Japan.

(52) *Dai Tōa Nyusu / Kabar Dai Tôa* (Greater East Asia News)
Type: News film (narrated in Indonesian).
Content: News film edited for people in Southeast Asia. It had different versions with narration in different languages according to the country for which it was intended.

In addition to these, there were also other documentary and culture films. Some of them concerned the following topics:

(53) The Japanese Red-Cross.
(54) The Enlightened Village (about the campaign against tuberculosis).
(55) The Campaign against Malaria in Japan.
(56) Training School of Sword-fighting.

Besides the above-mentioned films, it is quite likely that the following items were also shown in Java, although there are no sources to confirm this:

(57) *Marei no Tora* (The Tiger of Malaya)
Type: Feature film.
Produced: 1943.
Story: About a Japanese man who came to Malaya in prewar days and became a gangster. At the time of the Japanese invasion of Malaya, however, he cooperates with the Japanese and dies for the victory of his mother country.

(58) *Biruma Senki* (Military Operations in Burma)
Type: Documentary film on Japanese military operations in Burma.
Produced: 1942.

Sources:

Djawa Baroe (popular fortnightly magazine). This introduced, in almost every issue, new dramatic and cultural films with detailed descriptions of their contents.

Jawa Nenkan, p. 170. This gives the titles and brief contents of movies made in Java prior to 1943.

Film collection at Stichting Film en Wetenschaap (Foundation for Film and Science) in Utrecht.

Temporary catalogue of confiscated Japanese films at the Film Archive of the RVD (Rijks Voorlichting Dienst) in The Hague.

Catalogue of confiscated films compiled by the RVO (Rijksinstituut voor Oorlogsdocumentatie).

"Far East and World War II."

Nihon Eiga Hattatsushi III.

Nihon Eigashi.

Senchū Eigashi Shiki.

"*Sendenbu* Monthly Report."

"Japanese Films: A Phase of Psychological Warfare."

The scenarios of *Aikoku no Hana* and *AIUEO no Uta* by *Nippon Eigasha Bunka Eigabu* (Section of Culture Film, Nippon Eigasha).

Appendix II: Films Made in Java

1. DOCUMENTARY AND CULTURE FILMS (Unless specified, narrated in Indonesian)

The first 32 items are source material for content analysis in Table 2.4 on page 54. The letter at the end of the title, from (a) to (g), shows the classification in this table.

Films (1) to (19) are available at Rijks Voorlichting Dienst and were seen by the writer.

(1) *Dibawah Bendera Nippon* (Under the Japanese Flag) (a)
Produced: December, 1942.
Content: Recording the celebration of the first anniversary of the outbreak of the Great East Asia War on December 8, 1942 at Macassar, Celebes.

(2) *Tonari Gumi* (Neighborhood Associations) (g)
Produced: May, 1944.
Main theme: Political propaganda providing social education.
Content: Propaganda film emphasizing the merit of neighborhood associations through introduction of their various activities.

(3) *Pemakaran Tombak Bambu/Takeyari Jutsu* (The Use of the Bamboo Spear) (c)
Produced: 1943.
Main theme: Skills instruction.
Content: Teaches how to use a bamboo-spear. Also introduces Japanese battle tactics.

(4) *Indonesia Raya* (Great Indonesia) (a)
No narration but with the song of *Indonesia Raya* as the theme song.
Produced: After September, 1944.
Content: Film with purpose of teaching the Indonesian national anthem, "Indonesia Raya." The song is heard throughout the movie as background music while showing various scenes exalting the national spirit such as Borobudur, mass meetings and parades, the Great Mosque, PETA (Volunteer Army) garrisons, etc. In the middle of the film there is a scene of people in September, 1944 shouting for joy at the promise of independence.

(5) *Taiteki Kanshi* (Watching out for the Enemy) (c)
Produced: August, 1944.
Content: Emphasizes the importance of patrols. By contrasting peaceful scenes in daily life with tense scenes of patrol activities and fire watches, the film shows that danger is always near a peaceful life.

(6) *Tentara Pembela/Bōei Giyūgun no Uta* (Song of the Volunteer Army) (c)
No narration and only with the song of the Volunteer Army as background music.
Released: January 27, 1944.
Content: Introducing the process of recruiting and training the PETA soldiers using an example of one battalion in Priangan residency.

(7) *Oebi Djalar/Kansho* (Sweet Potatoes) (d)

Content: Emphasizing the necessity of increasing production and teaching how to plant sweet potatoes.

(8) *Tanaman Kapas/Wata o Tsukurimashō* (Let's Plant Cotton) (d)
Produced: August, 1943.
Content: Emphasizing the importance of planting cotton to alleviate the clothing shortage, and teaching how to plant it.

(9) *Kapas Taoen/Kimono o Tsukurō* (Let's Weave Clothing) (d)
Produced: August, 1944.
Content: Teaching how to plant and weave cotton.

(10) *Menoedjoe ke-arah Mengambil Bagian Pemerintahan Dalam Negeri/ Sansei e no michi* (The Way of Participation in the Government) (a)
Produced: December, 1943.
Content: Describing the development of Japanese military administration in Java from the outbreak of the Greater East Asia War up to the granting of native participation in administration. Introducing the announcement by Premier Tōjō at the Diet in Tokyo in June 1943 and the formation of the Central Advisory Council in October 1943.

(11) *Perdjoempaan Kaoem Moeslim Soematera Baroe* (Meeting of Moslems of New Sumatra) (a)
Produced: 1943.
Content: Describes a mass meeting held in Medan under the leadership of Hamka, a well known Muslim leader in Sumatra.

(12) *Heiho Angkatan Laut/Kaigun Heiho* (Navy Auxiliary Forces) (c)
Produced: 1943.
Content: Describes the day of family meetings at the *heiho* (Indonesian soldier of the Auxiliary Forces) barracks. Propaganda film for recruitment of navy *heiho*.

(13) *Ja'eshio/Ya'eshio* (The Song of the Boundless Ocean: *Ya'eshio*) (a)
No narration but with the song of *Ya'eshio* and speech by Sukarno in Indonesian.
Produced: 1942.
Content: Announcement of the first prize winner in the contest for composing the *Ya'eshio* song. Soekarno appears in the film and explains the meaning of this song.

(14) *Bekerdja/Kinrō no Uta* (The Working Song) (d)
No narration and accompanied by theme song of the same title which is introduced in *Djawa Baroe*, no. 1, January 1, 1944.
Produced: December, 1943.
Main theme: To exalt the working spirit.

(15) *Kinrō Butai* (The Labor Troops) (d)
Produced: February, 1944.
Content: Emphasizing the necessity of labor and introducing the process of recruiting *rōmusha* (forced coolie labor). Also depicts their life at the place of work. Propaganda film for *rōmusha* recruitment.

(16) *Tōa no Yoi Kodomo* (Good Child of East Asia) (f)
No narration, and the song of *Tōa no Yoi Kodomo* is used as a theme song throughout the film.
Produced: July, 1944.
Content: Introducing life at an elementary school in Jakarta. Scenes of

Indonesian pupils learning Japanese, singing Japanese songs, and having military training are introduced.

(17) *Djagalah Tanah Djawa/Mamore Jawa* (Defend Java!) (c)
Content: Describes the activities of *seinendan* (Youth Corps), *keibōdan* (Vigilance Corps), and PETA.

(18) *Penanam Bibit* (Planting Seeds) (d)
Narrated in Javanese.
Content: Describes how to plant rice.

(19) *Kesehatan Badan/Genki na Karada* (Healthy Body) (g)
Produced: March, 1944.
Content: Describing the healthy life of Indonesian children in a village.

Following are the films which have not yet been found but whose titles have been mentioned in one or more sources.

(20) *Kerdja dengan Gembira* (Work with Joy) (d)
Main theme: Economic propaganda.
Content: Encourages diligence in daily life by introducing industrial and agricultural activities in various parts of Java.

(21) *Pendjagaan di Oetara* (Guard at the North) (c)
Content: Describes the role of the Japanese Army in Indonesia.

(22) *Pembasmian Malaria/Mararia Bokumetsu* (Extermination of Malaria) (h)
Produced: March, 1944.
Content: Culture film to promote the extermination of malaria.

(23) *Jawa no Asa Bukuro* (Gunny [hemp] Sacks in Java) (d)
Produced: July, 1943.

(24) *Kimitachi wa Bōei Senshi Da* (You are Soldiers for Defense) (c)
Produced: September, 1943.

(25) *Hima o Zōsanseyo!* (Increase the Cultivation of the Castor-oil Plant!) (d)
Produced: March, 1944.

(26) *Rajio Taisō* (Warm-up Exercises with the Radio) (g)
Produced: March, 1944.

(27) *Jōgo Engo* (Assisting the Soldiers while We are behind the Front) (c)
Produced: April, 1944.

(28) *Bōkū Dokuhon* (Manual for Air Defense) (c)
Produced: November, 1944.
Content: Teaching the method for air defense.

(29) We Assault and Go Forward (Indonesian title unknown) (c)

(30) New Life in Java (Indonesian title unknown) (g)
Content: Describes various aspects of the life and work of the Javanese people.

(31) *Jawa no Tenchōsetsu* (Ceremony of Emperor's Birthday in Java) (a)

(32) *Di Kota* (In Town) (d)
Content: Campaign against the clothing shortage and promotion for production of clothing material.

The following films are recorded in one of the sources, but the content is not clear from the title and excluded from the samples in Table 2.4.

(33) *Furanbejia* (meaning unclear)
(34) *Sajap Baroe* (New Wing)
(35) *Mizuwata* (meaning unclear)

The following is also a documentary film produced in Java, but it seems to have been made for showing in Japan.

(36) *Jawa no Ryōyōjo* (Health Resort in Java)
 No narration but with Japanese subtitles.
 Content: Describes the recuperation of Japanese soldiers at Wonosari and Sukabumi.

2. FEATURE FILMS

(Only (1) and (2) are available at RVD and were seen by the writer. The others have not been found yet.)
 (1) *Berdjoeang* (Fighting) / *Minami no Ganbō* (Aspiration in Southern Area)
 Released: March, 1944.
 Main theme: Devotion and service to the nation.
 Story: About a young man who joins the *heiho* and his two friends and a girlfriend.
 The first film totally produced by Indonesians only.
 Note: The Indonesian title and Japanese title differ.
 (2) *Di Desa/ Mura nite* (In the village)
 Produced: October, 1944.
 Content: A PETA soldier goes home on leave and is welcomed by the villagers.
 (3) *Hudjan/Shū'u* (Rain)
 Produced: August, 1944.
 (4) *Ke Seberang* (Across the Sea)
 Produced: 1943.
 (5) *Djatuh Berkait* (Falling in Line)
 Produced: 1944.
 Content: Promotion of savings.
 (6) *Di Menara/Bōrō nite* (At the Tower)
 Produced: September, 1944.
 (7) *Kemakmoeran* (Prosperity)
 Released: January, 1944.
 (8) *Kris Poesaka* (Inherited Sword)/*Kurisu Monogatari* (Story of the Sword)
 Main theme: Political theme of "common prosperity in Asia."
 Story: Advocacy of unification of Asian nations under the leadership of Japan, a "nation of the Sun," emphasizing that all Asian nations are common in origin and equal in worshipping the Sun.
 (9) *Gelombang* (Wave)
 Musical film.
 Main theme: Political theme of "common prosperity in Asia." Describes the historical development of the Indonesian people, emphasizing Japan's role in saving Indonesia from Western rule.

(10) *Makazareba: Chokin Monogatari* (Preparation: Story of Saving Money)
(11) *Toekang Ngobrol/Oshaberi Pak Kromo* (Talkative Uncle Kromo)
Feature film using puppets (speeches in Indonesian).
Released: December, 1943.
Reviewed: *Djawa Baroe*, no. 26, December 1, 1943.
Main theme: Counterespionage precautions.
Story: A talkative man, Kromo, unconsciously gives information to an enemy spy and causes a serious situation.
(12) *Koeli dan Roomusha* (Coolies and *Rōmusha*)
Type: Feature film.
Written by J. Hoetagaloen (the scenario won first prize in a contest sponsored by *Rōmu Kyōkai*); introduced in *Djawa Baroe*, nos. 13 and 14, July 1945.
Story: Describing the difference between coolie laborers sent to Sumatra for plantation work in Dutch days and the *rōmusha* of the Japanese period, emphasizing how the latter are well-treated.
First performed as a theatrical play and then made into a movie.
(13) *Bei'ei Gekimetsu Odori* (Dance of Smashing America and Britain)
Produced: May, 1944.
(14) *Umi ni Hasete* (Going to the sea)
Produced: September, 1944.

3. NEWS FILMS

(Quite a few of them are available at RVD.)
(1) *Djawa Baroe* (New Java), Nos. 1–8
Type: News film (narrated in Indonesian).
Produced: August, 1942–March, 1943.
(2) *Berita Film di Djawa/Jawa Nyūsu* (Java News), Nos. 1–19
Type: News film (narrated in Indonesian and Japanese).
Produced: March 1943–December 1943.
(3) *Nanpō Hōdō* (Southern News) Nos. 1–43
Type: News film (narrated in Indonesian and Japanese).
Produced: January 1944–October 1945.

Sources:

Same as Appendix I, plus
"Filmographie Indonesienne," *Archipel*, no. 5 (1973), p. 64.
Nippon Eigasha Kaigaikyoku, "Kaigai Kyokuhō" (Report of Overseas Bureau) No. 11 (January 1945).

Appendix III: Newsreel Topics

Those with an asterisk are the 68 items reviewed by the author and classified in Table 2.4 on page 54. The letter after the asterisk shows the classification in this table.

July, 1942	Police school in Sukabumi.
August, 1942	Arrival of the Princes of Solo and Yogyakarta at Jakarta.
September, 1942	Athletic Meet of Indonesian Association of Sport.
December, 1942	New women teachers at Jakarta.
Djawa Baroe 2 (October? 1942)	*Hari Raya Idulfitri*. [Feast at the end of the Muslim Month of Fasting].*(e) Completion of repairs of railroad destroyed by the Dutch.*(d) Training in Japanese kendo [sword fighting] in Jakarta.*(f) Celebration of the Japanese Navy in Surabaya.*(b) Conquest of Aleutian Islands.*(b)
Djawa Baroe 4 (December ? 1942)	Celebration of *Kōa-sai*, one year anniversary of the outbreak of war.*(a) General situation in Tokyo.*(i) Learning Indonesian in Japan (at Kōnan school and Takushoku University).*(i)
Djawa Baroe 6 (February? 1943)	Japanese Emperor's visit to the Military Academy.*(i) Japanese Empress's visit to a military hospital.*(i) Anniversary of the outbreak of war in Japan.*(i)
Djawa Baroe 7 (March? 1943)	Sketches in Java on *Kigensetsu* Day.*(e) Campaign for saving.*(h) Reports from various places in Java: Ceremony to topple the statue of Jan P. Coen [the 4th Governor General of Dutch East Indies Company].*(a) Japanese sea battle at Rennell Island.*(b)
Jawa Nyūsu 1 (April 29, 1943)	Training of the Japanese Army in Malang. Japanese resolution. *Hōrai* Rice. Navy soldiers in the snowy mountains.
Jawa Nyūsu 2 (May 13, 1943)	Emperor's birthday in Java.*(a) "Destroy England and America!" [Speech of *Sendenbuchō*, the head of the Propaganda De-

partment.]*(a)
Birth of *keibōdan*.*(c)
Reopening of Jakarta Medical College.*(f)
Completion of repairs of the Tangeran bridge.*(d)
Birth of Magelang *Renseijo* [Center for Martial Arts].*(c)
Birth of *seinendan*.*(c)

Jawa Nyūsu 3 (May 23, 1943)	Kamikaze-Maru [a ship named *"Kamikaze Maru"*]. Judo training school. Castor oil plant. Navy Memorial Day.
Jawa Nyūsu 4 (June 10, 1943)	Asian students in Japan. Volunteer work (*kinrō hōshi*). Railway Japan. Soldiers and children.
Jawa Nyūsu 5 (June, 1943)	Granting native participation in administration.*(a) Ceremony of completion of new ship.*(d) Painting exhibition by Indonesian artists.*(e) Fishery by Japanese Army.*(b) Cultivation of cotton in Besuki, Java.*(d) Inspection of *keibōdan* and *seinendan* by 16th Army Commander.*(c)
Jawa Nyūsu 6 (July 9, 1943)	Appointment of new *Gunseikan* [military superintendent], General Kokubu.*(a) *Pasar Malam* [Night Market] in Jakarta.*(e) Construction of Neyama tunnel in Kediri.*(d) Indonesian ladies learn Japanese culture.*(f) Java defended by the inhabitants.*(c)
Jawa Nyūsu 7 (July 12, 1943)	Premier Tōjō's visit to Java.*(a) *Barisan Bekerdja* [Labor Troops], with the song, "Work, work, for the extermination of England and America."*(d) Sailor training school at Singapore.*(g) "Let's clean the well!" (Health Campaign)*(h).
Jawa Nyūsu 8 (July 29, 1943)	16th Army Commander-in-chief makes tour. March to destroy English and Americans. Anti-air raid maneuvers in Java.
Jawa Nyūsu 9 (August, 1943)	Instruction by Commander-in-chief. School. Student air force troops.
Jawa Nyūsu 10 (August, 1943)	Youth Training Meeting. Construction of military base. Cultivation of tobacco in Java.

Jawa Nyūsu 11 (September 9, 1943)

Night training of *seinendan*.
Tjipinan prison.
Athletic meeting.
Mass meeting of *keibōdan*.

Jawa Nyūsu 12 (September 23, 1943)

Production increase.
Kanuran gymnastics.
Defense at various places.

Jawa Nyūsu 13 (October 7, 1943)

Formation of Volunteer Army (PETA).
New Year in Java.
Ceremony to swear cooperation with the Japanese army.

Jawa Nyūsu 14 (October 21, 1943)

Opening of the Central Advisory Council.*(a)
"Work for intensifying military power!"*(d)
Recruitment of Volunteer Army (PETA).*(c)
"People's Health Day."*(h)

Jawa Nyūsu 15 (November 18, 1943)

PETA officer candidates enter training school.*(c)
Sketches of various places in Java:
Pasar Malam [Night Market] in Makassar.*(g)
Seinendan training in Surabaya.*(c)
Construction of air raid shelter on the island of Timor.*(g)
Mass meeting at Gambir Square in Jakarta.*(a)
All Java Athletic Meeting.*(e)

Jawa Nyūsu 16 (November 11, 1943)

Total mobilization for defense.
(Dates are as shown in the original Japanese.)

Jawa Nyūsu 17 (November 17, 1943)

Forced delivery of paddy.
The party visiting Japan came back from Japan.
Extermination of malaria.
Defense week.

Jawa Nyūsu 18 (December 8, 1943)

Fierce air battle.*(b)
Southern topics.*(g)
Appointment of native *shūchōkan* [Residents].*(a)
Sketches on December 8.*(e)

Jawa Nyūsu 19 (December 8, 1943)

Movie Festival.
Ceremony of *Kōa-sai*.
Soekarno returns from Japan.
Enthusiasm and unity of 5,000,000 in Solo.
Participation in labor work.

Nanpō Hōdō 1 (December, 1943)

Opening of uncultivated land.
Propaganda for food production increase and delivery of the product, and a Japanese shows how to plant rice.
Ship-building.
Training of *heiho*.

Nanpō Hōdō 2 (January, 1944)	Inspection team. Industries in Southern areas. Topics in Southern areas.
Nanpō Hōdō 3 (February 3, 1944)	Volunteer work by junior high school students. The Japanese Commander-in-chief and the *Gunseikan* visit a *tonarigumi* meeting.
Nanpō Hōdō 4 (February, 1944)	Opening of the second session of the Central Advisory Council in Java.*(a) Presenting of colors to PETA corps.*(c) Progress made by the Asiatic people. Planting of cotton by Prince of Solo and his wife and teaching of the planting of rice by the Mangkunegara Prince. Training of *keibōdan*, *seinendan*, and PETA.
Nanpō Hōdō 5 (March 2, 1944)	Second anniversary of fall of Singapore. Second anniversary of fall of Celebes.
Nanpō Hōdō 6 (March 11, 1944)	Celebration of the second anniversary of the foundation of New Java (Japanese conquest of Java). First mass meeting of the *Jawa Hōkōkai* at Jakarta. March past of Volunteer Army.
Nanpō Hōdō 7 (March 18, 1944)	Japanese army in Southern areas.
Nanpō Hōdō 8 (March 31, 1944)	Installation of Sumatera *Giyūgun* (Volunteer Army) on February 14, 1944, at Padang.
Nanpō Hōdō 9 (April 10, 1944)	News about construction. New creative ideas. Exhibition of children's work.
Nanpō Hōdō 10 (April 27, 1944)	Shooting down of enemy plane. Air-raids are unavoidable.
Nanpō Hōdō 11 (May 11, 1944)	Fatherland defense troops. Water patrol troops. Moving medical teams.
Nanpō Hōdō 12 (May 25, 1944)	Scientific youth. *Nōmin Dōjō* [agricultural training center].
Nanpō Hōdō 13 (June 8, 1944)	Bandjermasin. Salt farm. Marine youth. Training of Volunteer Army.
Nanpō Hōdō 14 (June 22, 1944)	Moving medical ship. Training of loading laborers. Cotton for clothing.

Nanpō Hōdō 15 (July, 1944)	Mass gymnastics. Volunteer work troops. Construction of railway.
Nanpō Hōdō 16 (July, 1944)	Hongō and Manabe: two heroes of Japan. Recruiting of Navy *heiho*. Production increase.
Nanpō Hōdō 17 (August, 1944)	Training school for railway staff. Sultan in North Borneo.
Nanpō Hōdō 18 (August, 1944)	Appointment of Volunteer Army officers. Indonesian students return from Japan. Textile industry. Coal mining.
Nanpō Hōdō 19 (August, 1944)	Irrigation work. Rice planting. Milling of paddy. Delivery of paddy.
Nanpō Hōdō Extra (September, 1944).	Granting of future independence to Indonesia.*(a)
Nanpō Hōdō 20 (September, 1944)	Soekarno joining *rōmusha**(d).
Nanpō Hōdō 21 (September, 1944)	Local civil defense in Greater East Asia. Ethnic festival. Ceremony to celebrate granting of future independence.
Nanpō Hōdō 22 (October, 1944)	Ethnic Festival in Makassar, Medan, Bukkittingi and Padang.
Nanpō Hōdō 23 (October, 1944)	Destruction of American warship. The new duty of the Volunteer Army.
Nanpō Hōdō 26 (December, 1944)	The 6th Session of the Central Advisory Council.*(a) Japanese speech contest.*(f) Brave *heiho* soldiers.*(c)
Nanpō Hōdō 37 (May? 1945)	New Life Movement.*(d) "Let's cultivate unused lands!" "Cotton planting." "Raising fish." Defense of village.*(c)
Nanpō Hōdō 38 (May? 1945)	Training of Japanese *kamikaze* pilots.*(b) Soekarno's visit to Celebes (April 29, 1945).*(a) Japanese Emperor's birthday in Borneo.*(g) Inauguration of *Kenkoku Gakuin* [Institute of Nation Building].*(f)

Nanpō Hōdō 43 (August, 1945)	Mass meeting in Celebes *(g) Coronation ceremony of Prince of Solo *(a) Our fatherland achieves more prosperity*(d)
Nanpō Hōdō 43 Extra (never released)	Granting of the formation of Committee for Preparation of Independence *(a)

The following are the items from *Dai Tōa Nyūsu* which the author has seen at RVD in The Hague.

Dai Tōa Nyūsu 38	Speech by the representative of students from Southeast Asia (*Nanpō Tokubetsu Ryūgakusei*). Burmese monks learning Japanese. Production increase in China. Anti-espionage Movement in Celebes.
Dai Tōa Nyūsu 45	A get-together with German navy sailors. Southeast Asian students arrive in Japan. Visit of Prime Minister Tōjō to Singapore.
Dai Tōa Nyūsu 47	Graduation ceremony at Officer Training School in Burma. Fighting at Yangtze river.
Dai Tōa Nyūsu 50	Women in Japan. Anti-air raid defense training in Japan. Enemy plane was shot down.
Dai Tōa Nyūsu 56	Premier Tōjō's speech at the 85th Diet in Japan. Wake up Asian people! Celebration of *Meijisetsu* [Birthday of the Meiji Emperor] in Japan. Ba Maw inspects Burma Independence Army. Youth Meeting at Tien-an-men in Beijing. Japanese navy.
Dai Tōa Nyūsu 61	Anti-air raid defense training: In Thailand. In Burma. In Japan. In Kwantung, China.
Dai Tōa Nyūsu	Foundation of a monument in Singapore commemorating the Dead Soldiers on September 10, 1942. Mass meeting of 3-A Movement in Jakarta. Sailor Training School at Makassar. Visit of Marshal Terauchi to Java in January, 1944.
Dai Tōa Nyūsu (October, 1942)	One-day experience at Tank Training School. Painting Exhibition in Japan. New-born Manila. Japanese submarine.

The following news items are known through archives, but it is not known where and in which news films they were reported.

"Birth of a New Java."
Monument commemorating the Japanese landing operation in Klagen, East Java.
Moslem meeting in Jakarta.
Opening of the Japan Club.
Meeting for construction of a New Java.
Dedication of a monument (a fountain) commemorating the inauguration of New Java (Yogyakarta).
Japanese Commander-in-chief and *Gunseikan* tour Java.

Sources:

K. A. de Weerd, "Description and text of six cinematographical films (newsreels), I–VI, which were made by the Japanese during the Japanese occupation of the East-Indies, and were seized by the Allied Forces on entering Batavia in September 1945" (unpublished document at Rijksinstituut voor Oorlogsdocumentatie No. 2760).
Collection of news films seen by the writer at Rijksvoorlichiting Dienst in The Hague.

3 Imperial Japan's Cultural Program in Thailand
E. Bruce Reynolds

INTRODUCTION

Although discussion of Japanese cultural activities in the areas of Southeast Asia colonized by the Western powers might logically begin with the arrival of Japanese troops during the Greater East Asia War, examination of Japan's cultural policy toward Thailand demands a longer perspective. The modern relationship between these two independent states dates from 1887 and has long had a cultural component, but this study specifically focuses on three distinct phases of cultural relations between Japan and Thailand: 1933 to 1941, 1942 to early 1943, and May, 1943 to the end of the war. During the first period the Japanese gradually intensified efforts to expand their cultural influence in Thailand. The war's early months saw the formulation of ambitious Japanese plans to shape cultural development there. However, during the last two years of the war the program lost its impetus due to resistance from the Thai authorities and negative developments on the battlefield which forced modification of Japanese policy.

JAPANESE CULTURAL OPERATIONS, 1933–41

Two events in the watershed year of 1933 brought an end to a period of stagnation in Japanese–Thai relations and initiated a phase of increased contacts in all realms. First, Thailand abstained when the League of Nations voted in February 1933 to accept the Lytton Commission Report, which criticized Japan's seizure of Manchuria. Then in June 1933 the younger members of the group which a year previously had overturned Thailand's absolute monarchy staged a second *coup d'état*. While the Thai abstention reflected a desire to stay out of the developing Sino-Japanese quarrel and to avoid gratuitous offense to a stronger Asian power, the Japanese chose to portray it as a brave act of pan-Asian solidarity and were effusive in their praise of Thailand. In the wake of this Japanese display of friendship for their country, the *coup* leaders, fearful of British or British–French intervention to restore their monarchist enemies, asked Minister Yatabe Yasukichi for Japanese support. Although Yatabe could not promise action to prevent European intervention – which as it turned out was not in the cards anyway – he offered welcome encouragement to the new regime.[1]

Subsequent trends further intensified ties between the two countries. Thailand assumed new importance in Japanese eyes as Tokyo's relations with the Western powers worsened, particularly after the outbreak of war with China in July, 1937. Not only did the isolated Japanese need friends wherever they might be found, but Thailand could supply rice, rubber, and tin if these commodities became unavailable from colonial areas, and could provide a vital strategic platform for launching an attack on British possessions in Southeast Asia. For the Thai, meanwhile, playing both sides of the developing rivalry between the Japanese and the British afforded rare diplomatic leverage. Also, some Thai leaders desired to emulate Japan's modernization techniques, particularly in the military realm. Japan's powerful armed forces – not to mention her links with the widely admired European fascist regimes – impressed many members of the increasingly dominant Thai military clique.[2]

In cultural affairs, the Japanese employed largely unexceptional devices in attempting to boost their nation's prestige in Thailand. These included the exchange of various delegations and exhibitions, the dispatch of Japanese experts to Thailand, and the promotion of Japan as a convenient location for higher education and technical training. The special aspect of the program lay in the Japanese stress on Asian linkages, including the claim that the two peoples were "blood relatives." The Japanese also emphasized a common Buddhist heritage, bilateral contacts in the early 17th century – when Japanese traders formed a community in Ayutthaya and the celebrated Japanese adventurer Yamada Nagamasa gained a high post at the Thai court – and the difficulties created for both countries by the advance of Western imperialism.[3]

However, this "pan-Asian" appeal notwithstanding, the Japanese did not make easy headway in the cultural realm. Only the flimsiest of evidence supported the "blood relatives" theory; Thailand's Therevada and Japan's Mahayana Buddhism offered little more basis for accord than Italian Catholicism and British Protestantism; the Thai could justifiably regard Yamada and his peers as nothing more than troublesome meddlers; and Thai leaders were certainly astute enough to recognize that Japan had long since joined the circle of imperial powers, a reality underscored by her long exercise of extra-territorial rights in Thailand.[4] Also, the Japanese, who liked to view other Asians as "younger brothers" in the Confucian sense of the term, ran up against a Thai unwillingness to accept unequal status. Since the Japanese commonly viewed this attitude as simple, unjustified national conceit on the Thai side, Yanagisawa Ken, director of Japanese cultural activities in Bangkok from 1942, showed unusual charity in ascribing it to "a strong sense of self-respect and self-confidence" which had limited Thai interest in foreign cultures for several centuries.[5]

Moreover, by their own admission the Japanese were late starters in promoting their culture in Thailand and despite Yanagisawa's perception of limited Thai interest in foreign cultures, the currents of Western influence ran deep in Bangkok.[6] Most influential Thais had studied in Europe, or in schools founded in Thailand by Westerners, and viewed the West as the wellspring of modernity. Even though the new Thai leaders hoped to increase their country's economic and political autonomy by reducing British influence and were quite willing to use the Japanese "card" to that end, their political ideas – whether inclined toward democracy or dictatorship – had been and continued to be shaped primarily by European models. They were nationalists, not pan-Asianists, and having just eliminated the "evil" of absolute monarchy one can easily imagine their lack of enthusiasm for such emperor-worship-based Japanese slogans as *Hakkō Ichiu* (the eight corners of the world under one roof) and *kōdō gaikō* (Imperial way diplomacy). Additionally, few Thai could speak Japanese and only a handful of Japanese knew Thai, so in personal contacts the Japanese were usually forced to deliver their "pan-Asian" message through the medium of Western languages.[7]

As the Japanese believed that the Thai generally failed to appreciate the scope of Japan's achievements,[8] they hoped that visits to Tokyo would convince influential officials that Japan offered the most appropriate model for Thailand's development. An early example of such a public relations effort came in 1934 when a group of hand-picked officials were sent on an expenses-paid junket to Japan, ostensibly to attend a Buddhist conference. The excursion, in fact designed to impress the participants with Japan's power and technological prowess, might be judged in retrospect as having produced rather mixed results. Two of the participants, Phraya Sarittikan

Banchong and Luang Chawaengsak Songkhram later played active roles in the Thailand–Japan Association, but one, Wilat Osathanon, came to be viewed as an enemy and was forced out of his position as Director of the Publicity Department at the beginning of the war at Japanese insistence. Two others, Sanguan Tularak and Chalo Srisarakon, later became key figures in the anti-Japanese Free Thai underground.[9]

Delegations more genuinely cultural in orientation were also exchanged by the two countries in the years leading up to the war, most notably a Thai musical and dance troupe which toured the Japanese Empire in 1935 and a similar Japanese group which visited Bangkok in 1937. The Thai group, numbering 35 members and led by the wife of Fine Arts Department Chief Luang Wichit Wathakan, spent 49 days in Japan, Korea, and Manchukuo. Yanagisawa, then head of the Foreign Ministry's Cultural Affairs Department, later recalled that he considered the tour's value in promoting Japanese–Thai relations well worth the 3,000 yen in red ink it produced. The Japanese troupe of 13 members, led by Professor Yoshida Seifu, spent a week in Bangkok.[10]

Although junkets to Japan and cultural exchanges were seen as short-term devices for increasing their nation's influence, the Japanese realized that education represented the best long-term means for overcoming their Western rivals' advantage in the cultural realm. However, the greater prestige attached to a Western education impeded efforts to lure Thai students to Japan, as the most able among them wished to study in Europe or the United States. While Japan could supply advanced education at a lower cost for the budget-minded student, the fact that few Thai students were proficient in the Japanese language posed an additional stumbling block. Schools in the Philippines offered a similar price advantage and instruction in the widely studied English language.[11]

While foreign students in Japan could be taught in English, in the Japanese view this seemed a short-sighted, stop-gap solution. As one educator noted, what would the Thai think of the efficacy of Japanese education if a returned student proved incapable of the commonly expected task of translating a document written in the language of the country where he had received his training?[12] Accordingly, it seemed better to meet the problem head on and insure that students achieved a good standard of language instruction. To facilitate this, the Japanese established a Bangkok language school, an institution which became the cornerstone of the prewar Japanese cultural program.

The first language program had begun in 1937 under the sponsorship of the local Japanese Association, but in 1938 the Cultural Affairs Department of the Foreign Ministry took over the effort, entrusting organization of the school to Matsunomiya Ichitada, previously the director of a language program in the United States. The school opened under the auspices of a Japan-Thailand Cultural Research Institute, which had the broader mission of stimulating Thai interest in Japan. Located in a two-story building at 21 Na Phra Lan Road, near the Chao Phraya River and opposite the Grand Palace, the Institute officially opened on November 22, 1938 with a ceremony attended by various dignitaries, including a member of the Thai Council of Regents. Later the organization changed its name to the Japan–Thailand Cultural Research Institute to give it an air of cooperative endeavor and assuage Thai nationalistic sentiments. Among other activities, the institute housed a small library of books on Japan and loaned out Japanese phonograph records.[13]

Initial plans called for two courses of language study – a three-year course of two hours study per day and a special course of four hours per day for one year. The staff included both Japanese native speakers and Thai with Japanese language training, but the program called for the sole use of the Japanese language in the classroom. Although 316 applications came in, the limited availability of classrooms and instructors permitted the acceptance of only 158.[14]

The students, predominantly young males, many of them government employees, were motivated primarily by a belief that knowledge of Japanese might further their careers, a point frankly acknowledged by Yanagisawa. He judged that 99 of every 100 students were enrolled for strictly pragmatic reasons, but he expressed no great concern over this, pointing out that knowledge of the language would naturally stimulate interest in things Japanese.[15]

The number of applications also reflected the sad state of Japanese language instruction in Bangkok at the time. The nation's oldest and most prestigious institution of higher learning, Chulalongkorn University, would not add a Japanese language course until 1942, and then in the evening program. When the Japanese began their own course, only the Thai government "Foreign Language School" offered Japanese. Hoshida Shingo, the first chief of the Japanese Cultural Research Institute, described this institution as merely a middle school with a language course during the last two years and noted that, without any prompting, its students abandoned it to join the new Japanese program.[16]

Not surprisingly, many students found the language course difficult and dropped out, leaving enrollment at 60 in March, 1939. A short-lived government policy tilt toward Japan in mid-1939 probably influenced an increase to 124 during the May to August term, but the numbers dropped off to 86 by the end of the next term in December, 1939 and stood at 77 in March, 1940.[17] A press report estimated the spring 1941 enrollment at 150, an increase certainly linked to Thailand's reliance on Japanese mediation of her border war with French Indo-China. The numbers naturally increased further when the arrival of Japanese forces in December, 1941 created an urgent demand for interpreters. A Japanese news story claimed that in April 1942 enrollment had surpassed 600, while a press report of November 1942 set the figure at about 400.[18] However, when the first three-year class held its graduation ceremony in March, 1942, a newspaper picture showed only 12 men and seven women graduates, a clear indication that very few students stayed the course.[19]

In the short-term, the effort to attract Thai students to Japan, backed by some scholarships and an increasingly organized program to provide accommodations, achieved considerable success. Two Western writers have suggested that as many as 200 Thai were studying in Japan in the late 1930s, but that estimate seems on the high side as several Japanese and Thai sources place the number at about 150, still second only to the approximately 200 students who were studying in the Philippines in the immediate prewar period.[20]

A NEW CULTURE FOR GREATER EAST ASIA, 1942–1943

The early months of 1942 were heady ones for the Japanese as their forces rolled through Southeast Asia and the South Pacific. A huge empire had fallen into their hands and "experts" emerged with various theories on the best way to consolidate Japanese control over the area's peoples and resources. Already, the perplexing problems posed by their attempt to establish hegemony over China had led the Japanese to adopt culturally oriented strategies as an adjunct to the application of military power.[21] Although their efforts had proved less than successful even in a region where a common form of written language provided something of a common denominator, rather than fundamentally reassessing their focus when the New Order in East Asia evolved into the large and heterogeneous Greater East Asia

Co-Prosperity Sphere, the Japanese made little modification in their cultural strategy.

The basic theme of Japan's cultural policy had become the creation of a "new East Asian culture" which would fuse traditional Asian values with modern technology and eventually provide the basis for a new "world culture." Ostensibly the "new" culture would evolve from joint research efforts by scholars of all Asian nations to establish its elements and to assess the aspects of local cultures worth preserving. However, Japanese were quick to point out that their nation, the "natural leader of Asia," remained the "repository" of the best of Asian culture – from both the Sinitic and Indic cultures – and had become the most successful assimilator of the positive elements of Western civilization. Japan, the argument went, had managed the remarkable feat of maintaining her own national essence while at the same time synthesizing the best elements of both Eastern and Western cultures.[22] In practice, therefore, creating a "new East Asian culture" actually meant the Japanization of East Asia as the first step toward Japanization of the world.

As its Foreign Ministry critics have noted, the Japanese strategy which led to the September 1942 decision to create the Greater East Asia Ministry amounted to applying the general mode of operations in occupied China to the rest of Greater East Asia.[23] The Japanese leadership spelled out this scheme as it applied to Thailand in a policy paper adopted by the Liaison Conference of September 29, 1942. This document declared Japan's intention to guide Thailand in every aspect of economic and financial affairs, including control of the nation's transportation system, industrial development, and trade.[24] Its counterpart in the cultural realm, a bilateral treaty drafted by the Japanese during the summer of 1942, aimed at facilitating the creation of the desired "new East Asian culture."[25]

However, despite the easy theorizing of "cultural experts," Japanese familiar with the situation in Thailand knew that cultural operations there would run into serious obstacles. The Thai, proud of their long record of national independence, were especially sensitive to the gap between the cooperative rhetoric of co-prosperity and the reality of Japanese domination. Moreover, Thai leader Field Marshal Phibun Songkhram had built his popularity on a strident nationalistic appeal and had already inaugurated his own cultural development program.

Before opening negotiations on the cultural treaty, the Foreign

Ministry had dispatched Yanagisawa to Bangkok to arrange for the expansion of the existing Japanese cultural institute, which he was expected subsequently to direct. Yanagisawa, who had spent most of his career serving in European posts and had once been chargé d'affaires in Lisbon, had left the Foreign Ministry during the stormy ministerial tenure of Matsuoka Yōsuke when his hopes for appointment to a higher diplomatic post were frustrated. As a published author and a former head of the Cultural Affairs Department in the mid-1930s, Yanagisawa felt he had been typecast as a cultural affairs specialist.

Given the fact that Yanagisawa had strong views on the complexities and limitations of cultural diplomacy and had to be coaxed out of retirement to take the Bangkok assignment, his appointment suggests that Foreign Ministry officials understood that the job demanded an experienced individual with few illusions about what might be accomplished. Even in the midst of the war Yanagisawa dared to make public his doubts about ill-thought-out, army-backed cultural schemes, noting that he considered the Thailand assignment primarily because of the Foreign Ministry's relatively strong foothold in that country. He also indicated that despite the reassuring presence in Bangkok of a former superior and a predecessor as chief of the Cultural Affairs Department, Ambassador Tsubokami Teiji, he undertook the initial mission reluctantly and without making a firm commitment to accept the directorship of an expanded cultural institute.[26]

Despite a bright facade of accord and friendship, Yanagisawa found Japanese–Thai relations strained when he arrived in Bangkok on May 6, 1942. Although the Thai had allied with Japan, they had resented the entry of Japanese forces into their country in December, 1941 and were upset about the economic dislocation caused by the war, the recent forced devaluation of the Thai currency, and the high-handed attitude displayed by the Japanese army. Yanagisawa's talks proved unexpectedly difficult and the sensitivity of his mission is reflected by the absence of any publicity about it in the Japanese-controlled English language daily, the *Bangkok Times*.[27]

Clearly, Prime Minister Phibun and other Thai leaders perceived the expansion of the cultural institute as the opening wedge in a campaign to further Japanese control and domination. Accordingly, Phibun's postwar claim that he pushed his own controversial wartime cultural program – which impacted many phases of social life and even included dress codes – to stave off Japanese influence is in large part true, despite the fact that the key elements of the program were in place before December, 1941 and reflected priorities and values unconnected with the Japanese presence.[28] Several actions taken during May and June, 1942 make clear that Phibun considered the intensification of his own cultural program the best means of "fighting fire with fire."

For instance, Phibun claimed that he undertook a much-criticized effort to reform the Thai language in order to provide a pretext to counter demands for the introduction of the Japanese language into Thai schools.[29] Skeptics might point out that Phibun's wife provided a more plausible explanation when she indicated years later that the program's main purpose was to encourage literacy by simplifying the language[30] and it is not improbable that Phibun hoped that as sponsor of this reform he might be seen as a latter day King Ramkhamheng, the revered monarch who reputedly developed the Thai written language. Nonetheless, the language reforms were hammered out, in apparent haste, in the very midst of Yanagisawa's negotiations. Phibun pointedly remarked at the reform committee's initial meeting on May 23, 1942: "Some nations have lost their independence because they have failed to promote their language."[31]

A parallel push to promote other aspects of the government's cultural program through the medium of the nightly broadcast dialogue between Radio Thailand announcers "Nai Man" and "Nai Khong" also reflected Thai unease about Japanese intentions. Phibun valued this propaganda forum so highly that he often provided or modified the program's scripts himself, so it can be assumed that the announcers were directly expressing his views when on the June 2 program they emphasized that "culture indeed is the soul of the nation, and when facing a crisis we have to be more attentive to culture to see to it that it is indeed deeply implanted in the minds of our compatriots."[32] On the program of June 5, 1942, the two exhorted Thai women to wear skirts and urged the people in general to use European-style eating utensils and to sleep on beds, warning that if the Thai were seen as lacking civilization, this would provide a pretext for outsiders to civilize them. That, they suggested, could force the nation into slavery.[33] A week later, a script contained the blunt remark that the country would live on despite military defeat if its culture remained strong. The broadcasters went on to describe culture as "the foundation of the nation's survival" and language as "the sign of the country's independence . . ."[34]

Eventually, on June 16, Yanagisawa reached an acceptable

compromise agreement which attempted to allay Thai fears by stressing reciprocity and mutual efforts in the cultural field.[35] He then returned to Tokyo to drum up support for cultural undertakings in Thailand. Yanagisawa would later write that he neither liked life in Bangkok nor saw any great prospect for success, but decided to accept the directorship of the expanded cultural institute out of a sense of patriotic duty. However, pride also influenced his decision as Yanagisawa felt that his diplomatic abilities and his previous strenuous efforts as chief of the Cultural Affairs Department had been insufficiently appreciated and clearly he now relished being called to step into a breach.[36] He revealed much about his own self-image and his desire to formulate his own program when he later wrote: "We must not lapse into a centralization of power culturally. In choosing those to do the work, we must avoid abstract theorists and choose realistic people who truly understand the circumstances. These realists should receive liberal authority."[37]

Drawing upon his literary skills, Yanagisawa sent forth a steady stream of articles expounding his views on the propagation of Japanese culture. Originally published by major Japanese newspapers and journals, in 1943 they were reissued in a 210-page volume entitled *Taikoku to Nippon Bunka* (Thailand and Japanese Culture). In his essays Yanagisawa paid ample lip service to the cherished goal of developing a "new Asian culture" and expressed support for the popular view that Japan's synthesizing ability guaranteed her the leading role in the process,[38] but he also warned his readers of the difficulties ahead. He expressed considerable understanding of the Thai position, did not hesitate to point out Japanese shortcomings, and, while speaking of new departures, actually advocated quite traditional programs. These, he frankly acknowledged, promised no quick results.[39]

Coercion must be eschewed, Yanagisawa cautioned, lest the Thai, like the Chinese, come to see Japanese activities as "cultural aggression." The Japanese also had to recognize, he added, that in the Southern region Japan lacked the cultural links which existed with Korea, Taiwan, Manchuria, and China. He wisely warned that efforts to utilize Buddhism as a common denominator risked generating conflict due to divergent practices in the two countries and sectarianism in Japan. Accordingly, Yanagisawa argued that the new Bangkok cultural center should have a major research component so that the local culture might be studied carefully. "We must face up squarely to evaluating the merits and demerits of the old forms of rule and avoid prejudice," he warned.[40]

Struck, as other astute Japanese observers were, by the parallels between Meiji Japan and post-1933 Thailand, Yanagisawa recognized the importance of accommodating Thai nationalist sentiment. He acknowledged that the Thai might be unduly conceited in praising the merits of their native culture, but pointed out that the Japanese also often displayed overweening national pride. Recalling that Germany had served as an important model for Japan during the Meiji period, he suggested that Japan might best help Thailand by assuming a similar role.[41]

Yanagisawa also became one of the first to promote a concept which should have been obvious to the Japanese, but which the highest authorities seemed slow in recognizing: that independent Thailand could serve as a useful model for other Southeast Asian states and that Japan's relationship with Thailand should be developed with that idea in mind. He added that since Japan's demands on Thailand in other realms were heavy during the wartime emergency, in the cultural field, where immediate results were less critical, the Japanese would have to show particular consideration for Thai sensibilities.[42]

Noting the deep influence of European culture on the Thai ruling class, Yanagisawa admitted that the common bond provided by his long experience in Europe amounted to his greatest asset in striking up relationships with Thai counterparts. He defended use of this tactic, explaining that he would later shift the topic of conversation to a common Asian heritage, but he went on to suggest that Japanese propaganda forgo blanket denunciations of democracy and other Western ideas, appraise them more reasonably, and even give credit where due.[43]

In meting out criticism to his countrymen, Yanagisawa expressed admiration for the unselfish work of American missionary doctors in Thailand and noted the absence of any similar humanitarian activity by Japanese. He described the Japanese residents in Thailand as rather individualistic and oblivious to the excellence of their own native culture. He charged that rather than engaging in constructive or invigorating activities, they whiled away their spare time in Chinese restaurants and dance halls. The former British Club boasted eight tennis courts, Yanagisawa pointed out, while the Japanese Association had only a billiard table or two. He lamented the lack of a good quality Japanese restaurant or tea shop in the Thai capital, as well as the poor facilities of the primary school established for Japanese children. Finally, he unfavorably contrasted the spiritless Japanese residents with the dedicated soldiers who had borne great hardships in the Burma campaign.[44]

Yanagisawa viewed the scientific and medical fields as areas of particular opportunity for Japanese initiative. The fact that during his first visit to Bangkok he himself had been confined to his room in the Oriental Hotel for more than a week with dengue fever no doubt reinforced his strong interest in promoting research on tropical diseases.[45]

According to Yanagisawa's plan, the expanded cultural institute would focus special attention on making Japanese media materials accessible to the Thai public. The provision of Japanese films seemed especially imperative, as, when Yanagisawa arrived in Bangkok, the two major Thai theaters were still recycling the largely Hollywood-produced films on hand when the war began.[46]

Given his mainstream background, it is hardly surprising that Yanagisawa, like his predecessors, placed strong emphasis on the importance of educating Thai youth and urged the expansion of the Japanese language program by the establishment of new branch schools in Bangkok, Chiang Mai, Songkhla, and Khorat, as well as through lessons by radio. He believed the number of language students could easily be doubled from the current level and favored establishing Japanese-style primary and middle schools to prepare Thai students desiring higher education in Japan. Once the students were ready, he suggested that instead of sending them to Tokyo they be placed in institutions in Taiwan and Kyushu where they would have an easier climatic adjustment. He also recognized the value of networking, stressing the need to encourage continued contacts with and among returned students. Finally, foreshadowing a postwar American development concept, he suggested that the Japanese educational program aim at encouraging the emergence of a middle class in Thai society.[47]

While Yanagisawa was formulating his plans, the Thai suggested establishing a joint Japanese–Thai cultural hall in the Wang Khun Phrom Palace on the banks of Bangkok's Chao Phraya River.[48] However, this July, 1942 proposal, clearly designed to forestall unilateral action by the Japanese side, was never implemented and the Thai decided to utilize the palace for their own National Culture Institute. Meanwhile, the Japanese established a separate, interim facility and Yanagisawa began promoting the construction of a grand new cultural center. In May, 1943 Yanagisawa spoke of a government allocation of 2,800,000 yen for this center and announced his intention to gather sufficient Japanese public donations within two months to meet the construction costs, an estimated three million yen according to one press report. This project enjoyed support at the highest level, as the Emperor's brother, Prince Takamatsu, was numbered among its patrons.[49]

Eventually the Japanese plan called for a cultural center containing two movie/lecture halls (one seating 1,000, the other 500), an industrial culture hall, a physical training room, a fine arts gallery, a room for photo displays, a dining hall, a tea room, and offices. A Buddhist hall would have a five-story pagoda modeled after the historic structure at Hōryūji Temple in Nara and constructed, like the rest of the buildings, of Thai teak. The compound, near Lumphini Park, would include a garden, a pool, tennis courts, an open air music hall, and perhaps even an ice skating facility. As a special feature, the center would house a library of 10,000 books to be provided by Japan's Society for International Cultural Relations, an organization headed by such luminaries as Marquis Tokugawa Yorisada and Count Kuroda Kiyoshi.[50]

As the Japanese formulated plans for the new cultural center, Japanese Foreign Minister Tani Masayuki and Thai Ambassador Direk Chayanam initialled the previously mentioned Japanese-drafted cultural treaty in Tokyo on October 28, 1942. The two sides exchanged ratifications in Bangkok on December 21 to commemorate the first anniversary of the alliance between the two countries. The cultural pact committed both countries to facilitating "institutions contributing to the promotion of cultural relations" and providing "every possible facility" for such purposes. Avenues of cultural exchange mentioned in addition to the cultural center included: cultural conferences, the establishment of chairs of culture in national universities, the exchange of experts and students, subsidies for culture-related publications, and exchanges of motion pictures and radio broadcasts.[51]

Indeed, specific student exchanges were already underway during 1942. The Japanese side particularly publicized the April, 1942 arrival in Tokyo of M. R. Wibun Warawan and Prasat Panyarachun, as attracting these two 19-year-old students to Japan seemed a major achievement. The former's father, Prince Wan Waithayakon, wielded considerable influence as advisor to the Thai foreign

Ministry, while the latter was a son of Prichanusat Panyarachun, head of the Thai Commercial Publishing Company and president of the Thai Press Association. In an initial interview M. R. Wibun stated their intention to stay for seven years in order to study at the prestigious Peers School and at Tokyo University.[52] Also in 1942, the Thai Ministry of Education dispatched four boys and two girls in their mid-teens to begin an eight-year course of study in Japan. Meanwhile, three Japanese academics were sent to Thailand to study language, history, and tropical medicine, respectively, for three years.[53]

Moreover, in an effort to promote educational exchange on a larger scale, the Japanese unveiled a plan to bring a group of 150 Thai students to Japan to board for approximately one year for language and cultural studies at a new, special school, Japan–Thailand Gakuin, which was to be built in Tokyo's Setagaya ward. After completion of the regular course the students would get a further taste of life in Japan through a home-stay with an "upper-class" family, after which they might seek entrance into regular Japanese educational institutions. A former prime minister, General Hayashi Senjūrō, served as titular head of this project which, according to press reports, dated from 1940. Yatabe, the former minister to Thailand, succeeded Hayashi when the General died on February 4, 1943. Newspaper accounts indicated that construction activities were underway during the spring of 1943.[54]

THE DREAM FADES AWAY, 1943–1945

Phairot Chayanam, director of the Thai Publicity Department during the war, described the cultural exchange agreement in retrospect as "not very effective" and recalled Yanagisawa's plans for the cultural center as a "dream" which never really materialized.[55] In fact, Japan's program in general and Yanagisawa's project in particular did not die suddenly, but instead withered on the vine in the face of Thai resistance and a shift in Japanese political strategy forced by the deteriorating war situation.

As previously explained, concern about Japanese cultural domination inspired Thai resistance. Thai Justice Minister Luang Thamrong Nawasawat acknowledged Thai apprehensions in a March 25, 1943 speech at a Chulalongkorn University assembly fêting the bilateral cultural treaty of the previous year. In remarks clearly intended both to reassure his countrymen and send a message to the Japanese in the audience, Thamrong admitted that "a great majority of the people" feared that the pact would force changes in Thai traditions and religious practices. However, he stated that this would not occur because of the reciprocal nature of the treaty. The pact, he explained

> avers that the two countries will respect the cultural aspects of the other, meaning that Thai culture will belong to the Thai people and Japanese culture to the Japanese people . . . the Thai people should endeavor to gain an insight into Japanese culture while the Japanese people would, on the other hand, endeavor to acquire a knowledge of Thailand.[56]

Such stress on reciprocity afforded the Thai a means of asserting their own cultural identity and underscoring their desire for equal status in relations with the Japanese. For example, Phairot told the press at the end of July 1942 that Thailand might "establish cultural institutions in foreign countries for the purpose of mutual cooperation in cultural matters," an indication that the Thai had ambitions of matching the Japanese overseas cultural promotion effort with one of their own.[57] Although no permanent Thai cultural center materialized in Tokyo, Ambassador Direk attempted to reach the Japanese public with a book comprised of speeches on his homeland and his successor, Luang Wichit, added eight "cultural experts" (two musicians, two singers, two dancers, a painter, and a scholar) to his entourage in Tokyo.[58]

Also, Phibun's decision to organize a National Culture Institute in September 1942, at the time the Japanese were pressing for conclusion of the cultural treaty, further demonstrated his determination to resist Japanese cultural domination.[59] In his speech at the Institute's dedication ceremony Phibun stated: "No country in the world can afford to shut itself to other countries, and in order to communicate with other countries we must be equal to them culturally, so as to preserve our national honor."[60] More than a year later, writing under a pseudonym, Phibun reminded his countrymen that the current hostilties included a "war of culture" and to win the people "had to uphold their own culture and see that it is not superseded by foreign elements."[61] Phibun, as Phairot later explained it, "wanted to show the Japanese that we had our own civilization."[62]

The official response to comments in an October 1942 press

interview by Byōdō Tsūshō, director of the existing Japanese–Thai Cultural Research Center, also reflected Thai sensitivity on the culture issue. Byōdō, a Buddhist studies expert who had been in Bangkok for two years, remarked that no traces of original Thai civilization remained and that most elements of Thai culture had been imported from India. After the story circulated, Byōdō and Embassy Information Chief Iwata Reitetsu were called on the carpet by a section chief in the Thai Publicity Department and pointedly reminded of the similar derivative nature of Japanese culture.[63]

Although they remained generally unwilling to regard Thai culture in any sense equivalent to their own, the Japanese did get the message that the Thai were attempting to convey. In a report to Tokyo in mid-1943 Ambassador Tsubokami acknowledged that Phibun's motives for the stepped-up cultural program included both a desire to deflect public discontent about wartime austerity and to elevate the "low tone" of Thai culture in order to counter the "stimulus for the advance of Japanese culture" provided by the cultural pact.[64] By the time of his departure in May 1943, Byōdō, who had come to consider the Thai "treacherous" and "superficial," had decided that prospects for successfully propagating Japanese culture seemed dim indeed, despite Yanagisawa's enthusiasm and optimism.[65]

In fact, May 1943 marked a major turn in Japanese policy which made the great cultural schemes of the previous year obsolete. As the Americans began their counterattack in the Pacific it became clear that Japan could not count on Japanizing all of Greater East Asia and that the deteriorating war situation demanded measures to win the immediate cooperation of the peoples of the region. New Foreign Minister Shigemitsu Mamoru, with the support of Prime Minister Tōjō Hideki, planned to achieve this result by offering such inducements as independence to Burma and the Philippines, the return of "lost territories" to Thailand, and the convening of a Greater East Asia Conference to affirm new and less selfish war aims.[66] With the outcome of the war hanging in the balance, it seemed less sensible than ever to irritate the Thai with cultural initiatives.

Nonetheless, Yanagisawa gamely kept up his publicity and fund-raising campaign for the new cultural center well into 1944, even arranging a competition among Japanese architects to develop the best design. An artist's conception of the winning entry appeared in the Japanese press on March 12, 1944. In late May of that year Yanagisawa, Prince Takamatsu, and other dignitaries gathered at the

Peers Club in Tokyo for a Thai cultural program, including a talk by the architect in charge of the cultural center's construction and the presentation of the design prizes.[67]

However, despite the fact that plans had called for a grand opening on December 8, 1944 – to coincide with the third anniversary of the beginning of the war and the annual Thai Constitution Festival, – the cultural center never advanced past the drawing board.[68] All along, the project had received more publicity in Japan than in Bangkok, but after May, 1944 references to it vanished even from the pages of the *Nippon Times*, the English-language mounthpiece of the Foreign Ministry.[69] Significantly, when the Japanese leadership drew up new guidelines for policy toward Thailand in September, 1944, these had nothing to say about propagating Japanese culture.[70]

Student exchange efforts also foundered as transportation between Japan and Thailand became increasingly perilous. The Japan–Thailand Gakuin plan apparently never materialized and the Japanese were embarrassed when M. R. Wibun and Prasat, the two most prominent Thai students in Japan, chose to leave before the end of 1943. Recalling the situation years later, Prasat indicated that frustration with the Japanese language was the overriding factor in the decision to return home.[71]

Under such unfavorable circumstances, Yanagisawa's accomplishments in Thailand were understandably modest. He did open a new "Culture House" on Petchburi Road (at the site currently occupied by the Indonesian embassy) adjacent to the residence then occupied by the Japanese ambassador. This new facility contained a library of books on Japanese subjects, served as the site for exhibitions, and sponsored at least two essay contests. Operations were disrupted when diplomatic and consular officers were transferred to "Culture House" after Allied bombs destroyed the Japanese Embassy in February, 1944, but the officials were subsequently relocated to the more spacious former British Legation on Ploenchit Road.[72] The Japanese Language School, meanwhile, continued to operate at its previous location, but also established a branch on Suriwong Road, a location convenient for Thai employees of Japanese companies.[73]

CONCLUSION

As they frankly acknowledged, the Japanese were late starters in attempting to expand their cultural influence in Thailand. At the end of the war, as the Thai scrambled to disassociate themselves from their erstwhile allies and to demonstrate full sympathy for the Anglo-American victors, all of Japan's cultural efforts seemed to have come to naught. Yet, in the late 1930s they had devised a sensible long-term strategy, centered on the Japan–Thailand Cultural Research Institute, to promote interest in Japan and to assist students wishing to study there. The postwar American success in implementing a similar scheme through the American University Alumni Association (AUAA) in Bangkok testifies to the viability and potential impact of such an approach. Although they were handicapped by the extreme nationalistic conceit common to many Japanese of the time and the fact that few Thai were familiar with their language, had their program been directed under peacetime conditions by a prudent man like Yanagisawa, surely the Japanese would have continued to make gradual headway in expanding their country's cultural influence.

Ironically, while Japanese military victories in 1941–42 cleared their Anglo-Americans rivals from Southeast Asia and inspired a spate of new schemes to spread Japanese culture throughout the region, military triumph created circumstances in Thailand which proved less than conducive to Japan's cultural initiatives. The Imperial Army's forceful entry into the country sparked nationalistic resentment and high-handed Japanese behavior fanned concerns about permanent subordination to the invaders. This led Prime Minister Phibun to intensify his own cultural program in a thinly-disguised effort to counter Japanese influence. Faced with such resistance and a deteriorating war situation, the Japanese logically chose to utilize their reduced leverage to induce Thai cooperation on vital military matters. Consequently, the propagation of their culture slipped to the bottom of the Japanese agenda and the grandiose plans of 1942 were relegated to the back shelf.

Notes and References

1. For fuller treatment, see: Edward Thadeus Flood, "Japan's Relations With Thailand: 1928–41," unpublished Ph.D. dissertation, University of Washington, 1967, pp. 52–65 (hereafter cited as: Flood dissertation) and Edward Bruce Reynolds, "Ambivalent Allies: Japan and Thailand 1941–1945," unpublished Ph.D. dissertation, University of Hawaii, 1988, pp. 40–3 (hereafter cited as: Reynolds dissertation).

2. Reynolds dissertation, pp. 43–64.
3. Reynolds dissertation, pp. 53–5 and Flood dissertation, pp. 102–5, 179–82.
4. Reynolds dissertation, pp. 64–74.
5. Byōdō Tsūshō and Byōdō Shōshin, *Waga Ya no Nittai Tsūshin* (Our Family Correspondence Between Japan and Thailand) (Tokyo: Indogaku Kenkyūjo, 1979), pp. 77, 131, and Yanagisawa Ken, *Taikoku to Nihon Bunka* (Thailand and Japanese Culture) (Tokyo: Fuji Shobō, 1943), p. 87.
6. For example, the South Manchurian Railway East Asia Economic Research Bureau (Mantetsu Tōa Keizai Chōsakyoku) volume *Shamu Hen* (Siam Volume) (Tokyo: Kaimeidō, 1941 [reprint of 1938 edition]), p. 523, noted: "The white men of various countries . . . from the distant past have been advancing culture in Siam, but Japan, which is close to Siam and is the East's advanced nation, has only recently made progress in this area. Moreover, this work is insignificant and lacking in spirit."
7. Reynolds dissertation, pp. 64–73. Hoshida Shingo, the first director of the Japan–Thailand Cultural Research Institute noted in "Taikoku ni okeru Nihongo" (The Japanese Language in Thailand"), *Shin Ajia*, January, 1942, p. 45, that the practice of using English for Japanese–Thai communication had become so ingrained that Japanese businessmen sometimes spoke in English even to those Thai employees who understood Japanese. A lack of English language facility sometimes complicated matters. In his autobiography *Gaikōkan no Isshō* (The Life of a Diplomat) (Tokyo: Chūo-Kōronsha, 1966 [reprint edition]), pp. 286–87, Ishii Itarō, who served as minister in Bangkok in 1936–37, relates the story of an English lecture by a visiting professor from Tokyo which no one, Ishii included, could comprehend.
8. For example, see the comments in Fukunaka Mataji, *Taikoku-Futsuin to Nihonjin* (Thailand, French Indochina and the Japanese) (Tokyo: Fujokaisha, 1941), p. 170–1.
9. Flood dissertation, pp. 103–4 and *Bangkok Times Weekly Mail*, May 22 and September 7, 1934.
10. *Siam Chronicle*, April 4, 1937 and *Japan Times and Advertiser* May 6, 1942.
11. Hoshida, "Taikoku ni okeru Nihongo," pp. 44–5; Byōdō and Byōdō, *Waga Ya no Nittai Tsūshin*, p. 105: and Mantetsu Tōa Keizai Chōsakyoku, *Shamu Hen*, p. 523.
12. Hoshida, "Tai ni okeru Nihongo," pp. 44–5.
13. Ibid., pp. 38–40; Hoshida Shingo, "Bankokku Nijūnenmae no Koborebanashi" ("Stories of Bangkok 20 Years Ago") in Taikoku Nihonjinkai (The Thailand Japanese Association), *Sōritsu Gojūshūnen Kinengo* (50th Anniversary Volume) (Tokyo: Shuryūsha, 1963), pp. 76–7; Yanagisawa, *Taikoku to Nihon Bunka*, pp. 83–5; and Byōdō and Byōdō, *Waga Ya no Nittai Tsūshin*, pp. 16–17.
14. Taishitsu Chōsaka (The Thai Room's Research Section), *1939nen Taikoku Seiji Keizai Jōsei* (Political and Economic Conditions in Thailand in 1939) (Tokyo: Taishitsu, 1940), p. 38 and Hoshida, "Taikoku ni okeru Nihongo," p. 43. When Byōdō Tsūshō, a scholar who had studied

in India and was an expert of Buddhism, arrived to head the institute in the latter part of 1940 he found three Thai instructors with reasonably good Japanese language skills: "Min," who had undergone naval training in Japan; "Suthet," a young woman whose brother worked as a Japanese interpreter for the Thai Foreign Ministry; and "Pan," "an older woman who had studied in Japan." In addition, he noted, there were two or three young Thai instructors whose Japanese he described as "faltering." (Byōdō and Byōdō, *Waga Ya no Nittai Tsūshin*, p. 17.)

15. Yanagisawa, *Taikoku to Nihon Bunka*, pp. 87–8. According to Hoshida, "Taikoku ni okeru Nihongo," pp. 41–2, of the 288 students who spent some time in the program during the December, 1938 to March, 1940 period, men outnumbered women 229 to 59 with the bulk of the students (some 200) coming from the 16–25 age group. By occupational background, government employees composed the largest group, totalling at least 108, with 20 each from the Army and the Ministry of Education. Students concurrently enrolled in other regular school programs numbered 63, while 57 students were unemployed middle-school graduates, and 32 enrollees were employed in private businesses. Teacher participants, presumably from both government and private schools, totalled 20, with seven nurses and a Buddhist monk rounding out the student body.

16. Hoshida, "Taikoku ni okeru Nihongo," p. 43. On the Chulalongkorn night school program, see *Bangkok Times*, May 28, 1942.

17. Hoshida, "Taikoku ni okeru Nihongo," p. 41.

18. *Bangkok Times*, April 8, 1942 and *Bangkok Chronicle*, November 11, 1942.

19. *Bangkok Times*, March 23, 1942. The accompanying news story, perhaps in order to avoid drawing attention to the small number of graduates, makes no mention of the size of the graduating class. The Japanese did their best to encourage the dedicated students, as ten were sent on a two-month tour of Japan in the spring of 1941. See: *Bangkok Chronicle*, April 29 and July 1, 1941.

20. Flood dissertation, p. 179 and Virginia Thompson, *Thailand: The New Siam* (New York: MacMillan Co., 1941), p. 135 use the 200 figure. Kenneth P. Landon, *Siam in Transition* (Shanghai: Kelly and Walsh, 1939), p. 111 does also, but in a footnote adds that Thai authorities in Japan put the figure at "about 100." Figures at or around the 150 mark appear in the *Siam Chronicle*, April 4, 1937; the *Japan Times and Advertiser*, November 20, 1940; the *Bangkok Times*, January 19, 1942; and the *Bangkok Chronicle*, July 21, 1942. The number for the Philippines appears in the *Japan Times and Advertiser*, August 1, 1942 and the *Bangkok Chronicle*, August 4, 1942.

21. See, for example: Akira Iriye, *Power and Culture* (Cambridge: Harvard University Press, 1981), pp. 41–3 on the operations of the *Hsin-min Hui* in North China.

22. Examples of this sort of theorizing can be found in the translated article from Ōkawa Shūmei in Joyce C. Lebra (ed.), *Japan's Greater East Asia Co-Prosperity Sphere in World War II* (Kuala Lumpur: Oxford University Press, 1975), pp. 38–40; by Kamei Kan'ichirō in his *Daitōa Minzoku no Michi* (The Path for the Greater East Asian People) (Tokyo: Shōki

Shobō, 1941), pp. 213–26; by Ishii Fumio in the *Japan Times and Advertiser*, December 15, 1941; by Count Kuroda Kiyoshi in the *Japan Times and Advertiser*, January 6, 1942; and Minowa Saburō in the *Japan Times and Advertiser*, March 29, 1942.

23. Tōgō Shigenori (trans. by Tōgō Fumihiko and Ben Bruce Blakeney) *The Cause of Japan* (New York: Simon & Schuster, 1956), p. 251. Shigemitsu Mamoru, later instrumental in changing the policy as Foreign Minister, described the policy which led to the creation of the Greater East Asia Ministry as "colonial" in nature. (Shigemitsu, *Shigemitsu Mamoru Shuki*, [Private Papers of Shigemitsu Mamoru] vol. 1 (Tokyo: Chūōkōronsha, 1986), p. 422.

24. The text is found in: Ōta Ichirō (ed.), *Nihon Gaikōshi, Daitōa Sensō Senji Gaikō* (Japanese Diplomatic History: Greater East Asian War Wartime Diplomacy) (Tokyo: Kajima Kenkyūjo Shuppankai, 1971), pp. 166–72.

25. The English text is found in the *Japan Times and Advertiser*, Dec. 22, 1942. The signing is reported in the October 29, 1942 edition of the same paper.

26. Yanagisawa, *Taikoku to Nihon Bunka*, pp. 1–6, 13–14 and *Japan Times and Advertiser*, April 24, 1942. Yanagisawa's pre-war publications included a book based on his experiences in Europe and a 1941 volume on Portuguese dictator Antonio Salazar.

27. Yanagisawa, *Taikoku to Nihon Bunka*, pp. 11, 172. The *Bangkok Times* did carry small stories from Japanese wire services noting Yanagisawa's appointment, but there was no news of his arrival, nor of his negotiations through the end of June.

28. On Phibun's cultural program, see: Thamsook Numnonda, "Pibulsongkram's Thai Nation-Building Programme During the Japanese Military Presence, 1941–1945," *Journal of Southeast Asian Studies*, vol. 9, no. 2 September, 1978, pp. 234–47. The text of Phibun's postwar explanation of his action is found in Thak Chaloemtiarana (ed.), *Thai Politics 1932–1957* (Bangkok: Social Science Association of Thailand, 1978), pp. 348–70.

29. Thak (ed.), *Thai Politics 1932–1957*, pp. 364–65.

30. Jayanata K. Ray, *Portraits of Thai Politics* (New Delhi: Orient Longman, Ltd., 1972), p. 198.

31. *Bangkok Times*, May 26, 1942.

32. *Bangkok Times*, June 3, 1942.

33. See the script in Thak (ed.), *Thai Politics 1932–1957*, pp. 308–11 and a somewhat different summary translation in the *Bangkok Times*, June 6, 1942.

34. Thak (ed.), *Thai Politics 1932–1957*, pp. 314–16.

35. Yanagisawa, *Taikoku to Nihon Bunka*, pp. 11–12. Although details of the agreement are lacking, a subsequent Thai announcement suggesting establishment of a joint Thai–Japanese cultural center in Bangkok suggests that they might well have pushed for such an arrangement during the negotiations. See pp. 107–08.

36. Ibid., pp. 4, 9–12, 112 and *Japan Times and Advertiser*, April 24 and May 6, 1942.

37. Yanagisawa, *Taikoku to Nihon Bunka*, pp. 70–1.
38. For example, Yanagisawa, *Taikoku to Nihon Bunka*, p. 151 and *Nippon Times*, March 12, 1944.
39. Yanagisawa, *Taikoku to Nihon Bunka*, pp. 118–19.
40. Ibid., pp. 55–7, 62, 70–1.
41. Ibid., pp. 22, 61.
42. Ibid., pp. 94–5, 100, 109, 147–8. Yanagisawa pointed out Thailand's potential as a model for other Southeast Asian states even before he went to Bangkok (*Japan Times and Advertiser*, April 24, 1942). Former Minister to Thailand Yatabe Yasukichi, who accompanied former Prime Minister Hirota Kōki on an official visit to Thailand in the summer of 1942 also issued a public plea that Thailand not be pressured in the cultural field (*Japan Times and Advertiser*, July 22, 1942).
43. Yanagisawa, *Taikoku to Nihon Bunka*, pp. 24–5, 57–8, 97, 185–8.
44. Ibid., pp. 100–1, 117, 185–8.
45. Ibid., pp. 101, 173, 190–8. Medical assistance also figured prominently in the cultural strategy advanced by Miyahara Takeo, head of Mitsui's Thai Room research unit in Tokyo. See his book: *Ataratanaru Tai* (The New Thailand) (Tokyo: Toshokenkyūsha, 1942), pp. 188–9. Considered a leading Japanese expert on Thailand, Miyahara served as an advisor to the Foreign Ministry, so his views probably influenced those of Yanagisawa, who had no previous experience in Southeast Asia.
46. Yanagisawa, *Taikoku to Nihon Bunka*, pp. 102–4.
47. Ibid., pp. 89–90, 97–8.
48. Ibid., pp. 11, 107–8.
49. *Bangkok Chronicle*, August 17, 1942, May 8 and June 14, 1943; *Japan Times and Advertiser*, August 19 and October 30, 1942; and *Nippon Times*, April 15 and May 6, 1943, March 12, 1944.
50. *Japan Times and Advertiser*, August 19, 1942; *Nippon Times*, April 15, May 6, and October 29, 1943; and *Bangkok Chronicle*, March 18, 1941 and June 14, 1943. Kuroda had visited Thailand in 1941 according to the *Bangkok Chronicle* of April 22, 1941.
51. The text appears in the *Japan Times and Advertiser*, December 22, 1942.
52. *Japan Times and Advertiser*, April 25, 1942. The Japanese press story botched several names and stated that M. R. Wibun was the younger brother of Prince Wan. A correction appears in the *Bangkok Chronicle*, April 29, 1942.
53. *Bangkok Chronicle*, October 15, 1942 and *Japan Times and Advertiser*, June 30, 1942. The three Japanese were: Kawabe Toshio, then an assistant professor at Tōhoku University, Tomita Takejirō of the Osaka School of Languages, and Mori Yoshio, a specialist on tropical medicine who worked for the South Manchurian Railway. In the postwar period, Kawabe became a professor of Thai language at Tokyo University of Foreign Languages (*Tokyo Gaikokugo Daigaku*) and currently teaches Southeast Asian studies at the graduate school of Tokyo International University (*Tokyo Kokusai Daigaku*). He has published various books and articles on Thailand and Southeast Asia. Tomita, who established Thai language studies at Osaka University of Foreign Languages (*Osaka*

Gaigo Daigaku), recently completed his *magnum opus*, a Thai–Japanese dictionary of more than 2,000 pages. Tomita's project is described in a special supplement to *The Nation* (Bangkok), September 26, 1987, although the dates given in the article are badly muddled.

54. *Japan Times and Advertiser*, December 11, 1942 and *Bangkok Chronicle*, December 24, 1942 and May 26, 1943.
55. Phairot Chayanam, "Kromkhotsanakon" ("The Publicity Department") in *50 pi Kromprachasamphan* (50 Years of the Public Relations Department) (Bangkok: Kromprachasamphan, 1986), p. 54 and interview with Phairot Chayanam, November 16, 1987. (The wartime Publicity Department subsequently was redesignated as the Public Relations Department.)
56. *Bangkok Chronicle*, March 27, 1943.
57. *Bangkok Chronicle*, July 31, 1942.
58. Direk's book was entitled *Taikoku o Kataru* (Speaking of Thailand) and one copy is in the National Diet Library. On Wichit's cultural team, see: *Nippon Times*, January 23, 1944.
59. Although of course he did not acknowledge that the purpose was to resist the Japanese, Thai Foreign Minister Luang Wichit Wathakan admitted the direct connection between the establishment of the National Culture Institute and the cultural treaty to Ambassador Tsubokami. See: "Tsubokami to Tokyo," September 29, 1942, File A600 1–27, vol. 2, Japan Foreign Ministry Archives, Tokyo.
60. *Bangkok Chronicle*, October 2, 1942.
61. *Bangkok Chronicle*, December 21, 1943.
62. Interview with Phairot Chayanam, November 16, 1987.
63. Byōdō and Byōdō, *Waga Ya no Nittai Tsūshin*, pp. 319–21. The article based on the interview appears in the *Japan Times and Advertiser*, October 29, 1942.
64. "Tsubokami to Tokyo," June 2, 1943, File A600 1–27, vol. 2, Japan Foreign Ministry Archives, Tokyo.
65. Byōdō and Byōdō, *Waga Ya no Nittai Tsūshin*, pp. 158, 334.
66. For a fuller discussion, see Reynolds dissertation, pp. 489–500.
67. *Nippon Times*, December 20, 1943 and March 12 and May 30, 1944.
68. *Bangkok Chronicle*, June 14, 1943.
69. In fact, stories about Thailand in general largely disappeared from the Japanese press after the fall of the Phibun government in July 1944. Evidence of this appears in an index of wartime articles on the countries of the Greater East Asia Co-Prosperity Sphere in the Japanese language daily newspaper *Asahi*. This reference book, compiled by the Research Section of the *Ajia Keizai Kenkyūjo* (The Institute of Developing Economies), *Asahi Shimbun (Tokyo han) ni Miru Daitōakyōeiken – 1941–45*: *Kiji Sakuin* (The Greater East Asia Co-Prosperity Sphere as seen in the *Asahi Shimbun*, 1941–45 [Tokyo Edition]: News Article Index) (Tokyo, 1983), indicates that in 1942 there were 202 days in which the newspaper published at least one story relating to Thailand, and this increased to 205 days in 1943. In contrast, Thai-related stories appeared on only 72 days in 1944 and on a mere 13 days after the end of August. During the

period from the beginning of 1945 until the end of the war there were a mere six days when the *Asahi* carried Thailand-related stories and the last appeared on May 5.

70. The text of this document is found in: Ōta (ed.), *Nihon Gaikōshi, Daitōa Sensō Senji Gaikō*, p. 182.
71. Interview with Prasat Panyarachun, February 17, 1988. Prasat suggested that few of the Thai students in Japan approved of the policies of the Japanese government, although "they liked the girls and their friends." He emphasized that he was very well treated while in Tokyo.
72. Interview with Nishino Junjirō, July 28, 1989. The *Bangkok Chronicle*, February 12, 1943 and April 11, 1944 report the results of the contests, the latter co-sponsored by the Thai Cultural Institute. In neither case did the judges find an essay worthy of the announced first prize, although in both contests second and other prizes were awarded.
73. *Bangkok Chronicle*, April 20, 1944 and Nishino interview.

4 Japanese Cultural Policy in Malaya and Singapore, 1942–45

Yoji Akashi

Among the territories in Southeast Asia occupied by Japan in 1942–45, until the end of war the military government of Japan retained direct control of British Malaya and Singapore (renamed Syonan, the Light of the South) as permanent possessions of the Empire. This was done because Malaya and Singapore are located in a strategic region that, linked by the Malacca Straits, connects the Indian Ocean with the Pacific Ocean, and because Malaya and Singapore were rich in natural resources necessary for Japan's defense and for the construction of the *Daitōa Kyōeiken* (Greater East Asia Co-Prosperity Sphere). Furthermore, the indigenous people, in Japan's judgment, had not developed their cultural sophistication to a level deemed worthy of independence and nationhood. Since their personal allegiances had largely remained with the sultans of their respective states,[1] the Japanese had decided to indoctrinate them to become subjects of *Tennō Heika* (the Emperor) through "Nipponization" and *kōminka kyōiku* (education for transforming citizens into the Emperor's subjects). Moreover, Japanese government leaders made the decision in May 1943 that Malaya and Syonan as well as Indonesia were to be incorporated into "permanent possessions of the Empire," while Burma and the Philippines were promised independence.[2] Official policy drafts prepared by the Ministry of Foreign Affairs in February 1945 reconfirmed the territorial disposition of the former British colonies.[3]

Two studies prepared by the Total War Institute were explicit in defining the role of cultural and educational policy to achieve the objectives of "Nipponization" and *kōminka kyōiku*. *Basic Plans for Establishing the Daitōa Kyōeiken* said that the *Daitōa Kyōeiken* ideology would be the instrument through which Japanese moral principles should be propagated, and that Japan, with the Emperor as the fountainhead of all moral principles, ought to be the leader of an Eastern moral and cultural revival; therefore, the Japanese had a

117

historic mission to create a new moral order in the *Daitōa Kyōeiken* and to eradicate "Western individualism and materialism."[4] Through a reorganization of the Western-style educational system and curriculum and through teaching Japanese *seishin* (spirit) by means of *Nippon-go* (Japanese language) and cultural programs, all Asian people should be taught to follow the Japanese Imperial Way.

Establishment of East Asia: Maneuvers for the First Period of Total War spelled out in detail for whom this cultural and moral educational policy should be implemented.[5] It stressed the need through a leadership exchange program to convert intellectuals to the Japanese way of life from their Western orientation in which they were so deeply immersed and their Western way of thinking and habits with which they were tainted. The Total War Institute documents set forth the policy for establishing a new educational program based on the ideologies of the *Daitōa Kyōeiken* and *Hakkō Ichiu* (Eight Corners of the World Under One Roof). To this end, native teachers should be retrained and promising young men sent to Japan for further leadership education and indoctrination in *Nippon seishin*, i.e., absolute love of *Tennō Heika*, absolute loyalty to him, absolute willingness to die for him, and iron discipline. In short, the Japanese educational and cultural policy intended to inculcate the Emperor cult and *Nippon seishin* through *Nippon-go* as the *lingua franca* and to train young leaders spiritually and physically fit for military and national service to be useful subjects for the *Tennō Heika* and Japan.

As noted elsewhere in this book, the Japanese military, based upon lessons of their propaganda campaign in the Sino-Japanese War, felt the need for organizing a propaganda unit as a part of psychological warfare essential to a successful modern war. This was believed to be significant not only in order to report the war situation to the people on the home front, but also to propagate Japan's messages of the *Daitōa Kyōeiken*, *Hakkō Ichiu*, and "Asia for the Asians" to try to win the support of the populace under occupation. Accordingly, in September 1941 the Army General Staff established a Propaganda Unit in the Second Bureau charged with intelligence.[6]

The General Staff and the War Ministry, assisted by Nakajima Kenzō who was then a lecturer in French literature at Tokyo Imperial University, began recruiting *bunkajin* (intellectuals including novelists, poets, painters, journalists, cartoonists, cameramen, movie directors, university instructors, etc.).[7] Several hundred such individuals were drafted at two separate times for the propaganda service and were assigned, with a budget of 3,000,000 yen each, to one of the four armies that were given the task of conquering British Malaya and Singapore, the Philippines, Burma, and the Dutch East Indies. About 150 *bunkajin* were assigned to the 25th Army of Lt. General Yamashita Tomoyuki, whose army was to lead the assault upon the British colony. Among the prominent *bunkajin* in the Propaganda Unit assigned to the 25th Army were: Ibuse Masuji, Jimbo Kōtarō, Kitagawa Fuyuhiko, Nakajima Kenzō, Nakamura Jihei, Sakai Seiichirō, Satomura Kinzō, Kaionji Ushigorō, Terasaki Hiroshi, Kurihara Makoto, and Oguri Mushitarō.[8] Together with other *bunkajin* assigned to the other invading armies, they truly represented the best minds of the day. The first group of the unit left Japan in mid-November accompanying the 25th Army and entered Syonan on February 17, 1942, two days after the city fell into Japanese hands, while the second group sailed for Syonan on February 18 and arrived there on March 15.

With the arrival of the second group, propaganda activities of the 25th Army *Gunseibu* (military government, *Gunseikambu* after July 1942) went into full swing for the "Nipponization" programs. Setting up headquarters in the Cathay Building in Singapore, the Propaganda Unit (abbreviated as *Marusen*)[9] launched a campaign for the propagation of *Nippon-go* aiming at making it the *lingua franca* of Malaya, Syonan, and Sumatra.[10] An editorial in English (!) of *The Syonan Times* edited by Ibuse made the policy clear:[11]

> One of the first considerations in the construction of mutual well being and prosperity in Asia is that of introducing a common language. The suggestion therefore that the language of Nippon becomes the lingua franca of Malaya while startling at first becomes an obvious necessity . . .
>
> The substitution of Nipponese for English as the lingua franca in Malaya is but the natural recognition of a nation which has stood up for things Asian and which is now in the process of saving Asians from continuing to be the victims of the British strategy to squeeze the wealth and culture of Asians.
>
> As a preliminary step it is suggested that shop signs and street names be substituted by Nipponese signs and names as a material indication that Malaya is included in the new order of things.

Meanwhile *The Syonan Times* had started a daily column of *Nippon-go* lessons beginning February 23. In support of the "Nipponization" programs and the popularization of *Nippon-go*, the War

Ministry laid out a general principle of education for the occupied territories of Southeast Asia. It said that the principal objective of education was to teach *Nippon-go* and to propagate Japanese culture.[12]

It was Colonel Watanabe Wataru, the new *Gunseibuchō* (chief military administrator) in Malaya, effective March 1, 1942, and the author of the two Total War Institute studies, who was to implement the policy of the"Nipponization" programs.[13] A devotee of the Imperial cult, Watanabe carried out the policy with determination and vigor to transform the native people into *Tennō Heika*'s useful subjects through teaching *Nippon-go* and Japanese culture and moral principles which were, in his view, far superior to "materialistic western culture."[14]

His idea was echoed by two prominent and influential Japanese. In an interview with a reporter of *The Syonan Times* while visiting the city, Yamamoto Sanehiko, publisher-president of *Kaizō*, a monthly Japanese magazine catering to the intelligentsia, expressed his "desire of seeing Nippon culture introduced into Syonan as one of the essentials in eliminating all traces of Western domination here, even to the extent of importing and planting Nipponese flowering plants and other aesthetic amenities so that the whole atmosphere of Syonan may breathe of Nippon ideals, Nipponese culture, and all the high ideals which Nippon's mission of Greater East Asia Co-Prosperity implies."[15] Another article signed by a certain Obara, presumably a staff editorial writer in the *Sendenbu* (the Military government's propaganda department), declared that the first imperative of the New Order was to break down the "habits and customs left behind by the British" and to revive Oriental culture based on moral and spiritual principles.[16] "The Nippon spirit," he concluded, "contains such great virtues as bravery, loyalty, propriety, faith, simplicity and self-sacrifice. To act and exhibit these virtues as practiced by the Nipponese should be the aim of every Asiatic not only to make them upright citizens but also to create a superior race . . ."[17]

The first occasion for the "Nipponization" of indigenous people through "spiritual purification" and the propagation of *Nippon-go* took place on April 29, 1942, the birthday of the Emperor. The *Gunseibu* ordered citizens of Syonan and Malaya to hoist Japanese flags and to participate in a mass ceremony in which they were required to pay respect with a deep bow in the direction of the east where the palace of *Tennō Heika* was located. The *Sendenbu* took the occasion to proclaim the "Declaration for the Popularization of the *Nippon-go* Movement." "On the auspicious occasion of the Emperor's birthday," the opening statement of the Declaration said, "we set forth the path to follow for residents of Malaya and Sumatra. As Commanding General [Yamashita] said in his speech, the people of both territories have now become His Majesty's subjects." Nakajima, who authored the Declaration, exhorted officers and soldiers of the Japanese Army that it was their "sacred duty to teach indigenous people *Nippon-go* and to make them use it." "In order to guide them to become His Majesty's subjects," he urged, "we must teach them our language as the *lingua franca* so that it will remove differences in customs and habits of various ethnic races in Malaya and Sumatra."[18]

The timing for announcing the Declaration coinciding with the Emperor's birthday was well calculated because it was the biggest festive day for the Japanese, a day when the *Sendenbu* could mobilize a great mass of people for implanting in their minds the cult of Emperorism. In a special edition for the Emperor's birthday, *The Syonan Times* carried feature articles on the Imperial Household, Japanese patriotism and reverence for the Emperor as well as speeches by General Yamashita and Colonel Watanabe. Riding high on the crest of military fame as the "Tiger of Malaya" who conquered Singapore, the ebullient general called upon "the newly joined Nippon subjects of Malaya and Sumatra" to understand "the superior national spirit of Dai Nippon . . . symbolized by the unique combination of two factors in our relations with *Tennō Heika* – that of lord and vassal and at the same time of father and children." The inhabitants of Malaya and Syonan were fortunate, he said, in becoming "glorious new imperial subjects." Therefore, they should prove themselves "worthy subjects of this great Empire and *Tennō Heika*" by working hard and devoting themselves to establishing peace founded upon righteousness and morality. Elucidating the cult of Emperorism, Watanabe said that for the Emperor the Japanese would cheerfully lay down his life. To die for Him and in His service was the "greatest privilege" that would come to a Japanese. This devotion and loyalty to the Emperor made the Japanese different from the Britons and Americans and superior to them.[19]

On this most important day of felicitations, the *Sendenbu* organized a variety of events such as photo exhibits of Japan, a Japanese Navy Band march and concert, a parade of school children carrying Japanese flags and singing "*Aikoku Kōshinkyoku*" (a patriotic marching song), marching along the streets bedecked with flags of the rising sun, specifically at General Yamashita's request. The *Sendenbu* also authorized the reopening of movie theaters where films of Japanese culture, industry, and the magnificence of the Japanese Imperial Forces were presented.

Two days after the massive celebration, the *Sendenbu* opened the *Syonan Nippon Gakuen* for teaching *Nippon-go* and Japanese culture to adults, and the *Syonan Jidō Gakuen* for children.[20] Jimbo Kōtarō, a poet and a scholar of German literature, became the principal, and Nakajima and Ibuse advisors. Nakajima coined the campaign slogan *"Manabe! Takae! Nippon-go!"* (Study, Use, *Nippon-go*) for recruiting students. More than 370 people applied for the adult school. Seizing a surging tide of interest in *Nippon-go*, Nakajima, Jimbo, and Ibuse planned an intensive *Nippon-go* Week in June.

"Manabe! Tukae! Nippon-go!" With this slogan the *Sendenbu* launched on June 1, a massive campaign with the mobilization of mass media for the *Nippon-go* Week.[21] To promote the campaign, the *Sendenbu* printed leaflets and picture posters with the slogan in English, Chinese, and Malay. 500,000 copies were distributed to government offices, schools, churches, movie theaters, and shops in Syonan, Malaya, and Sumatra. Newspapers in Japanese, English, and Chinese editions printed the slogan in large bold letters across the front page every day of the Week and carried a series of articles about Japanese culture, history, and institutions. The *Sendenbu* also published the *katakana* (Japanese syllabary) newspaper *Sakura* designed for children, recruited teachers from the garrison army for expanded *Nippon-go* classes, programmed *Nippon-go* lessons broadcast for schools, and organized programs of children's songs, dramas, and fairy tales in *Nippon-go* presented at the *Daitōa Gekijō* (formerly Cathay Theater). *Kana* was printed alongside *kanji* (Chinese characters) names of theaters, and *kana* was introduced to identify trolleys' destinations as well. Trolleys, automobiles, and rikshas plastered with the posters also helped to disseminate the slogan for promoting *Nippon-go* Week.

Despite the elaborate programs accompanied by a fanfare of events, the campaign had not produced the expected response by the end of the Week. An editorial of *The Syonan Times* complained of a lack of enthusiasm on the part of "a large portion of the public" who made hardly any effort at all to commence the study of *Nippon-go*. "Without a knowledge of Nippon-go," it said, "your future in this country will be beset with difficulties, hardships and even unemployment and destitution . . ."[22] To generate enthusiasm, the *Sendenbu* mobilized the literary talents of Nakajima, Jimbo and Ibuse to popularize *Nippon-go* by extending the campaign for two more weeks. Jimbo gave a discourse on *Nippon-go* saying that to learn *Nippon-go* was not only "a duty but also a glorious opportunity given by Heaven." "Through Nippon-go," Jimbo explained, "the beauty of *Nippon-go* can become clearer in your mind and you can appreciate the feelings which are in the hearts of all Nippon-zin."[23] Emphasizing the importance for all people of learning *Nippon-go*, Ibuse suggested an easy way of learning *Nippon-go* by studying *waka* (5-7-5-7-7 syllable poem) and *haiku* (5-7-5 syllable poem), because once thoroughly conversant with *waka* and *haiku* one would be "sure to become anxious to further his study of *Nippon-go*."[24] Nakajima composed an ode in which the initial letters of lines were vertically arranged in such a way as to be read as the slogan "Why You Must Learn Nippon-go."[25] Only with the intensive campaign extended for two weeks could the *Nippon-go* Emphasis Week be declared "a great success."[26]

Equally disappointing were the results of an essay contest on Japanese culture which was held in conjunction with the *Nippon-go* Week. There were no essays deserving of the first or second prizes. According to the opinions of the contest judges, entrants failed to appreciate Japan's scientific and engineering achievements such as the completion of the underground tunnel connecting Honshū and Kyūshū and Japan's excellent educational system, triumphs which were touted in feature articles in the daily newspapers.[27] Accordingly, *The Syonan Times Saturday Supplement* greatly expanded the space for introducing Japanese culture and history as well as industry.

The role of *Nippon-go* taught at schools through the *kōminka kyōiku* program was the essence of "Nipponization" and, accordingly, was considered extremely important. The need for *Nippon-go* as a tool of *kōminka kyōiku* in Greater East Asia, as had been the case in Taiwan and Korea, was recognized as early as June, 1939, when the Ministry of Education deliberated what should be the role of *Nippon-go* education in any national policy for the "Nipponization" of a would-be occupied area of Asia. Following recommendations of the Council for National Language Policy, the Ministry created in 1940 a section charged with the teaching of *Nippon-go* and helped organize the Association for the Promotion of *Nippon-go*.

In a message for the publication of the first issue of the Association's journal *Nippon-go* (April, 1940), the chairman of the Association elaborated upon the mission of the Japanese. He said that it was to "establish a Co-Prosperity Sphere in Asia," which in short meant the "formation of an Asian cultural sphere" under Japan's leadership. "We [as *Nippon-go* teachers and educators] must never cease our utmost efforts," he declared; "for the popularization of *Nippon-go* and the promotion of *Nippon-go* education."[28]

This monthly periodical was an authoritative and influential medium through which Education Ministry officials and literary critics often expressed opinions on teaching *Nippon-go* and its role in creating and shaping a *Daitōa Kyōeiken* culture under *Hakkō Ichiu*. For example, Kugimoto Hisaharu, an Education Ministry official, set forth his view that *Nippon-go* had much to contribute to the realization of *Kōdō Seishin* (Imperial way spirit) for the peoples of the *Daitōa Kyōeiken*. "The concrete experience of *Kōdō Seishin*," he said, "can be imparted only through *Nippon-go*."[29] Matsumiya Kazuya, an official of the Society of Japanese Culture, considered it imperative that *Nippon-go* should become the "foundation for understanding and experiencing the essence of *Daitōa Kyōeiken* culture.[30] Tsurumi Yūsuke, who was typical of the best minds of the *bunkajin* and of the prewar pro-American establishment, asserted that the most important problem confronting Japan for the construction of a *Daitōa* culture was how to make *Nippon-go* the *lingua franca* of Greater East Asia. "I have been waiting for that day to come," he said, "for thirty-one years and I have been thinking about this problem as my dream."[31] In a dialogue with Kugimoto, Satō Haruo, an important poet, novelist, short story writer and translator of Chinese literature, maintained that it was essential for the "*Nipponzin* to make native people of the Southern region understand *Kōdō Bunka* (Imperial Way Culture)" through *Nippon-go* for the construction of a Japanese culture.[32] Kaionji Ushigorō, a prize winning author of historical novels and historical biographies and a staff member of the *Sendenbu*, elaborated that *Kōdō Bunka* was "the essence created out of a refining process in the crucible of Chinese, Indian, and Western thoughts." Japan, he proclaimed, ought to teach it to all Asian people. As the first step to do so, "the pride of Asian people in their own cultures" had to be "destroyed completely by condemning theirs as being useless in the present age." "The essence of modern culture is Japanese culture, that is the *Kōdō Bunka*," Kaionji said, "which is the most useful for the present and future generations." Indigenous people ought to be indoctrinated in the *Kōdō Bunka* for their own happiness, and, accordingly, "Confucianism, Taoism, Buddhism, Brahmanism, and Hinduism should face severe and merciless criticism. Otherwise, the superiority of the *Kōdō Bunka* cannot be made understandable to native people."[33]

Cognizant of the importance of *Nippon-go* education for Japanization and *Kōdō Bunka*, the government advisory body *Daitōa Kensetsu Shingikai* (Council for the Construction of Greater East Asia) created a department charged with the task of developing policies for education, culture, and religion. It presented recommendations, adopted by the cabinet in late May, 1942, that the fundamental policy of education and culture should be founded upon the ideology of *Hakkō Ichiu*, i.e. Japan as the center of morality, aimed at making the indigenous people aware of being citizens of Asia and of the nature of the *Daitōa* War as a Holy War for the liberation of Asia. At the same time it was agreed that all vestiges of Anglo-American ideas should be removed through a quick popularization of *Nippon-go* as the *lingua franca* and that English should be abolished as soon as possible, because there was no further reason to use English since it was only an obstacle to the propagation of *Nippon-go*.[34]

At the recommendation of the Council for the urgency of *Nippon-go* education and the training of *Nippon-go* teachers, the government on August 18 established a fundamental policy of education for the Southern region. The Ministry of Education, at the request of the War Ministry, was to formulate the policy for *Nippon-go* education and propagation. Also the Ministry of Education organized the Council for the Popularization of *Nippon-go* charged with the task of editing and publishing textbooks necessary for language instruction and the training of *Nippon-go* teachers to be dispatched to the Southern area.[35]

While the fundamental education policy was being deliberated in Tokyo, *Nippon-go* education and "Nipponization" programs, boosted by the Emphasis Week, were well under way. Primary schools, now renamed *Futū Kō Gakkō* (Common Public Schools) and modeled after the Japanese system, had been reopened in Syonan, Malaya, and Sumatra, and enrollment had been increasing although it was still short of the prewar level.[36] English had been discarded as a subject in the curriculum of schools, and *Nippon-go* had replaced it as a compulsory language, being taught on the average of seven hours a week of reading, writing, and conversation. In Perak and Penang, as much as fifteen hours of *Nippon-go* instruction were crammed into a weekly school timetable.[37]

Nippon-go had also spread to the rural areas of Malaya, where "whole families, including grandparents, parents, children and relatives, have taken to the study of Nippon-go under Nippon volunteers and soldiers . . ."[38] *Nippon-go* was so effectively taught with Japanese songs to musically inclined Malays that "Japanese tunes were everywhere to be heard on the lips of young people who a few months earlier had been whistling or singing the latest hit from Hollywood."[39] Jimbo's *Syonan Gakuen* also had been receiving more applications seeking admission to the second term which started in August, 1,386 people having applied for the maximum capacity of 427 students.

Apart from the immediate aim of popularizing *Nippon-go*, the supposed spiritual value of education received much attention. Jimbo, who said that he changed after December 8, 1941, from the quiet poet–scholar that he was before that day to an activist for "Nipponization" programs, criticized British education in Malaya for having neglected spiritual indoctrination, and he ridiculed the cultural level of British colonial administrators as being "second or third class." This was evident, he said, in the seeming ill-mannered behavior of students at *Syonan Gakuen* where the students could be seen eating snacks and drinking soft drinks in classrooms, littering the floor, and sitting on classroom desks or books, as well as in jazz music records seized from the houses of British officials and in the poor facilities of Raffles College which was the highest institution of learning in the British colonial period.[40] He rectified the students' poor manners, which he regarded as vestiges of *laissez-faire* British education and of a "lopsided emphasis on material culture and de-emphasis on spiritual culture," and he introduced Japanese manners for their deportment in the classroom. Now the students stood at attention when a teacher entered and left the classroom and bowed to him, and they performed in perfect unison at the commands spoken by the class monitor in *Nippon-go*: "*Kiritsu*" ("Stand At Attention"), "*Rei*" ("Bow,") and "*Chakuseki*" ("Be Seated"). This custom was adopted in all schools throughout Syonan and Malaya.[41]

Jimbo's educational philosophy appeared to be unadulterated "Nipponism," believing that the *Yamato* (Japanese) "race" was superior. "It is a heaven sent mission," Jimbo declared, "for the *Yamato* race to guide the indigenous people." In a speech to graduates of *Gakuen*'s first class, he urged them to appreciate "the reality of Nippon," i.e., "Nippon's strength, Nippon's beauty, Nippon's great spirit." To learn *Nippon-go*, he exhorted, was a process through which they were to be assimilated into superior *Yamato* culture, whereas the Malayans "did not have a culture worthy of the name." "You must show your real and pure feelings and love Nippon-go. You cannot master Nippon-go without love. To love Nippon means you have won the distinction of being a glorious and good Nippon-zin," he admonished the students.[42]

Elaborating on the spiritual value of education, a *Syonan Times* editorial on education and a new national consciousness said that once the evils of the "European Christianized and bureaucracy-planned controlled system" had been destroyed, the mind of the child would have to be "gradually cleansed of all its old shibboleths, superstitions and loyalties and won over to new beliefs and new loyalties," the most important of which would be an abiding faith in his future as a member of the New Order and as a unit in a new civilization. The objective of the Japanese education system was the "creation of a new national consciousness" in the rising generation as "co-partner . . . in the New Order created by the Nippon Empire."[43] Needless to say, the national consciousness did not mean national awareness for independence, which Japan did not intend to grant to the Malayans.

Under the auspices of *Syonan Gakuen* and the *Sendenbu*, a series of lectures on Japanese culture and history were presented by Ibuse, Jimbo, Fukuda Hajime, deputy chief of the *Dōmei* Wireless Service in Syonan, and Tanakadate Hidezō, curator of the Syonan Museum. Ibuse delivered lectures on history beginning with the divine origins of Japan founded by *Amaterasu Omikami*. He emphasized the uniqueness of the founding of the nation, the first Emperor Jimmu's eastward expedition conquering barbarians, and his accession to the throne at Kashiwabara where he was enshrined. After completing the lecture series, Ibuse said that the experience had "made his life worth living."[44]

Nakajima, in his speech on Japanese culture given at the *Daitōa Gekijō*, characterized the present time as a turning point into "a new modern age" when Eastern culture, which had been sleeping for a long time, woke up and began to have "the power of a universal influence." The *Daitōa* War, he said, was a catalyst for the turning point, and the ultimate intent of the *Daitōa Kyōeiken* was to prove "the first step to the fundamental construction" of the new modern age and the opportunity to display the Asian aptitude for it. To achieve that ideal Malayans ought to change their way "from a consuming life to a creative life" depending less on their rich natural resources and more on their creative will and industry. Unless they were willing to deal with this "unreasonable urge," they would not be able to escape from their "colonial character forever." His declaration, "the British will not come back," evoked the loudest applause and cheers from the audience.[45]

Jimbo exhorted the audience by exclaiming that since the previous December the world had been undergoing the painful labor of creating a new history. Of course he said, in this process everyone was expected to make great sacrifices. New things would "not emerge without the heavy pain of creation." "The many tragedies which we are experiencing nowadays," he continued, "are nothing but the significant phenomena through which the new world is coming out." He assured the audience that Japan's culture would mold the new history of the world.[46]

With the shortage of foodstuffs in mind, Fukuda asked the crowd to be "patient and endure any hardships and trials."[47] It was all for preparing ourselves, he said, to continue the war and to achieve victory. He advised the listeners to learn *Nippon-go* in order to get to know more about Japan and the Japanese who were always friendly and loyal towards them.[48]

In his discourse on Japanese culture, Tanakadate gave unstinting praise to the code of bushido and such virtues as self-sacrifice, loyalty, patriotism, and *harakiri* (ritual ceremony of disembowelment) as well as the Japanese love of nature, as expressed in their poems. The Japanese, he stated, were imbued with the great qualities of self-sacrifice, loyalty, and patriotism and, governed by the Emperor, were determined to defend the country against the Western aggressors and to construct a "Utopia" for the peoples of East Asia.[49]

With the repatriation from India in August 1942, of a dozen Japanese school teachers who had taught in the prewar Japanese communities in Singapore, Kuala Lumpur, and Penang and with the drafting of soldiers and officers who had had teaching experience in Japan,[50] the teaching staff of *Nippon-go* in Malaya was strengthened to intensify *Nippon-go* education and "Nipponization" programs. For two months from late September to early November, the *Gunsei-kambu* launched an intensive editorial campaign for Japanization. In the editorial "Trust Nippon & Nippon-zin," *The Syonan Times* said

this is a heaven-sent opportunity to all men to turn away from lives of aimless search for worldly riches and to apply themselves to their own spiritual upliftment and spiritual upliftment of their fellow Asians. Once they develop such a broad, spiritual outlook, they will begin to appreciate Nippon's mission, which simply means bringing contentment and everlasting peace and prosperity.[51]

It called upon everyone to play his role for the construction of the *Daitōa Kyōeiken*, especially upon teachers and those in executive positions to help impart Japan's message to the indigenous people: "Trust Nippon and the Nippon-zin" for the reconstruction of Malaya into "a paradise for all Asiatics."

Expounding the "Trust Nippon and the Nippon-zin" theme, the newspaper editorialized on September 29 that Malayans ought to absorb the dynamic spirit influencing the Japanese.[52] By uplifting their spiritual quality, it admonished, they would "appreciate Nippon's mission" and awaken to "a new national consciousness" that would "inspire in all Malayans a willingness to share gladly in all the trials and sufferings" which were now "being borne by the Nippon-zin" and which "all Malayans should bear as a test of their fitness for a place in the New Order." Get rid of the colonial mentality of indifference and apathy implanted by the British, it said, and prove through spiritual uplift that you are "suitable for acceptance as subjects of *Tennō Heika* and the Nippon Empire and as members of the New Order in East Asia."

The editorial of October 2 directed a scathing attack at the evil effects of Western civilization upon Malaya.[53] British colonial rule and its influence not only made the Malayans forget their spiritual values and caused them to be absorbed in material pursuits but also to scorn their own cultural heritage and language as well as their customs. The Christian religion of the West with its "black magic" of rites and rituals robbed the Malayan character of discipline for strengthening body and soul.[54] Malayans influenced by Western civilization had no feeling for their fellows who were starving and dying, while they enjoyed drinking and dancing in cabarets. The British had denied the right of the Malayans to be happy and to prosper. Instead they had "enslaved and oppressed the peoples of Malaya . . . to an existence on the borderline of starvation, merely to ensure the freedom and advancement of the people of Britain." The Malayans should, the editorial said, "eradicate every trace of this spurious Western civilization" which degraded the people and encouraged in them a "callous disregard to the sufferings of their fellowmen." There was no better way for their cultural transformation than a close study of the culture of the East" and a culture which had assimilated all that was "best of the civilizations and cultures of the West with the spirit of *Hakkō Ichiu* as its paramount driving power." It was Japanese culture, it concluded, to which Malayans ought to "look for guidance out of darkness and despair of their condition."[55]

The fourth in the series of the editorial campaign called upon the Malayans to rise above selfish motives, to devote themselves to greater service, and to sacrifice their "energy, time, money, and if necessary life to assist the new government in its endeavours to create a New Malaya." The Malayans, welded by the spirit of *Hakkō Ichiu*, were to be prepared for service and sacrifice that were heretofore lacking in them, in order to reconstruct Malaya together with the *Gunseikambu*. Otherwise, they had no right to be subjects of the Imperial Japanese Empire and of the New Order.[56]

Editorials on education of October 23 and November 10 emphasized not only the importance of intellectual advancement but also of moral and vocational education as well as physical training. The object of moral education was to be aimed at creating an understanding of the "purport underlying Nippon's sacred mission to liberate Asia;" the realization of "the principle of the 'oneness in virtue and spirit'" between Malayans and Japanese and of racial harmony by getting rid of inter-racial prejudices and jealousies; the creation of a spirit of goodwill and cooperation; and the clarification of "the principles of loyalty and filial piety to the State based upon one virtue and one spirit."[57]

Physical training was absolutely necessary for building "an indomitable mind and a good character" for the creation of a new national consciousness.[58] Paralleling physical training was an emphasis on vocational education, which was spelled out as one of the principles of educational policy for the occupied territories of the Southern region.[59] The British produced more clerks in Malaya than were necessary but fewer blue collar workers. The *Gunseikambu*, the editorial said, would educate the growing generation of Malayans in the dignity of labour and of never being "afraid of soiling their hands."[60] Hereafter, the *Gunseikambu* established more vocational schools for practical training combined with physical exercise.

The editorial series on "Nipponization" inevitably ended with a call upon Malayans for *Hakkō Ichiu*, specifically upon Malays, who were left by the British in the state of "the most backward of all races of Malayans," to awaken to their national consciousness and to prepare for sharing hardships in order to earn the right for the future happiness and prosperity of Malaya under *Hakkō Ichiu*, in which "all the peoples of Malaya, irrespective of their races or creeds are one people under the aegis of Nippon."[61]

Because British Malaya was the first enemy territory in the Southern region which Japan conquered and in which Japan established a military government, the *Gunseikambu* was determined to make its administration a model for the rest of Southeast Asia. Colonel Watanabe, executive officer of the *Gunseikambu*, was eager to implement and carry out the policy of "Nipponization" and its indoctrination that was to transform the native people into Imperial Japan's good citizens, who would be able to "comprehend the supernatural will of *Tennō Heika.*"[62] Executing the policy, Watanabe went so far as to eliminate the residue of Western influence by changing the names of schools, hotels, theaters, bridges, and so forth, and the *Gunseikambu* even adopted Tokyo standard time in Malaya, turning back the clock two hours. Watanabe also attempted in vain to change street names and to ban the use of English in official documents, newspapers, postal services, road signs, and advertisements[63] in order to implement the policy adopted by the cabinet in May, 1942.[64] Colonel Ōkubo Kōichi, chief of the *Sendenbu*, scoffed that "speaking English is to bow our heads to the English people. There is nothing to be proud of in speaking English but . . . it is considered disgraceful."[65] Marquis Tokugawa Yoshichika, senior advisor to the 25th Army, who was fluent in Malay, had at first frowned upon imposing *Nippon-go* on occupied populations, but he too became an advocate of *Nippon-go* education reversing his previous position. Writing an article in February 1942, Tokugawa maintained that it was "absurd to coerce South Sea peoples to learn *Nippon-go.*"[66] In July he reversed his view by advocating that *Nippon-go* had to be "made the *lingua franca* through a proper *Nippon-go* education."[67]

The *Gunseikambu* also introduced Japanese national holidays and special commemoration days which it forced Malayans to observe often disregarding their religious beliefs.[68] Japanese at offices and schools observed such occasions with solemn ceremonies. Japanese and local people assembled and, at a command of an officer, they sang *Kimigayo* (national anthem) and bowed deeply to the *hinomaru* (national flag) and to the Imperial Palace in the East. Invariably, a ranking Japanese official would make a speech exhorting citizens to emulate the diligence, bravery, loyalty, and patriotism of the Japanese. The celebration would end with three cheers of "*Tennō Heika Banzai*" and "*Dai Nippon Teikoku Banzai.*"

There were two special days of commemoration for people in

Syonan and Malaya – the day Japan declared war against the Axis Powers (December 8) and the day the British at Singapore surrendered to the Japanese Army (February 15). On the former day, with a solemn ceremony, the *Gunseikambu* held a big celebration for the commencement of the *Daitōa* War. Newspapers printed statements of military commanders, *gunseikan*, governors and mayors, sultans, and local leaders, each stressing the significance of the war for the liberation of Asia. Also during the ceremony a Japanese official would recite the Imperial Rescript of the Declaration of War reminding people of the *Daitōa* War as a holy war for the establishment of the *Daitōa Kyōeiken*. Reading of the Rescript was regularly observed on the eighth day of every month at schools and offices, as it was done in Japan. Also the fourth day of the month was designated as the day for hoisting the *hinomaru*.[69] February 15 in every year was a day of gigantic celebrations. Local residents of Syonan and Malaya were reminded by dignitaries of the Japanese military government and local communities of the significance of the day as the occasion for liberation from the yoke of British colonial rule and were urged to rid themselves of vestiges of the Western way of life. On these days, too, they were required to pay a visit to Syonan *Jinja* (Shinto shrine) and *Tyūreitō* (war memorial) irrespective of their religious beliefs. Sultans were not exempted from the rule.[70]

Motion pictures were another medium through which the *Sendenbu* propagated Japan's culture for "Nipponization." Following the British surrender, the *Sendenbu* seized more than 50,000 reels of British and American produced movie films.[71] After censoring them, ideologically harmless and purely entertaining films were released for the general public. Before the arrival of Japanese films shipped from Japan, the *Sendenbu* showed films of current news and of an edifying nature introducing Japanese culture and the reconstruction of Malaya.[72] Beginning in late 1942, Japanese-made feature films were released to local theaters, and then after April 1943 they were shown regularly following the government's decision for systematic distribution of motion pictures to the occupied territories.[73] They were an effective means to "wipe out the indigenous people's mistaken notion of Japan and to convey Japan's true picture" to a captive society for whom movie-going was one of the few recreational pastimes in a controlled society.[74] Films like "Modern Japan," "Industry in Nippon," "A Glimpse of Nippon," and "Tokyo Symphony" struck viewers with amazement and disbelief about modern and industrialized Japan and even the beauty of Japanese women, because the

Malayans had been indoctrinated by the British about Japan's backwardness in modernization and industrialization and their image of Japan had been distorted by British propaganda.[75]

Selection of films after April 1943 was decidedly propagandistic, designed to prove the superiority of Japanese culture, self-sacrifice, patriotism, and diligence and to portray the evils and weaknesses of the British.[76] For example, the film *"Sora no Shinpei"* ("Divine Soldiers of the Sky") impressed the young cadets at *Kōa Kunrenjo* (Rising Asia Training School designed to train future middle-ranking staff members to assist Japanese officials) creating the desired effect. Inspired by the rigorous training of the paratroopers, they wrote essays stating that they discovered in the training the "essence of the *Nippon seishin*" and the secret of Japanese strength. Some of them expressed their desire to volunteer to go through the same hard training emulating the spirit of the paratroopers and to "die for the defense of *Daitōa*."[77] In such films as "Opium War" and "The Day the British Surrendered," the British were depicted respectively as despicable people exploiting the vice of opium smoking of the Chinese and as cowardly soldiers ignominiously surrendering to the Japanese Army.

With an increased supply of Japanese movies, the *gunseikambu* announced on July 31, 1943 that no Western films would be shown to the public, effective from September 1.[78] Whenever a new movie was released for public showing, government controlled local newspapers introduced the story to the public and urged them to see it in order to appreciate Japan's culture and *seishin*. Although some films were of good quality, most of them were not of a quality worthy of cultural propaganda nor could they rival a film like "Gone With the Wind," that was seized by the *Sendenbu* but banned from public release. Stating his impression of one movie after seeing it in a private presentation, a *Sendenbu* staff member deplored the low quality of Japanese films used for cultural propaganda. "Japanese films," he lamented, "are not serving the purpose for achieving the objectives of cultural activities. We must introduce quality films that will move the viewers. Otherwise, our cultural activities cannot be expected to improve."[79]

There was no let-up in the campaign for "Nipponization" through *Nippon-go*. The government in Tokyo, in cooperation with the Association for the Promotion of *Nippon-go*, started in early 1943 a program for training *Nippon-go* teachers to be sent to the occupied Southern region. Nakajima, who had returned from a tour of duty with the *Sendenbu* in late December 1942, served as one of the regular guest speakers lecturing on Malayan affairs for trainees.[80] *Nippon-go* education, strengthened by the arrival of trained teachers, was further emphasized with the commencement of the Second *Nippon-go* Week beginning November 14, 1943. During the Week the state government of Selangor sponsored a program consisting of speech-making, essay-writing, and slogan competitions as well as discussions and a concert. For the essay contest in *katakana* and *kanji*, entrants were requested to write on one of the following topics: Construction of Malaya, Our Self-Awareness, and Our Daily Life. Every day during the Week slogans written in bold letters appeared on the front page such as "Hallmark of Loyalty: A Knowledge of Nippon-go," "*Nippon no Nampō no Kokumintachi Kokugo wo Manabe*" (Citizens of Nippon in the Southern Region Learn the National Language), "Your Part in *Daitōa Kyōeiken*: The Mastering of *Nippon-go*," "Concentrate Your Energy on *Nippon-go*," "*Nippon-go*. The Lingua France of *Daitōa Kyōeiken*," and "Malayan Employees! Learn *Nippon-go* for Efficiency."[81] The All-Malay *Nippon-go* Week was concluded with an elocution contest in *Nippon-go* held at the *Daitōa Gekijō* which was filled to capacity.

Thanks to *Nippon-go* teachers who taught with "an almost missionary zeal,"[82] the introduction of *Nippon-go* as the *lingua franca* was a considerable success, although the military government failed in the end to establish it as the common language of Syonan and Malaya. Given more time and less unsettled conditions, the Japanese might have been successful as one Chinese writing in 1946 argued:

> Given a further five years, [Japan's] programme of Nipponization would be so consolidated that all East Asia would be thoroughly conquered politically, economically and culturally.[83]

Another Chinese writing a letter to the Editor of *The Straits Times* about a year after the war was over recalled:

> Every conceivable facility was given to those who wished to study the Japanese language. Scholarships, allowances and even remunerative posts were given to those graduated. Credit must be given to the Japanese for the fact that their efforts were wholehearted and they achieved not a little success.[84]

Many Malayans had gained a reasonable degree of fluency in

Nippon-go while others had achieved a remarkable degree of eloquence by the end of the war, as prize winners of oratorical contests testify.

On the other hand, some local Chinese had unpleasant recollections of *Nippon-go* education and "Nipponization" programs. A young Chinese named Tan Chia-ch'ang recalled slaps on his face that were associated with *Nippon-go* lessons. Being only a 13-year old boy, he could not resist giggling when a *Nippon-go* teacher read on the eighth day of every month the Imperial Rescript of the Declaration of War, because it started with a sentence, "*Chin omou ni* . . . [I think]" that had a sound similar to his name, since Tan is pronounced Chin in Japanese. He could hardly comprehend the meaning of the Imperial Rescript written in classical style. For him the *kōminka* education was nothing but a memory of the pain of being slapped in the face.[85]

Another former student remembered an incident that took place when a high ranking Japanese education official visited his school. The visiting officer asked the pupils who was the greatest man in China today, and two Chinese boys replied to the consternation of the principal that it was Chiang Kai-shek. The expected correct answer, of course, was Wang Ching-wei, chairman of the Japanese-sponsored Nanjing government. The *Gunseikambu* severely reprimanded the Chinese principal for the failure of having properly indoctrinated the children.[86]

No doubt there were many inhabitants who consciously rejected the study of *Nippon-go*. Negative feelings toward cultural indoctrination were sometimes expressed by young children in their thoughtless exuberance. Thio Chan Bee, a former schoolmaster, recalled an incident:

> At one school playground, as they sang Japanese songs and tried their new Nippon-go phrases on one another, they began to chant in unison, "Nippon-go! Yankee Come! Nippon-go! Yankee Come!" Horrified, the adults quickly stopped the children from continuing with their dangerous sing-song. Nevertheless the story of this episode was passed from one person to another in Syonan, and it cheered the hearts of many.[87]

The most intensive "Nipponization" program was seen in the curriculum of *Kunrenjo* (training school) of various kinds,[88] of which the *Kōa Kunrenjo* is an outstanding example.[89] It was the brain child of

Colonel Watanabe, executive officer of the *gunseikambu*, who wanted to train promising young men of 17–25 years old at a special academy for future staff members. The *Syonan Kōa Kunrenjo* located near the former Japanese Cemetery in Yeo Chu Kang Road was established on May 15, 1942, and was opened with an enrollment of 84 cadets of Malays, Chinese, and Indians. Living together with Japanese instructors, they were to "receive a rigid training in moral discipline." The objective of the scheme was to "give the cadets a complete course in Nippon-go, develop a spiritual outlook, and a general Nippon education."[90] Speaking at the opening ceremony to the trainees who were to assume a greater responsibility in their future work, Watanabe advised them to "forget individual matters and understand the meaning of spiritualism and its principles," remembering that they had to endure hardships and to obey without questioning.[91]

The cadets were selected by education department officials and recommended by governors of their respective states (mayor in the case of Syonan) and appointed to the *Kōa Kunrenjo* by the superintendent of the *Gunseikambu*. There were no specific rules for selecting candidates other than that they ought to be "promising young men who want to become responsible middle ranking staff members."[92] An examination of their employment, family, and educational backgrounds reveals that a great majority of them had worked for Syonan city or state governments, had come from prominent and well-to-do families, and had received higher education at such schools as Raffles College, Clifford Secondary School, or the Sultan Idris Training College.[93]

In the actual process of selecting candidates, there was neither a written nor an oral examination given by state governments or by the *Kunrenjo*, because they had been carefully screened by Japanese officials who had first-hand knowledge of their nominees. Some, however, did have an interview with the governor and a physical examination. The governor asked, for instance, such simple questions as follows: Would you help Nippon to fight against the Western colonial powers?; Would you cooperate with the Nippon-jin for building the Co-Prosperity Sphere?; Who do you admire most?[94]

The rigorous training program modeled after the education of the first-year draftees in the Japanese military was entirely a new experience and a culture shock for the cadets. On the first day at the *Kunrenjo*, their long hair was cropped to the scalp. Attired in a khaki uniform and wearing a cap, they stood erect at attention to listen to a stern welcome speech given by Captain Ogawa Tokuji, Director of the *Kunrenjo*. After congratulating them for having been chosen, he warned that they had come to the *Kunrenjo* to study the *Nippon seishin* discipline as well as to learn the dignity of labor and to get rid of the lazy habits that the British had instilled in them. He told them that the life at the *Kunrenjo* was strictly regulated by codes of conduct allowing no nonsense.[95]

From the first day at the *Kōa Kunrenjo*, the students lived in a world of controlled existence designed to give them a complete program of *seishin*. From morning till night they breathed *seishin*; they ate, played and sang, worked and slept with *seishin*. If they were not allowed to do something it was because of *seishin*. If they were made to do something which almost broke their back, it was still because of *seishin*. In short, *seishin* was to make them tough, fearless, and above all, men. That was what their instructors kept ceaselessly telling the cadets. "If you have *seishin*, you are a man. Without it, you are a mouse."[96] The teachers were determined to drum *seishin* into the minds of every one of the students. A day's program was full of activities and study from sunrise to sunset, and cadets hardly had time to rest. The following description conveys a glimpse of a typical daily schedule:

Reveille was at 6:00. At the sound of the bell the students had to get up and put away their own beds which had to be folded neatly. They rushed to a basin to brush their teeth, while Islamic cadets ran to a room especially provided for a morning prayer. Putting on their uniforms, they raced outside for a roll call. Students who were late for it were deprived of the privilege of a Sunday leave for that week. The roll call was followed by flag raising ceremonies and a deep bow in the direction of the Imperial Palace in Tokyo, and radio *taisō* (calisthenics). After that they recited in unison *Seito Shinjo* (Student's Creed), which underscored strict observance of rules, sincerity, diligence, discipline of mind and body, frugality, cooperation, integrity, justice, and loyalty to Imperial Japan.[97] Before breakfast at 7:30, the trainees cleaned up the lavatories, swept the drains around the buildings and compound, collected litter, and finally jogged around the field for four miles.

After breakfast, they assembled on the parade ground to go to classes on the double for morning lessons in *Nippon-go* and Japanese studies which consisted of learning *katakana*, *hiragana*, and *kanji*, history, geography and mathematics as well as listening to recitation and singing songs. The *Nippon-go* textbooks compiled by the staff of the *Kunrenjo*, were designed to inculcate *seishin*. Of 35 chapters in one of the texts, 23 were edifying stories extolling *Nippon seishin* and military virtues. In *Kunrenjo* life the common language was *Nippon-go*, the use of English being forbidden. Cadets were penalized by a fine for speaking English.[98] Occasionally, visiting dignitaries lectured on Japanese history, culture and ethics emphasizing the *Yamato damashii* (Japanese spirit) or memorializing a war hero who fought and died gallantly for the Emperor.

Much of the afternoon hours was spent for military training and physical exercise that were an important part of the curriculum. Some trainees fainted during a marching drill under the blazing tropical sun. They were not carried to a dispensary but were punished by being assigned to the "suicide squad" as cadets called it. Punishment included running around the field for two hours after the military drill was over. Afternoon gymnastics and sports consisted of bayonet practice, vaulting over wooden horses, and working out on parallel bars as well as kendo (Japanese fencing), sumo (Japanese wrestling) or judo. Martial sports were taken seriously. For instance, the instructor forced physically weaker trainees to remain in the sumo ring until they either would win a match or pass out from exhaustion. In this way the students developed and acquired physical stamina and agility as well as prowess.[99]

At the end of the day's activities the trainees assembled for flag lowering ceremonies. Until dinner at 17:30, they had a free period during which they bathed and relaxed. Taking a shower communally was a new experience, and many found it hard to get used to, particularly the Malays whose customs were contrary to such activities.

Roll call was at 20:30 and lights-out at 23:00. Students took turns on night watch. Once in a while, there was an emergency call without warning. The trainees were awakened from their sound sleep and were expected to assemble on the parade ground for a roll-call. On the first few occasions, it was a hilarious sight. The cadets had to put on their clothes and shoes in pitch darkness. There was confusion and chaos in which they, bumping and knocking into each other in the pitch darkness, tried to search for their underwear, socks, shoes, uniforms, and caps. Some came out to the field with two different shoes and in someone else's shirt and trousers. After frequent practice, they learned to be more alert and agile as well as self-confident in order to cope with the situation. Soon they were able to assemble outside in a few minutes for a roll call.

Integrated into the curriculum were an excursion to Syonan, a field day, and a 40-mile round trip march. The trip to Syonan was primarily for indoctrination. During a four-day tour, the cadets paid a courtesy call at *Gunseikambu* headquarters, where they were greeted by the chief executive officer, and went to pay their respects to such sacred places as Syonan *Jinja*, *Tyūreitō* built on the top of Bukit Timah where a fierce battle took place in the conquest of Singapore, and the Ford Automobile Plant where General Percival, the British commander, surrendered to General Yamashita. In the evening hours they saw a Japanese war movie. As one cadet said, a visit to the *Tyūreitō* was unforgettable when they saw British and Australian POWs, who only several months before ruled Singapore and Malaya, doing menial work that only indigenous people had done, and begging for cigarettes. The sight impressed the cadet reminding him of the dawn of a new era in Asia and of a new Malaya for which he had trained.[100]

Field day competition was not only for recreation but was also an occasion to develop group solidarity and a competitive spirit. In the games of *tunahiki* (a tug of war), *bōtaoshi* (game of knocking over a pole guarded by rows of defenders), and *kibasen* (game of mounted soldiers), as well as in marathons, the students demonstrated a fighting spirit and an *esprit de corps*. In the athletic contests they proved to themselves and to officers of the *Kunrenjo* that they could win against odds. In a field day competition of 1943 the cadets put up a good fight in *bōtaoshi* against a team of Japanese garrison army soldiers.

The third major event that was held just before the end of the training period was a 40-mile march. This was the occasion to test endurance and perseverance as well as strengthen group responsibility and solidarity. Up early in the morning, cadets, equipped with full military gear, walked in intense heat a distance of 40 miles between Malacca and Tampin and back. They covered it in 15 hours with brief rests, singing the song of the *Kōa Kunrenjo* and military songs. Very few dropped out of the trek. Persevering in the intense heat and enduring painful sore feet, thirst, and fatigue, they made it, while stronger cadets helped weaker ones to complete the march. A whole group might be punished for leaving behind drop-outs.

What was most impressive during the march was that the Director and the instructors, too, walked with the students every inch of the way. The British, they thought, would have driven in a car. They felt much closer to the instructors who shared the rigors of the march with them.[101]

As has been described in the preceding paragraphs, the *Kunrenjo* was intended to groom a middle-ranking leadership corps thoroughly immersed in Japanese ideals and ethos – *seishin*, discipline, perseverance, sacrifice, frugality, obedience, devotion to moral goals, responsibility, and the like. By undergoing the training, the cadets indeed acquired these qualities and matured physically and psychologically. One former trainee recalled an incident in which he was involved. During physical training he fell on the ground scraping one side of his face. He cried out in pain expecting sympathy from an instructor, who instead of offering comforting words, slapped him hard on the other cheek, barking "nobody cries in pain in this school!" The lesson taught him to be strong. Far from creating hostile feelings, this kind of discipline and self-control seemed to have encouraged the cadets to emulate their instructor's toughness.[102]

Discipline was not to be flouted without punishment. To break rules would invite severe chastisement. One cadet, caught redhanded by an instructor, was smuggling bread across the fence surrounding the *Kunrenjo* compound violating student codes. He was punished mercilessly. The instructor pounced on the trainee like a sack of potatoes; he kicked, slapped and threw the poor fellow on the floor several times until the boy lay bleeding. The teacher ordered the student to be confined in a cell for three days provided only with newspapers for bedding and no solid foods but a cupful of water twice a day.

Fellow students were stunned by the brutal treatment administered by the instructor, who otherwise had been known to be a moderate teacher. Had the bread been stolen, they would have understood the severity of the punishment, but the boy had paid for the bread. Where then was the offence? Could not a person buy anything with his own money? One thing they had overlooked – *seishin*. Yes, *seishin* was what was expected of them, and the cadet failed the expectation. To repress hunger is *seishin*, as the *Bushidō seishin* extolled. To fill your stomach, even with food bought with your own money, was not *seishin*. Not to have *seishin* was an unforgivable crime of the worst kind one could commit at the *Kunrenjo*.[103]

On the other hand, honesty and courage were valued and admired. One former student recollects an incident where his entire squad was ordered to line up for an offence committed by one of the cadets in the group. An instructor demanded to know who was the guilty person and asked him to identify himself voluntarily. The culprit fearing severe discipline was too frightened to come forward and confess his crime. Finally, summoning up his courage, he stepped out expecting a blow in his face. The teacher, much to his surprise, bear-hugged the student commending his honesty and courage as exemplary conduct.[104]

The systematic indoctrination program had indeed created an impact on cadets at the *Kunrenjo*. One student said that one thing he learned at the *Kunrenjo* was a *"gambari seishin* (spirit of endurance)" which meant "never give up on anything no matter how difficult" a task was.[105] Another trainee declared that by the time the training period was over he had changed "all his old habits and ways of thinking" and learned "something of the Nippon spirit . . . ready to serve in the reconstruction of a New Malaya."[106] Still another cadet asserted that the *Nippon seishin* was "supreme in the world" and that all the people of Greater East Asia should be "loyal to the Emperor and work hard for the construction of the Greater East Asia Co-Prosperity Sphere."[107]

The Japanese government also created a much more intensive program of "Japanization" for Malay youths who were to be trained in Japan for three years under the *Nanpō Tokubetsu Ryūgakusei* program (Special Overseas Students from the Southern Regions). It was established in February 1943 by the Greater East Asia Ministry in order that students from the occupied countries of Southeast Asia would be trained in acquiring the essence of *Nippon seishin* to become "useful leaders of their countries for the construction of the *Daitōa Kyōeiken*" in cooperation with Japan. Specifically, they were to be indoctrinated in enhancing the spirit of Oriental morality, bringing about a greater understanding of and trust in "Imperial Nippon," promoting a correct understanding of the construction of Greater East Asia, strengthening their desire for it with dedication, and acquiring the superior science and technology of "Imperial Nippon."[108] Elaborating in much more concrete terms, Tōkō Takezō, an official of the Greater East Asia Ministry, explained that the objective of the program was to train capable young men who, through indoctrination in *Nippon seishin*, would think and behave like the Japanese, renouncing their blind adoration of the Anglo-American way of life and truly understanding Japan in order to cooperate with it for the construction of a Greater East Asia.[109]

Under this program 12 students from Syonan and Malaya came to Japan in two groups in 1943 and 1944 (eight in 1943 and four in 1944).[110] In addition, five more Malay youths came to Japan under the Tokugawa Scholarship established by Marquis Tokugawa Yoshichika himself. *Nanpō Tokubetsu Ryūgakusei* or *Nantokusei*, as the term was commonly abbreviated, were chosen from various social strata and educational backgrounds, while the Tokugawa Scholarship recipients were selected from families of royal houses and *orang besar* (distinguished people).[111] The students of both groups went through one month of special training at the *Kōa Kunrenjo* to prepare themselves physically and psychologically for a much more rigorous indoctrination program in Japan.

The Tokugawa Scholarship students arrived in Tokyo on January 6, 1943 and were housed with the Tokugawa family. In a press interview held a few days after their arrival, Ungku Aziz declared that "Malais, young and old alike, irrespective of the class distinction, today are conscious of a new and better life and are striving for a still better life by collaborating with Nippon military administration." Ungku Mushin stated that Malay youths of today were, without exception, proud of being Asians. Wan Abdul Hamid said emphatically that ". . . new and bright days dawned upon the Malais."[112] The three young men studied at Waseda University and the Tokyo College of Agriculture. Although they were enthusiastic at first for the opportunity to be able to study in Japan, their enthusiasm began to wane creating some serious problems in late 1944. After returning from Syonan, Marquis Tokugawa discussed the future of the five students with officials of the Ministry of Education. In his diary he expressed his disappointment at the Ministry's lack of support for his scholarship project, saying that he would not be able to take care of the scholarship students properly.[113] Partly because of complaints from the students of little official support and little educational opportunity and partly because of the deterioration of the war situation, it was decided to send them home in February 1945, cutting short their original plan to study in Japan for three years.

Nantokusei received much more proper treatment from the Japanese government.[114] Disembarked in Moji in northeasternmost Kyushu,[115] the first group of *Nantokusei* stayed overnight at a Japanese inn, where they encountered the first cultural shock of communal bathing. They had not been accustomed to bathing together in the nude. Only after repeated orders of a Japanese instructor did they enter into a communal bath with great hesitancy.[116]

On the following day they travelled by train to Tokyo and arrived on June 30 at Tokyo Central Station. They were greeted by representatives of the Army, the Greater East Asia Ministry, and the *Kokusai Gakuyūkai* (International Students Institute).[117] Dressed in army khaki uniforms they snapped to attention at a command in *Nippon-go*, and their precise and energetic movements pleased the Japanese officials no end. Kanazawa Hitoshi of the *Kokusai Gakuyūkai* could not help but marvel at the military-like discipline which they had acquired in a few months of training at the *Kunrenjo*, though he was apprehensive whether these indoctrinated students could adjust themselves to a liberal educational environment at the Institute.[118]

Following the ceremony at the station, they were immediately led to the grounds of the Imperial Palace where they cheered "*Tennō Heika Banzai* (Long Live the Emperor)" and a few days later to the Yasukuni Shrine and the Meiji Shrine – sacred Shinto shrines consecrated to the memory of the war dead and the Emperor Meiji, respectively. Writing of their visit to the Imperial Palace grounds, the *Asahi* newspaper reported that the awe-inspiring ceremony "visibly moved the students."[119]

The Malay group was housed in the *Kokusai Gakuyūkai*'s dormitory at the former American School in Meguro, where they stayed until March of the following year, for 10 months of intensive *Nippon-go* training, studying five hours a day. The daily program of the *nantokusei* was similar to that of the *Kōa Kunrenjo* and their daily life to that of the Military Academy.[120] The supposedly liberal educational environment that characterized the *Kokusai Gakuyūkai* notwithstanding, the objective of the training was to wipe out thoroughly the students' so-called "Anglo-Saxon ideology" and to implant in them an awareness of being citizens of Asia. Okamoto Senmantarō, *Kokusai Gakuyūkai*'s councillor, had elaborated the objective of *Nippon-go* education by articulating that what had to be taught through *Nippon-go*, the *lingua franca* of all peoples of *Daitōa* for appreciating Japan's culture, was to develop the diligence and studiousness which had facilitated Japan's modernization. In addition, he said that *Nippon-go* education should be aimed at inculcating Japanese *seishin* which was the bedrock of "*Nippon* culture symbolized by the unbroken line of *kokutai* (national polity), loyalty and patriotism, and the simple but refined way of life and arts epitomized in Shintoism." *Nippon-go*, he said further, should be the instrument through which "*Nippon-seishin*" was to be infused through instructional and inspirational lectures on *kokutai*, the forty seven *rōnin*, bushido, the Meiji Restoration, and Japanese arts.[121] This kind of educational philosophy steeped in spiritualism was accentuated further by the appointment, insisted upon by the Army Ministry, of a retired army general, who was once the Principal of the

Military Preparatory School and the commanding general of the Kwantung Army's Military Police, to be the Principal of the *Kokusai Gakuyūkai's Nippon-go* School. The appointment, according to Kanazawa, was intended to keep the *Nantokusei* from being tainted by "liberal" influences of the regular staff of the *Kokusai Gakuyūkai*.[122]

Class room study of *Nippon-go* was interspersed with lectures on culture, history, and the arts and visits to such sacred places as the Grand Shrines of Ise and the Tōgō Shrine as well as museums, the military academy, steel mills, a broadcasting station, department stores, and so on.[123] In short, "the final product was expected to be so saturated with Japanese ideologies, Japanese habits and customs, Japanese discipline and the Japanese outlook, that he was considered a new human being – a newly manufactured 'Japanese.'"[124]

At the end of the ten-month training in *Nippon-go* and physical exercise at the *Kokusai Gakuyūkai* in late March, 1944 the *Nantokusei* took a series of examinations (*Nippon-go*, history, mathematics and physics) preparatory to entering colleges and universities located in the western part of Japan. Taking their wishes and academic achievements into consideration, the government sent the students variously to Hiroshima Higher Normal School, Miyazaki Higher School of Forestry and Agriculture, Kumamoto College of Medicine, and Kanagawa Police Training School.[125]

A few months after the first group of the *Nantokusei* enrolled in their respective schools, the second batch consisting of 89 students from Southeast Asia arrived in Tokyo in June 1944. Four of these were from Malaya, and two were from North Borneo. They, too, entered schools of their choice in April 1945, but two of them – one each from Malaya and North Borneo – enrolled in the Military Academy.[126] There was no recruitment for a third group in 1945 perhaps because of the deteriorating situation of the war. In the meantime, the government had decided to relocate all foreign students including *Nantokusei* to a few selected schools in accordance with the policy, *Principles of Emergency Measures for Foreign Students*, adopted by the cabinet on December 29, 1944,[127] partly for their safety and partly because of the serious problems arising from the discontents being accumulated on the part of the *Nantokusei* about isolation, difficult relations with Japanese supervisors and local people, and communications gaps, that "contributed to complications causing emotional flareups."[128] In April 1945, the Malay students were transferred to Kyoto Imperial University, Hiroshima University of Humanities and Sciences, Fukuoka Higher School,

Tokushima College of Technology, and Kumamoto College of Medicine. They continued to study at these institutions until the end of the war in special classes of private lessons with professors, because most schools suspended regular classes after April 1, 1945, and Japanese students were either drafted for military service or mobilized for ammunition factories.[129]

When the atomic bomb was dropped over Hiroshima on August 6, there were three Malay *Nantokusei* studying at Hiroshima University of Humanities and Sciences. Two of them died of the effect of its radiation – Nik Yusoff died instantly and Syed Omar passed away on September 3 at a hospital in Kyoto, where his remains were interred.[130] The third student, Abdul Razak, together with five other *Nantokusei*, miraculously survived. Another Malay student, Syed Mansoor, who studied at Kumamoto College of Medicine, died of tuberculosis at the University Hospital of the Imperial University of Kyushu on December 21, 1946, and he was buried in Fukuoka.[131] Nine other Malay *Nantokusei* returned home in September, 1945.[132]

The students who studied at the *Kōa Kunrenjo* and in Japan were by and large positive in evaluating the program as useful for developing their self-discipline, self-reliance, self-respect, and *gambari seishin*. Asked to evaluate how the *Kunrenjo*'s programs helped change their character, former students replied in interviews stating their reactions. The following statements represent their retrospective evaluations: "The *Kunrenjo* training has taught me to be self-reliant and to take the initiative and has helped me prepare to work hard and never to give up something that I set out to accomplish."[133] "The *Kunrenjo*'s training is a great help to achieve my success today."[134] "The *Kunrenjo* program is really beneficial for trying to test one's ability, and the Malaysian government should adopt a similar program for training government officials."[135] "I realize that no work is too difficult to accomplish, and I would not have risen that fast in my career, if it were not for my Japanese training."[136] "The training has taught me to be more diligent in my work and has enabled me to solve problems and make a good decision."[137] "Definitely, it has helped me change from being materialistic to being spiritualistic."[138] "The training is especially profitable for having acquired a quick action without wasting time in carrying out any given task."[139] "The programs have taught me to work hard. It is the *seishin* that taught me to do best in my endeavors."[140] "The *Kunrenjo*'s training has made me confident, resilient, and unafraid to take on responsibilities, especially not to consider the white man as a superior race. I have become proud myself of being an Asian."[141] "The *Kunrenjo*'s programs have helped me consolidate my own views of a good way of life and have taught me to be able to socialize and to be friendly to others beside my own people."[142]

When former cadets were asked whether the wartime training changed their attitude towards Asian solidarity and towards their own country, the overwhelming majority replied affirmatively. They were most emphatic that the Japanese had "instilled national solidarity and consciousness."[143] The *Kunrenjo* training served as a catalyst for them in the development of their own nationalism.

These postwar statements of former students 32 years after their experience echoed wartime sentiments expressed by the cadets about the *Kunrenjo* training then. One of the cadets of the wartime Japanese training program proudly said: "I feel as if I were reborn and [I am] a new man possessing new culture and greater ambition."[144] Another trainee said in 1943: "I learned the dignity of labour when I cultivated land and grew vegetables in the *Kunrenjo* ground. In the British period, the educated never held a *chungkul* (hoe). To hold it meant you were a labourer and lost dignity. In the Japanese period, everyone was equal and there was no class discrimination."[145]

Every one of the *Nantokusei* was even more affirmative in evaluating his experiences in Japan and their impact on his personal life. One former student said that he owed what "he has achieved today to the training and experience in Japan."[146] Another *Nantokusei*'s opinion represents the prevailing view of his fellow students. Asked to make an assessment of his experience in wartime that contributed to changing his personal traits, Tungku Abdullah listed the following points: (1) sense of almost military-like discipline; (2) *gambari seishin*; (3) work ethic – dedication to work and achievement; (4) respect for elderly persons; (5) punctuality; (6) politeness and understanding the other person's problems and feelings; (7) love for nation; and (8) orderliness in life style.[147]

These positive evaluations notwithstanding, critical comments are not lacking from former students, particularly those who had had higher education at British schools in prewar days. One former graduate of the *Kōa Kunrenjo* and also an alumnus of Raffles College said that the Japanese teachers "did not seem to understand that many cadets were degree holders of such higher institutions of learning as Raffles and King Edward VII Medical College, the highest educational establishments in British Malaya." He had a skeptical view of Japanese cultural indoctrination.[148] Another gradu-

ate of the *Kōa Kunrenjo* reported that he did not believe the myth-
ology about *Amaterasu Omikami* (Sun Goddess who was supposedly
the ancestress of the Imperial Family), the divinity of the Emperor,
and the like. If the Japanese accepted them as their own beliefs, he
said, it was "their business and not mine."[149] Still another graduate
managed to evade nomination for an opportunity to study in Japan
because he did not want to be indoctrinated in the cult of Emperorism about which he was also skeptical.[150]

Although these young men were mostly around 20 years old and
certainly susceptible to Japanese propaganda and indoctrination,[151]
most of them maintained the mentality that they had acquired in
prewar British education steeped in free inquiry. This helped them to
sustain a sense of balance enabling them to keep from being completely Japanized and to hold an arm's length view of Japanese
cultural indoctrination.

Japan's cultural indoctrination programs came to an abrupt end
with its defeat giving the occupied Malayans immediate relief from
the strict regimen imposed upon them every day. No sooner had the
war ended than they longed for the return of the British, discarding
everything that was associated with Japan and its imposed culture; no
traces of the Japanese presence were left in Singapore and Malaya
except such hated words as "*kempeitai*" (military police), "*bakaya-
rō*" (idiot), "*rōmusha*" (forced laborer), "*binta*" (slap in the face),
and the like that harassed and tormented people in daily life during
the occupation period.[152] To that extent, the Japanese cultural policy
of imposing its own value system upon indigenous people, which was
implemented too hastily and too crudely and clumsily, was a failure
even discounting the fact that it was implemented in a short span of
less than four years under the unusual circumstances of war in which
by the second year Japan was fighting a losing battle. As a result,
instead of winning popular support for ideals and objectives of
Daitōa Kyoeiken, generic Japanese cultural policy and its programs
seemed to have left a legacy of bitter hatred toward the Japanese that
lingered for some years in the postwar period not only in Malaya and
Singapore but also elsewhere in Southeast Asia.[153]

Many of the cultural programs geared to "Nipponization" seemed
to be contrary to the principles laid out in *Senryōchi Gunsei Shori
Yōkō* (Outline of Military Administration of Occupied Areas) of
March 14, 1942, that warned of the dangers of interference in
customs and religion of the indigenous people. Forced Emperor
worship, Syonan Shinto Shrine, and *Tyūreitō* all created resentment

toward the Japanese. Furthermore, Japanese cultural and *Nippon-go* education policies were paternalistic if not undisguisedly racist. Military authorities presented Japan as a superior nation founded upon the cult of Emperorism and depicted the Japanese themselves as big brothers and people with an outstanding quality of leadership. Conversely, occupied people and their cultures were seen as inferior and backward. Therefore, it appeared logical for the Japanese to assume that the indigenous people should be subservient to Japanese masters and should emulate the superior Japanese way of life that was presented in the *Hakkō Ichiu* ideology and *kōminka* and *kōdō* education. Worse yet was the attitude of Japanese officials including *bunkajin* engaged in propagandizing Japanese culture. Most of them, without seriously studying the culture of the indigenous people, had a preconceived notion that these other Asians had no culture worthy of the name. To propagate cultural programs with such arrogance could in no way, of course, win the support of the occupied people, who, having been liberated from colonialism by the Japanese, expected an equality of partnership that they thought was the spirit of *Daitōa Kyōeiken*. When they encountered the reality of the harsh and brutal military administration and the crude cultural programs of *kōminka* education implemented by arrogant officials, their disappointment was so great that they simply turned away from responding to Japan's propaganda messages.

However, the specific training at various *Kunrenjo* in Singapore and Malaya as well as in Japan was individually certainly a useful experience and a unique educational opportunity for those young men who participated in the programs. As has been discussed, the *Kunrenjo* training not only strengthened body and soul and solidarity but also significantly augmented their self-confidence, in particular eliminating lingering fears of *orang puteh* (white man). Favorable responses of former trainees are certainly indicative that the *Kunrenjo* training had an impact upon their future careers in the long run, though some did question Japanese cultural propaganda and Japanese sincerity. Nonetheless, former cadets appeared to have learned what was best from the training and surely for the most part made excellent use of what they acquired for their careers.

The *Nanpō Tokubetsu Ryūgakusei* system was Japan's first national educational policy under which a large number of young scholarship students from the occupied areas in the Southern region were systematically invited to Japan for further education and training as well as indoctrination.[154] The program itself was abandoned unilaterally by the Japanese government upon the termination of the war forcing the students without financial security into a chaotic and confused postwar Japanese society in which they literally had to live on their own until their departure. The Japanese government deserves much criticism for this irresponsible decision that resulted in much hardship for many *Nantokusei*. This arbitrary policy of termination of the program, however, does not mean that the *Nantokusei* program was a failure.

Indeed, the *Nantokusei*, among all the indigenous Asian people who received wartime Japanese education and training, place the highest value on their experiences as well as on the Japanese with whom they came into contact. "It was the best kind of education," one former student said, "that no money could buy and changed my outlook for the better."[155] "I am aware that the program was a part of Japanese occupation policy," another one declared, but "it was the most valuable and precious experience in my life."[156] Not only do they evaluate the training favorably, but they also sincerely appreciated the many kindnesses with which Japanese hosts treated them and the sacrifices which these same Japanese made in trying to make these young men's lives in Japan comfortable under adverse wartime circumstances. All of them, including the Malay trainees, are indeed nostalgic for the wartime Japanese life of less food, comfort, and amenities, because under those conditions the Japanese treated the *Nantokusei* as if they were family members sharing what little they had.[157] *Nantokusei* and the Japanese during World War 2 were mutually poor in material life but were rich in their human relations, because they were bound together by "*kokoro-to-kokoro no tsunagari* (linked by heart-to-heart relationship)". This was the consensus of 67 former *Nantokusei* who gathered in 1983 in Tokyo for the 40th anniversary of their arrival in Tokyo.[158]

It is for this reason, then, that "none of the *Nantokusei* returned home with bitterness toward Japan and its people."[159] Today they remain most understanding friends of the Japanese, forming in their respective countries the core of the ASEAN Council of Japan Alumni, which was organized in 1977 for a deeper understanding and friendship between Japan and ASEAN. In contrast to their feelings the Japanese today are criticized for being arrogant toward other Asians whom they look down upon with disdain. As a result, many current Asian students return home with anti-Japanese sentiments. A significant lesson can perhaps be drawn from the wartime experience for improving Japan's present foreign student program and contemporary Japanese attitudes toward Asians.

Evaluating the impact of the *Kunrenjo* training and the *Nantokusei* programs, it may be argued whether there is a correlation between the programs and postwar careers of former cadets. Although there has not been a thorough study of the individual participants concerning this question, it is tentatively concluded, based upon a study of limited samples of Tokugawa scholarship students, former *Kōa Kunrenjo* students, and *Nantokusei* in Malaysia, that there seems to be some correlation between the training and successful careers.[160] Practically all of these men attributed their postwar career successes to *gambari seishin* (never-give-up-spirit). Ungku Aziz, former Vice Chancellor of the University of Malaya summed up the impact of the Japanese cultural indoctrination policy upon postwar careers when he replied in an interview with the author: "Many Malayans who received the Japanese training at the *Kunrenjo* and in Japan are very successful. There are hardly any leaders in Malaysia today who were not trained at the *Kunrenjo* and in Japan and hardly any of those trained by Japanese at the *Kunrenjo* and in Japan did not become leaders."[161] This conclusion, however, must be somewhat qualified since many of the former students, particularly *Nantokusei* and Tokugawa scholarship students who were selected largely from prominent families, were likely to have succeeded in their chosen careers with or without the Japanese training. Until a more thorough and systematic investigation of the individual participants is done, a positive evaluation must remain tentative.

As was also discussed at the beginning of this essay, the cultural programs were organized by the military and carried out by *bunkajin* for the systematic indoctrination of the occupied people. To implement these programs the military mobilized several hundred *bunkajin*.[162] During their service and afterward, until the war was over, they produced hundreds of reports, essays, novels, poems, speeches, films, paintings, and musical compositions to propagate Japanese culture.[163]

These drafted *bunkajin* may be classified into several categories. Some volunteered for service with the *Sendenbu*; others joined it with reluctance; still others participated in it with naiveté or curiosity; and some seemingly joined it against their wishes. It is difficult to ascertain now which *bunkajin* belonged to which category, because most of them have passed away and most of the surviving *bunkajin* are reluctant to talk about their wartime role in propaganda activities, and, even if they do talk, the truth is difficult to determine.

I would like to discuss briefly the role of certain *bunkajin* who were active propagandists in order to evaluate the cultural policy in occupied Syonan and Malaysia.

Nakajima Kenzō, a former leftist liberal, played a prominent role in the *Sendenbu*'s campaign for the popularization of *Nippon-go* in which he declared that people of Syonan and Malaya should be "taught to learn and speak *Nippon-go*" and "when they are able to speak, even broken *Nippon-go*, will the *Daitōa Kyōeiken* be established . . . and will Malaya and Sumatra be incorporated into Japanese territory."[164] Also in his speech to graduates of the Syonan *Nippon Gakuen*, Nakajima, without having much knowledge of educational problems in a plural society, criticized the British *laissez-faire* policy of primary-school education which he said had no principles and neglected to build moral character.[165]

After his return to Japan from Malaya and Syonan, Nakajima delivered a number of speeches on *Nippon-go* education and *Daitōa Kyōeiken* and spoke regularly to students of the government-operated *Nippon-go* Teachers' Training Institute emphasizing the importance of teaching and propagating the language in the Southern region. Also in January 1943 he joined the Army-financed *Tōhōsha* to engage in anti-British propaganda activities. Judging from his wartime record, Nakajima worked closely with the military serving as a mouthpiece for *Hakkō Ichiu* propaganda. Writing in 1957, however, he was apologetic implying that "what appeared to be an activist role played in wartime" was against his wishes and was forced upon him at gun point, and that he himself, too, was a victim of militarism.[166]

Until 1982 he had kept silent about most of his wartime activities, and only then Nakajima revealed in his autobiography in detail his wartime record in Syonan as a member of the *Sendenbu*. By that time, the former wartime activist Nakajima had established his reputation as a progressive liberal and as the director general of the Japan–China Association for Cultural Exchange in which he served since 1956. The book was Nakajima's apologia for "what appeared to be a wartime activist role." For example, he wrote that he refused to rewrite the first draft of a speech that was to be delivered by General Yamashita on the Emperor's birthday after it was rejected by military authorities as the "writing of a liberalist."[167] He also said that he was "fed up with composing slogans for the *Nippon-go* Emphasis Week," and that he resisted a military order to propose new Japanese names for the streets in Syonan.[168] That may be so. Nonetheless, his literary career and political orientation did fluctuate from left to right and right to left through the years since the 1930s, not dissimilar to many of his contemporary *bunkajin* drafted to work on cultural policy.

Jimbo Kōtarō, a poet and a Germanic scholar, is a much more interesting case of a *bunkajin* as propagandist. Before he was drafted into the *Sendenbu*, he was an apparently innocent *bunkajin* having no interest in cultural propaganda. Once he assumed the post as the principal of Syonan *Nippon Gakuen*, however, as he wrote, Jimbo transformed himself into an activist agitated by an "uncontrollable urge to do something for the nation."[169] Based upon his experiences in Syonan and Malaya, he wrote four books – memoirs, essays, and collected poems – that exalted the virtue of the Japanese spirit which Jimbo wanted to impose upon the indigenous people. He was very "glad to be given the opportunity to engage in the *bunkajin* service in the war" and was proud of "being selected" to work on cultural policy.[170] Commenting on Jimbo's radical spiritual transformation, one critic attacked him with scathing words:

It may be a bit of an exaggeration to say that he is an example of how stupid a poet is. I wonder how his mental faculty with which he has imposed without hesitation Japan's virtues and beauty upon men who are not Japanese operates. This book [*Syonan Nippon Gakuen*] lays bare the shame of Japan's *bunkajin* who have carried out such policies with audaciousness.[171]

The criticism is harsh, but Jimbo's wartime books and poems, studded with rabid anti-Western passages and ultranationalistic lines, contrast sharply with his prewar anti-war and romantic sentiment.[172] Jimbo's transformations from anti-war and pacifist poet to a romantic realist, to an extreme nationalist poet, and to an innocent poet in the postwar years is unusual, to say the least. Jimbo's anti-Westernism and racist strain may well have been amplified by the background of his Germanic scholarship and his fondness for German music of which his preference was for that of Richard Wagner, Adolf Hitler's favorite composer. Jimbo's case is that of the romantic naiveté of an innocent poet who allowed himself to be used as a mouthpiece of the cultural policy for *kōdō* and *kōminka* education as well as "Nipponization." Once he became a spokesman for military propaganda and held authority over what he regarded as inferior people with backward cultural standards, Jimbo, intoxicated with the anticipation of victory, turned himself without ideological preparation into an ultra-nationalist *bunkajin*.[173] With the same ease Jimbo, without the slightest compunction, returned again in postwar years to being an innocent and passive poet.

Ibuse Masuji, the doyen of the literary world, a prolific and popular writer, and a recipient of the Order of Cultural Merit, unlike many of his contemporary colleagues, in his writings does not evidence ideological meandering in the interwar years. His numerous writings published during and after the war were purely literary. *Hana no Machi*, his major novel, based upon his experiences in Syonan and published in 1943, is a satirical work in which Ibuse supposedly having distaste for a warlike spirit tried to show the qualms of his conscience for having cooperated with the cultural policy aimed at "Nipponization." Nonetheless, Ibuse found some satisfaction as a member of the *Sendenbu* in propagating the virtue of Japanese culture and of the Emperor cult. As he said, the experience of giving lectures on Japanese history to Malayan students of *Nippon-go* "made his life worth living." Though he may have been less compromising with the military, Ibuse, as a member of the occupying forces, can be held responsible for imposing Japanese cultural values upon the indigenous people.[174]

I have discussed the wartime activities of three *bunkajin* engaged in the propagation of "Nipponization." They were not an exceptional group of *bunkajin* who cooperated with the military. Practically all of them were drafted for *Sendenbu* activities and, in one way or another, did serve as mouthpieces for the military propaganda of "Nipponization." Some went further than Nakajima, Jimbo, and Ibuse, while others passively followed the military policy of spreading *Nippon-go* as the *lingua franca* and of propagating Japanese culture, and few resisted it.[175] In military-dominated Japan fighting for its survival, even the most liberal *bunkajin* such as Tsurumi Yūsuke and Miki Kiyoshi served the military.[176] Such was the political and intellectual atmosphere of wartime Japan in which *bunkajin* had seemingly little alternative but to comply with the demands of the military, although it was clearly against their wishes for some *bunkajin*.[177] These men could, of course, be kept in military service as a punitive measure, as was the case of Satomura Kinzō who was drafted for military service in 1937 and kept in it until he died in the Philippines in February 1945 because he was a runaway soldier and a former proletarian writer.

It was certainly natural for the military to seek the services of intellectuals like the *bunkajin* to assist in the formulation and execution of Japanese wartime cultural policies. For their part the *bunkajin*, whose intellectual roots were relatively shallow at best, were often flattered to have the opportunity to "serve the nation" and were also often intoxicated by the semblance of power which their new "importance" seemed to bestow upon them. Accordingly, it is perhaps not so surprising that a significant portion of the *bunkajin* recruited for propaganda work in the Southern regions were profoundly committed to it and worked very hard at it.

Notes and References

1. For a study of Malay nationalism, see William R. Roff, *The Origins of Malay Nationalism* (Kuala Lumpur, Malaysia: University of Malaya Press, 1976).
2. "Daitōa Seiryaku Shidō Taikō" ("Basic Principles for the Political Strategy of Greater East Asia"), May 31, 1943, adopted by an Imperial Conference, in *Sambō Honbu* (Army General Staff) (ed.), *Sugiyama Memo* (General Sugiyama's Memorandum) II (Tokyo: Hara Shobō, 1967), pp. 352–3.
3. Gaimushō, Seimu Dai Ni-ka (Foreign Ministry, Political Affairs Bureau Second Section), "Marai no Dokuritsu Mondai" ("On the Problem of Malaya's Independence"), February 20, 1945; "Marai Dokuritsu no Kanōsei ni tsuite" ("On the Possibility of Malaya's Independence"), July 1945, in *Senryōchi Gyōsei Kankei. Daitōa Sensō Kankei Toji* (Administration of Occupied Areas. Greater East Asian War File).
4. *International Military Tribunal for Far East, Exhibit 1336*. Dated January 7, 1942.
5. Ibid., *Exhibit 1335*. Dated February 18, 1942.
6. Machida Keiji, *Tatakau Bunka Butai* (Fighting Cultural Unit) (Tokyo: Hara Shobō, 1967), pp. 19–20; Tsuneishi Shigetsugu, *Shinri Sakusen no Kaisō* (Reminiscences of Psychological Warfare) (Tokyo: Tōsen Shuppan, 1978), pp. 5–7. The Propaganda Unit was modeled after J. Goebbels's P. K. (*Propaganda Kompanie*) at the recommendation of General Yamashita Tomoyuki, who visited Nazi Germany in early 1941 as head of a military mission.
7. Machida, *Tatakau Bunka Butai*, p. 20. In cooperation with Major Fujiwara Iwaichi and Major Katō Katsuo of the 8th Section (Propaganda and Espionage), General Staff, Nakajima, a part-time employee, helped prepare a list of *bunkajin* to be drafted. Some of them volunteered for the service. For example, Hayashi Fusao, a nationalist writer converted from Marxism, offered himself to the Press Department of the War

Ministry because of his strong ideological commitment to the cause of the war. After the war, Hayashi published in 1963 the controversial book *Daitōa Sensō Kōtei-Ron* (An Affirmative Discourse on the Greater East Asian War). The final selection of the personnel was made jointly by the chiefs of the Eighth Section and the Press Department of the War Ministry. Ibid., p. 363.

8. Machida, *Tatakau Bunka Butai*, pp. 15, 24, 299; Nakajima Kenzō, *Shōwa Jidai* (The Shōwa Era) (Tokyo: Iwanami Shoten, 1957), p. 155; Nakajima Kenzō, *Uka Tensei no Maki: Kaisō no Bungaku* (Literary Reminiscences of Nakajima Kenzō) vol. 5 (Tokyo: Hiebonsha, 1977), pp. 12–14, 30, 73, 78, 151, 175: Kuroda Hidetoshi, *Gunsei* (Military Government) (Tokyo: Gakufū Shoin, 1952), pp. 73, 74–5; Ibuse Masuji, *Ibuse Jisen Zenshū* (Ibuse's Selected Works) vol. 10 (Tokyo: Shin-chōsha, 1986), p. 257. Some *bunkajin* considered the draft as a punishment for their anti-military attitude. They sarcastically remarked that it was *chōyō* (punishment) rather than *chōyō* (draft). Nakajima denied that it was meant to be a punishment, but he characterized it as a mandatory recruitment and admitted that the appointments of the *bunkajin* to various positions in propaganda operations was not a case of the right man in the right post. Some military officers, however, understood that it was a disciplinary measure against the *bunkajin*. Among those who were drafted as a punitive measure were former liberal leftists (Miki Kiyoshi, Ōya Sōichi, Nakajima), Marxists like Shimizu Ikutarō, or a deserter from military service like Satomura Kinzō.

Ibuse is the doyen of Japanese novelists and a winner of many literary awards including The Japan Art Academy Award in 1956. He is today a member of the Japan Art Academy and is a recipient of the Order of Cultural Merit (*Bunka Kunshō*), the highest medal the nation bestows upon a person who distinguishes himself in humanities and sciences. He has written several works based upon his experiences in Syonan including *Syonan Nikki* (Syonan Diary), *Hana no Machi* (The City of Flowers), and *Marai no Tsuchi* (The Soil of Malaya). Jimbo Kōtarō, a poet and a scholar of German Literature, has published *Syonan Nippon Gakuen* (Syonan Japanese School) and *Fudō to Aijō* (Climate and Love) based upon his experiences in Syonan. Kitagawa Fuyuhiko is a poet. Nakamura Jihei, a novelist, has written *Marai Dengekisen* (Malayan Blitzkrieg) and *Marai no Hitobito* (Malayan People). Sakai Seiichirō, a novelist, has published *Kinabaru no Tami* (People of Kinabalu). Satomura Kinzō, a former proletarian writer and a deserter from military service, was redrafted into the service after having recanted in 1937. During his service in the Southern region, he published *Marai Senwashū* [Collection of Battle Reports on the Malay Operations] and *Kawa no Tami* [People of the River]. He was not permitted to return home like some of the others and was dispatched in 1945 as a war correspondent to the Philippines, where he died in action on 23 February. Kaionji Ushigorō, a historical novelist, has published *Marai no Kakyō-ki* (Chinese in Malaya). Terasaki Hiroshi, a university instructor and a playwright, has written *Kaju Kiraku* (Flame of a Forest of Blossoms). Kurihara Makoto,

156   *Japanese Cultural Policy in Malaya and Singapore*

a water color painter, has published *Rokunin no Hōdō Shōtai* (Six-War-Correspondent Platoon). Oguri Mushitarō is a mystery fiction writer.

9. *Sendenhan* was known by its nickname *Marusen* coined by a member of the 25th Army *Sendenbu*. Its members wore an armband designed with the Chinese character *Sen* (Propaganda) written in black on a white fabric. The letter was surrounded by a circle made by the words *Barisan Propaganda* written in red cloth. Machida, *Tatakau Bunka Butai*, pp. 347–8.

10. Sumatra was incorporated into the area administered by the 25th Army until March 1943, when the 25th Army was transferred to Sumatra to administer the island, while Syonan and Malaya were placed under the direct command of the Southern Army for military administration.

11. *The Syonan Times*, February 28, 2602 (1942). Ibuse assumed the editorship of *The Syonan Times* on February 19 and served for three months. The first day's edition was mastheaded as *Shonan Times* instead of *Syonan*. It was corrected in the second day's edition to *Syonan* in conformity with the spelling in the 1923 edition of *Sanseido's Dictionary*. Ibuse, *Ibuse Jisen Zenshū* vol. 8, pp. 88–9, 232.

12. War Ministry, Secretariat, *Senryōchi Gunsei Shori Yōkō* (Principles for the Disposition of the Occupied Areas under Military Administration), March 14, 1942. "Secret"

13. Watanabe spent most of his military career in the 1930s in China engaging in political affairs. He was appointed in 1940 to the Total War Institute, where he prepared *Basic Plan for Establishing the Dai Tōa Kyōeiken* and *Establishment of East Asia: Maneuvers for the First Period of Total War*; see notes 4 and 5. Watanabe was the architect of *budan gunsei* [government by bayonet] in the first year of military government from March 1942 to March 1943. For Watanabe's *budan gunsei*, see Iwatake Teruhiko, "Shoki Gunsei no Futatsu no Taipu. Yamashita-Watanabe Gunsei (Marai) Imamura-Nakayama Gunsei (Jaba) ("Two Types of Military Government in the Early Stages: The Yamashita-Watanabe Military Government in Malaya and the Imamura-Nakayama Military Government in Java"), *Tōnan Ajia Rekishi to Bunka* vol. 12 (1983), pp. 91–138.

14. Watanabe Wataru, *Nampō Gunsei no Kaiko* (Memoirs of the Military Government in the Southern Region), unpublished ms.

15. *The Syonan Times*, March 9, 2602 (1942).

16. Prime Minister Lee Kuan Yew of Singapore, who was then 17 years old, was working for the *Sendenbu*.

17. *The Syonan Times*, March 14, 2602 (1942).

18. *Jinchū Shinbun*, April 29, 2602 (1942) in Jimbo Kōtarō, *Syonan Nippon Gakuen* (Syonan Japanese School) (Tokyo: Ai-no-Jigyōsha, 1943), pp. 260–1. The Declaration was authored by Nakajima. Writing his memoirs in 1977, Nakajima said that he was disgusted with the Declaration when he was asked to draft it. Nakajima, *Uka tensei*, p. 98. For a critical comment on Nakajima's active role in propagating *Nippon-go* for the Army, see Tanaka Hiroshi, "Marai Gunsei to Sengo Nippon – Nakajima-shi no 'Sengen' to Shinozaki-shi no 'Kaisōroku' wo meguru Kōsatsu" ("The Military Administration of Malaya and Postwar Japan –

An Observation on Nakajima's 'Declaration' and Shinozaki's Memoirs"), *Kiyō*, no. 14 (1981), Chiiki Kenkyū Kanren Shokagaku-hen, Faculty of Foreign Languages, Aichi Prefectural University, pp. 73–97.

19. *The Syonan Times*, April 29, 2602 (1942).
20. Jimbo, *Syonan Nippon Gakuen*, p. 38.
21. *The Syonan Times*, June 1, 2602 (1942): "Marai no Nippon-go" ("Japanese Language in Malaya"), *Nippon-go* (May 1943), p. 37. This is the verbatim record of a roundtable discussion in which Nakajima and Jimbo participated. Matsumoto Naoharu, *Marai no Hyōjō* (Faces of Malaya) (Tokyo: Chōyōsha, 1943), pp. 147, 158.
22. *The Syonan Times*, June 6, 2602 (1942).
23. Ibid., June 9, 2602 (1942).
24. Ibid., June 11, 2602 (1942).
25. Ibid., June 16, 2602 (1942) See Appendix I.
26. Ibid., June 19, 2602 (1942).
27. Ibid., June 18, 2602 (1942).
28. Matsuo Chōzō, "Hakkai no Ji" ("An Opening Message"), *Nippon-go*, April, 1940, p. 1.
29. Kugimoto Hisaharu, "Shisōsen to Nippon-go Kyōiku" ("Ideological Warfare and Japanese Language Education"), Ibid., July, 1943, pp. 11–12.
30. Matsumiya Kazuya, "Kyōeiken Bunka no Kakujū to Nippon-go" ("Expansion of Co-Prosperity Sphere Culture and Japanese Language"), Ibid., May, 1942, p. 77.
31. Tsurumi Yūsuke, "Daitōa Bunka Kensetsu no Kadai" ("Construction of Greater East Asian Culture and Its Problems"), Ibid., March, 1943, p. 8. Tsurumi was elected to the House of Representatives in 1928 and was appointed as Executive Director of the *Taiheiyō Kyōkai* in 1942.
32. Satō Haruo and Kugimoto Hisaharu, "Nampō wo Kataru – Bunka Kensetsu no Shomondai [Dialogue on the Southern Area – Problems of Constructing Culture]," Ibid., October, 1944, p. 14.
33. Kaionji Ushigorō, *Marai Kakyō-ki* (Chinese in Malaya) (Tokyo: Tsuru Shobō, 1943), pp. 87–88.
34. Kikakuin Kenkyūkai, *Daitōa Kensetsu no Kihon Kōryō* (Basic Principles for the Construction of Greater East Asia) (Tokyo: Dōmei Tsūshinsha, 1943), pp. 31–62. Daitōa Kensetsu Shingikai, "Daitōa Kensetsu ni Kansuru Bunkyō Seisaku Tōshin" ("Report Concerning Education Policy for the Construction of Greater East Asia") May 21, 1942, in Ishikawa Junkichi, (ed.), *Kokka Sōdōinshi Shiryōhen* (Documents of the History of National General Mobilization) No. 4 (Tokyo: Kokka Sōdōinshi Kankōkai, 1976), pp. 1,295–9.
35. Kikakuin, *Daitōa Kensetsu no Kihon Kōryō*, p. 57.
36. Department of Education Notice, *The Syonan Times* June 30, 2602 (1942). Enrollment of Chinese and Indian language schools was low, 24.5 percent and 55.7 percent respectively, in 1943 compared to prewar figures. For a detailed study of Japanese education policy, see my article, "Education and Indoctrination Policy in Malaya and Singapore under the Japanese rule, 1942–45," *Malaysian Journal of Education* 13, nos. 1/2 (December 1976). A Chinese source, however, contends that enrollment

158 *Japanese Cultural Policy in Malaya and Singapore*

in Chinese language schools during the occupation period in Singapore only reached six percent of prewar figures. Shu Yun-t'siao and Chua Ser-koon, ed. *Nihongun senryōka no Shingapōru* [Singapore Under the Japanese Occupation] trans. Tanaka Hiroshi (Tokyo: Aoki Shoten, 1986), pp. 214–15. The book is a partial translation of *Sin Ma-Hua-jen K'ang-jih-shih-liao* [Singapore-Malay Chinese Anti-Japanese Resistance History – Documents] (Singapore: Cultural and Historical Publishing House, 1984).

37. Nagaya Yūji, *Senryōgo ni okeru Marai no Shotō Kyōiku* (Primary Education in Malaya After Occupation), 1943?, n.p.
38. *The Syonan Times*, July 2, 18, 2602 (1942).
39. Sybil Kathigasu, G. M., *No Drum of Mercy* (London: Neville Spearman, 1945), p. 46.
40. Jimbo Kōtarō, *Fūdo to Aijō – Nampō bunka no tsuchikai* (Climate and Love – Cultivation of Culture in the Southern Region) (Tokyo: Jitsugyō-no-Nipponsha, 1943), pp. 47–8, 154, 259–60; Nippon bungaku Hōkoku-kai (ed.), *Shinsei Nampō-ki* (Record of New Born Southern Region) (Tokyo: Hokkō Shobō, 1944), pp. 178–9.
41. Jimbo, *Syonan Nippon Gakuen*, pp. 55–6. Jimbo. *Fūdo to Aijō*, pp. 49–50, 152–58. Nippon Bungaku Hōkoku-kai, *Shinsei Nampō-ki*, p. 184. *The Syonan Times*, September 24, 2602 (1942).
42. *The Syonan Times*, June 9, 11, 13, 2602 (1942). Characterizing the Malay culture in Syonan, Jimbo said that the indigenous culture was "boorish" and that there was no cultural atmosphere in the Malay culture which would "enrich the heart of the Japanese," Jimbo, *Fūdo to Aijō*, p. 15; Jimbo, *Syonan Nippon Gakuen*, p. 69.
43. Editorial of *The Syonan Times*, August 27, 2602 (1942).
44. Jimbo, *Syonan Nippon Gakuen*, pp. 96–7; Sekidōhyō Kinen Shuppan Henshū Iinkai (ed.), *Sekidōhyō* (The Equator) (Tokyo: Sekidōkai, 1975), p. 87.
45. *The Syonan Times*, September 10, 2602 (1942).
46. Ibid., September 12, 2602 (1942).
47. Fukuda was until 1990 a member of the Liberal Democratic Party and served as Speaker of the House of Representatives, 1980–83.
48. *The Syonan Times*, September 15, 2602 (1942).
49. E. J. H. Corner, *The Marquis. A Tale of Syonan-tō* (Kuala Lumpur, Malaysia: Heinemann Asia, 1981). Appendix 5, pp. 173–80; *The Syonan Times*, October 14, 2602 (1942).
50. Corporal Sunakawa and Sergeant Kunitani were graduates of Normal School and were assigned to *Syonan Nippon Gakuen* and later *Kokumin Gakkō* (primary school); Lieutenant Torii and Lieutenant Mori, university instructors, taught at *Kokumin Gakkō* and later at *Kunrenjo*; Lieutenant Ogawa, a graduate of the University of Pennsylvania and a university instructor, served as Director of *Syonan Kōa Kunrenjo*; and Miss Misawa and Mrs. Sakai, former teachers in English Schools in Singapore, taught at *Kokumin Gakkō*.
51. *The Syonan Times*, September 26, 2602 (1942).
52. Ibid., September 29, 2602 (1942).
53. Ibid., October 2, 2602 (1942).
54. Ibid. Nakajima said teaching such an abstract subject as religion was "of

no practical use to the inhabitants of the city." Ibid., August 26, 2602 (1942).
55. Ibid., October 2, 2602 (1942).
56. Ibid., October 7, 2602 (1942).
57. Ibid., October 23, 2602 (1942), November 10, 2602 (1942).
58. Ibid.
59. Ibid., November 10, 2602 (1942).
60. Ibid.
61. Ibid., November 5, 2602 (1942).
62. Ibid., April 29, 2602 (1942).
63. Raffles Hotel was changed to *Syonan* Hotel. Penang was at first named *Tōjōtō* (Tojo Island), but it was so ostentatious that it was dropped.
    Chin Kee Onn, *Malaya Upside Down* (Singapore: Jitts & Co., 1946) p. 143; Marai Gunseikambu, *Senji Geppō* (Monthly Report), October and November 1942; *Tokyo Asahi Shimbun*, January 14, 1943; Ōdate Shigeo Denki Kankōkai, *Ōdate Shigeo* (Tokyo: Ōdate Shigeo Denki Kankōkai, 1956) Shingapōru Shiseikai (ed.), *Syonan Tokubetsu-shi. Senjichū no Shingapōru* (Syonan city. Wartime Syonan City) (Tokyo: Nippon Shingapōru Kyōkai, 1986), pp. 208–9; Marai Gunseikambu, *Marai Kōhō Gōgai* (Malay Official Bulletin Extra), May 5, 1943; Marai Gunseikambu, *Showa 18-nen 5-gatsu Kaisai Marai Kakushū (shi) Chōkan Kaigi Kankei Shorui Toji* (File of Official Papers concerning a Conference of Governors and Mayors held in May 1943), n.p. (secret); Nakajima, *Uka Tensei*, pp. 102–3; Interview with former Major General Fujimura Masuzō, July 11, 1966. Fujimura was the superintendent of the Malay Military Administration.
    The *Gunseikambu* decided to remove road, traffic, and public signs written in English by the end of 1942, English store names and advertisements by March 1943, and English in official documents and letters by June 1943. English newspapers were also to be discontinued but no definite deadline was set.
    The decision to abolish English was so unpopular that the Municipal Office of Syonan, directed by Mayor Ōdate Shigeo, sabotaged it by refusing the shipment of paint from a paint plant that it administered. Staff officers of the 25th Army also demanded that street names of Syonan be changed into Japanese. Nakajima and Hirano Naomi of the *Sendenbu* also sabotaged that demand by supplying commonplace names that the 25th Army would not accept. Some states like Johore did change street signs into Japanese.
64. See Footnote 34.
65. *The Syonan Times*, January 14, 2603 (1943).
66. Tokugawa Yoshichika, "Nampō keiei shiken" ("A Personal View Concerning the Administration of the Southern Region") *Taiheiyō* V (February 1942), p. 62. He also opposed the policy supposedly aimed at destroying the White Man's exploitative maladministration and establishing a Japanese system to replace the former. He was reported to be reluctant to force indigenous people to learn *Nippon-go* but encouraged his staff to learn Malay. E. J. H. Corner, *Omoide no syonan Hakubutsu-kan Senryōka no Shingapōru to Tokugawakō* (Memoirs of the Syonan

Museum. Wartime Singapore and Marquis Tokugawa), Ishii Michiko trans. (Tokyo: Chūo Kōronsha, 1982), p. 132.

Tokugawa thought that it was "a mistaken policy to conclude that foreign languages including English are no longer necessary," recommending that Japanese students learn foreign languages. *The Syonan Times*, October 7, 2602 (1942).

67. Tokugawa Yoshichika, "Nampō kensetsu no shinten" ("Progress in the Construction of the Southern Region"), *Taiheiyō* V (July 1942), pp. 87, 90. In November 1942, Tokugawa reiterated that the British education system had to be replaced by a new one that would fully develop the mental and physical facilities of the people. *The Syonan Times*, November 1, 2602 (1942).

68. New Year's Day (January 1), New Year's Day in the Court (January 3), National Foundation Day (February 11), Empress's Birthday (March 6), Army Day (March 10), Day commemorating the Emperor Jinmu (April 3), Spring festival for the Yasukuni Shrine (April 10), Emperor's Birthday (April 29), Navy Day (May 27), Empress Dowager's Birthday (July 25), Day of Offering Wine Made of Newly Harvested Rice to the Grand Shrines of Ise (October 17), Fall Festival for the Yasukuni Shrine (October 23), Day Commemorating the Birthday of the Late Emperor Meiji (November 3), Day Offering Newly Harvested Rice to Ancestral Gods (November 23), and Day Commemorating the Birthday of the Late Emperor Taishō (December 25).

69. Jimbo, *Fūdo to Aijō*, p. 167. Ibuse Masuji, *Ibuse Masuji Zenshū* (Ibuse Masuji's Complete Works) (Tokyo: Chikuma Shobō, 1965), p. 61.

70. During a conference of Sultans of Malaya and Sumatra held in Syonan on January 20–21, 1943, they were led to Syonan *Jinja* and *Tyūreitō* and offered prayers in a Shinto style.

71. Ibuse, *Ibuse Jisen Zenshū* X, pp. 270–1; Koide Hideo. *Marai Engekiki* (Motion Pictures and Dramas of Malaya) (Tokyo: Shin Kigensha, 1943), p. 4–5.

72. "Modern Japan," "A Glimpse of Japan," "Japanese Youth," "Industry in Japan," "The Japanese Navy" were representative of propaganda and cultural films shown to the public in the early days of the Occupation.

73. Machida, *Bunka Butai*, p. 22. Nippon Motion Picture Co. and Motion Picture Distribution Co. were given by the government the exclusive right for the production and distribution of motion pictures.

74. Tōkō Takezō, "Tai Nanpō Bunka Seisaku" ("Cultural Policy Toward the Southern Region"), *Nippon Bunka* (1944), No. 23, p. 108. Tōkō was chief of the Cultural Affairs Section, Secretariat for the Southern Region, Greater East Asian Ministry until November 1942, and thereafter chief of the Political Affairs Section of the same Secretariat. He was the principal official concerned with establishing the *Nanpō Tokubetsu Ryūgakusei* (Special Overseas Students from the Southern Regions) program and formulating its policy.

75. Machida, *Bunka butai*, p. 223. Koide, *Marai Engekiki*, p. 106.

76. "Kagirinaki Zenshin" ("Endless Advance"), "Hawaii, Marei Oki Kaisen" ("The War at Sea from Hawaii to Malaya") and "Sora no Shinpei" ("Divine Soldiers of the Sky") were typical films of this kind.

77. Tokioka Shigehide. "Eiga to Nippon-go" ("Motion Pictures and the Japanese Language"), *Nippon-go* (October 1943), pp. 59–61.
78. *Malai Sinpo*, July 31, 1943.
79. Terasaki Hiroshi, *Marai no Jōmyaku* (Malaya's Vein) (Tokyo: Shunyōdō, 1943), p. 147.
80. Beside serving as a regular speaker, Nakajima joined *Tōhōsha*, a dummy publishing house operated by the 8th Section (Propaganda and Espionage), General Staff, and frequently gave lectures and participated in roundtable discussions on the propagation of *Nippon-go*. Tsuneishi, *Shinri Sakusen no Kaisō*, pp. 163–4. Also see, *Nippon-go* (May, December 1943), *Nippon Hyōron* (February 1944).

One of the qualifications for selecting *Nippon-go* teachers to be sent to the Southern region was that he ought to have *Nippon seishin*. Mori Takashi, "Nampō Haken Nippon-go Kyōshi no Senkō wo Oete" ("An Observation on Screening Japanese Language Teachers to be Sent to the Southern Region"), *Nippon-go* (April 1943), p. 46.
81. *Malai Sinpo*, November 14, 1943.
82. N. I. Low and H. M. Cheng, *This Singapore* (Singapore: Ngai Seong Press, 1946), p. 90. Interviews with Mr. M. Manickavasagar, Singapore, December 23, 1972, and with the Rev. T. R. Doraisamy, Singapore, January 10, 1973. Manickavasagar gave the language training credit for his "reasonable degree of fluency in Japanese by the end of the war." The Rev. Doraisamy, former Principal of Teachers' Training College, Singapore, who was a teacher at the Bras Basah Road Boys' School during the Occupation, "confirms that the standard of language instruction was 'excellent,'" quoted from H. E. Wilson, *Social Engineering in Singapore. Educational Policies and Social Change 1918–1972* (Singapore: Singapore University Press, 1978), p. 104. Their views are corroborated by John Bertram van Cuylenburg, a medical practitioner, who said that *Nippon-go* classes were "conducted . . . by well-qualified Japanese teachers, mostly civilians." *Singapore Through Sunshine and Shadow* (Singapore: Heinemann Asia, 1982), p. 166. For an opposite view, see O. W. Gilmour, *With Freedom to Singapore* (London: Ernest Benn Ltd., 1950), p. 114. Shu Yun-t'siao and Chua Ser-koon (ed.), *Nihongun Senryōka no Shingapōru*, pp. 214–15.
83. Chin, *Malaya Upside Down*, p. 144.
84. *Straits Times*, October 26, 1946, quoted from Wilson, *Social Engineering*, p. 103.
85. Suzuki Shizuo, Yokoyama Michiyoshi (eds), *Shinsei Kokka Nippon to Ajia. Senryōka no Han-Nichi no Genzō* (Sacred Nation of Japan and Asia. A Portrait of Anti-Japanese Feelings During the Occupation) (Tokyo: Keisō Shobō, 1984), p. 172.
86. Kobayashi Masahiro, *Shingapōru no Nippon-gun* (The Japanese Army in Singapore), (Tokyo: Heiwa Bunka, 1986), p. 181.
87. Thio Chan Bee, *Extraordinary Adventures of an Ordinary Man* (London: Grosvenor Books, 1977), p. 43.
88. There were *kunrenjo* for railways, fishing, agriculture, technology, electric and telecommunications, postal service, police, etc. The Japanese educational objective was to train indigenous people to be tech-

nicians. See Daitōa Kensetsu Shingikai, "Daitōa Kensetsu ni kansuru Bunkyō Seisaku Tōshin," ("Report on Educational Policy for the Construction of Greater East Asia") in Ishikawa, *Kokka Sōdōinshi*, No. 4, p. 1,298.

89. *The Syonan Times*, May 22, 2602 (1942). The Syonan *Kōa Kunrenjo* closed in July 1943 and moved to Malacca. The training period was later extended to six months. For a study of the *Kunrenjo*, see my article, "The Kōa Kunrenjo and Nampō Tokubetsu Ryūgakusei: A Study of Cultural Propaganda and Conflict in Japanese Occupied Malaya, 1942–1945," *Shakai Kagaku Tōkyū* (Waseda University) XXIII, No. 3, pp. 39–66.

90. *The Syonan Times*, May 22, 2602 (1942).

91. Ibid.

92. Marai Gunseikambu, *Senji geppō*, May 1942.

93. Akashi, "Kōa Kunrenjo," pp. 42–3.

94. Ibid., p. 43.

95. Abdullah Hussain, *Terjebak* (Kuala Lumpur, Malaysia: Pustaka Antara, 1965), pp. 206–7. Abdullah was a Syonan *Kōa Kunrenjo* trainee, and *Terjebak* is his autobiographical novel.

96. Interview, Koh Kam Watt, *Bahasa* instructor at the University of Malaya, September 6, 1976.

97. Akashi, "Kōa Kunrenjo," pp. 46–7.

98. "Waga Kokoro no Hiroshima. Aru Malaysia-jin Hibakusha no Seishun ("My Love of Hiroshima. The Youth of a Malaysian Who Suffered from the Atomic Bomb"), NHK Special TV Program, August 6, 1988. The person featured in the program is Abdul Razak.

99. Similar training was conducted elsewhere at *kunrenjo*. At Johore Central Agricultural Training Institute, the training motto was "Fight until you die." Uchida Hidenobu, Tsukuda Tomeo (ed.), *Takunan Juku-shi* (History of *Takunan* School) (Tokyo: Seikei Shinsha, 1978), p. 221.

100. This is reconstructed in interviews conducted in September–October, 1976 with former *Kunrenjo* students.

101. Akashi, "Kōa Kunrenjo," p. 50.

102. Ibid., p. 51.

103. Ibid.

104. Ibid., p. 52.

105. *Syonan Sinbun*, April 21, 2603 (1943).

106. Nampō Gunsei Sōkambu Chōsabu, *Marai ni okeru Rensei Kyōiku* [Training Education in Malaya] *Sōchōshi* No. 4 (June 1943), p. 31.

107. Ibid.

108. Daitōashō Nampō Seimukyoku, *Nanpō Tokubetsu Ryūgakusei Ikusei Jigyō* (Program for the Training of Special Students from the Southern Region), February 1943. For the study of this subject, see Akashi, "Kōa Kunrenjo," Grant K. Goodman, *An Experiment in Wartime Intercultural Relations. Philippine Students in Japan, 1943–45*, Data Paper No. 46, Southeast Asia Program, Dept. of Asian Studies, Cornell University, 1962; Kanazawa Kin, *Omoidasu Kotonado* (My Recollections) (Tokyo: Kokusai Gakuyūkai, 1973); Kadono Hiroko, *Sugao no Nanpō Tokubetsu Ryugakusei. Tōnan Ajia no Otōtotachi* (Special

Yoji Akashi 163

Students from the Southern Region As They Are. Younger Brothers from Southeast Asia) (Tokyo: Sankōsha, 1985); Murakami Hyoe, *Ajia ni Makareta Tane* (Seeds Sown in Asia) (Tokyo: Bungei Shunjūsha, 1988); Goto Ken'ichi, "Nippon Tokubetsu Ryūgakusei ni tsuite no Oboegaki – Indonesia Ryūgakusei no Baai" ("A Memorandum About Special Students from the Southern Region – The Case of the Indonesian Students") in Shiraishi Shirō (ed.), *Tōnan Ajia no Keizai Gaikō to Anzen Hoshō* (Economic Diplomacy and Security of Southeast Asia) (Tokyo: Gakuyō Shobō, 1984); Leocadio de Asis, *From Bataan to Tokyo Diary of a Filipino Student in Wartime Japan 1943–1944*, International Studies, East Asian Series Research Publication, No. 10 (Lawrence, Kansas: Center for East Asian Studies, the University of Kansas, 1979). This book is translated into Japanese and titled *Nanpō Tokubetsu Ryūgakusei no Tokyo Nikki – Firippin-jin no Mita Senjika no Nippon* (Tokyo: Shūei Shobō, 1982); Hirakawa Sukehiro, "Leocadio de Asis no Nanpō Tokubetsu Ryūgakusei Tokyo Nikki to Mori Ōgai no Doitsu Nikki – Ryūgaku Taiken to Kindaika Undō (Leocadio de Asis's Tokyo Diary and Mori Ogai's German Diary – Experiences of Study Abroad and the Modernization Movement);" Tsuchiya Kenji, Shiraishi Takashi (ed.), *Tōnan Ajia no Seiji to Bunka* (Politics and Culture in Southeast Asia) (Tokyo: Tokyo Daigaku Shuppankai, 1984); Suwa Toshio, *Nanpō Tokubetsu Ryūgakusei ni kansuru Ki* (Recollections About Special Students from the Southern Region) unpublished manuscript, 1983; Matsuura Yasushi, *Nanpō Tokubetsu Ryūgakusei ni tsuite no Shiteki Kōsatsu* (A Historical Study of Special Students from the Southern Region) BA thesis, Faculty of Arts and Sciences, Waseda University, 1984; Egami Yoshirō, "Daitōa Sensō Makki ni okeru Ryūgakusei no Ukeire ni tsuite" ("The Administration of Foreign Students in the Last Stages of the Greater East Asia War – Admission of Special Students from the Southern Region to Gifu Agricultural College"), *Kanoya Taiiku Daigaku Kenkyū Kiyō*, No. 2 (March 1987); Egami Yoshirō, "Nanpō Tokubetsu Ryūgakusei Shōhei Jigyō ni kansuru Kenkyū (1) Nanpō Tokubetsu Ryūgakusei Shōhei Jigyō Hossokuji ni okeru Mondaiten" ("A Study of Scholarship Programs for Special Students from the Southern Region (1) Problems at the Outset Concerning the Scholarship Program for Special Students from the Southern Region"), *Kanoya Taiiku Daigaku Kenkyū Kiyō* No. 3 (March, 1988); Egami Yoshirō, "Nanpō Tokubetsu Ryūgakusei Shōhei Jigyō ni kansuru Kenkyū (2) – Shōwa 18-nen Shōhei Nanpō Tokubetsu Ryūgakusei no Firippin ni okeru Boshū to Junbi Kyōiku ni tsuite – Suita Taisukeshi kara no Kikigaki ("A Study of Scholarship Programs for Special Students from the Southern Region (2) – Recruitment and Preparatory Education for Filipino Special Students in 1943 – Interview with Suita Taisuke"), *Kanoya Taiiku Daigaku Kenkyū Kiyō* No. 4 (March, 1989).

109. Tōkō, "Tai-Nanpō Bunka Seisaku," *Nippon Bunka*, p. 107. See footnote 74 for Tōkō's biography.
110. In addition to the 12 students from Malaya, there were two students from North Borneo (See Appendix II). It should be noted that neither

Chinese nor Indians were selected as *Nanpō Tokubetsu Ryūgakusei*, although 45 Malayan Indians were enrolled in the Japanese military Academy as Indian National Army cadets. Perhaps the Japanese military authorities did not fully trust the Malayan Chinese. See my article, "Japanese Policy towards the Malayan Chinese, 1941–45", *Journal of Southeast Asian Studies*, I, No. 2 (September, 1970).

111. The students from the Philippines, Indonesia, and Burma generally came from prominent families, but in the case of the Malay students some came from ordinary families and one from an extremely poor family. However, the Tokugawa Scholarship students were selected from prominent families in Johore – three boys (Ungku Abdul Aziz, Wan Abdul Hamid, Ungku Mushin) were relatives of the Sultan of Johore, and two girls (Cheah binti Yahya and Rosan Mahyuddin) also came from well known families in Johore. (See Appendix III.)

112. *Malai Sinpo*, January 2603 (1943).

113. *Tokugawa Nikki*, August 31, September 14, October 12, 1944. Unpublished diary.

114. *Nantokusei* received a monthly allowance of 100 yen, which was increased to 200 yen in 1944. This was a generous stipend considering that the average monthly income of a first-year university graduate at the time was 70 yen. Moreover, the *Nantokusei* were frequently lionized by prominent and wealthy Japanese families.

115. Arriving aboard the ill-fated *Awa Maru*, which was sunk by an American submarine on April 1, 1945, while carrying Red Cross materials for Allied POWs in Japan, they were led by one Sera Takuma. According to Corner, Sera was extremely anti-British when he served temporarily as Director of the Syonan Museum in March 1945 for three months. He threw out of the director's office everything British and replaced them with Japanese things. Corner, *Omoide no Syonan Hakubutsukan*, pp. 155–6.

116. Some *Ryūgakusei*, perhaps Filipino students, complained of their being cropped to the scalp, saying that only convicted men would have such hair-cuts. Nakayama Shirō, *Ten no Hitsuji, Hibakushi shita Nanpō Tokubetsu Ryūgakusei* (Sheep in Heaven. A Special Overseas Student from the Southern Region Who Died of the Effects of the Atomic Bomb) (Tokyo: Sankōsha, 1982), p. 107.

117. Kanazawa, *Omoidasu Kotonado*, p. 62; Egami Yoshirō, "Nanpō Tokubetsu Ryūgakusei Rai-Nichi" (The Arrival of Special Students from the Southern Region to Japan) *ISI Kaihō*, No. 46 (1985), p. 12.

118. Kanazawa, *Omoidasu Kotonado*, pp. 62–3. In a postwar interview, Kanazawa went so far as to say that they were "a sort of hostages," though outwardly the government had invited them to study in Japan. Nakayama, *Ten no Hitsuji*, p. 101.

119. *Asahi Shinbun*, July 1, 1943 (evening edition).

120. For the daily life of the *Tokubetsu Ryūgakusei*, see de Asis, *From Bataan to Tokyo*.

121. Okamoto Senmantarō, "Nippon-go Kyōiku to Nippon Bunka" ("Japanese Language Education and Japanese Culture"), *Nippon-go* (March 1942) pp. 40–4.

122. Kanazawa, *Omoidasu Kotonado*, pp. 71–2.
123. Military policemen kept a close surveillance upon the activities of the *Nanpō Tokubetsu Ryūgakusei*, and the Army Ministry dismissed a liberal minded dormitory supervisor as being unfit for the post. Nakayama, *Ten no Hitsuji*, pp. 154–62.
124. Chin, *Malaya Upside Down*, p. 138.
125. Egami, "Nanpō Tokubetsu Ryūgakusei no Rai-Nichi," *ISI Kaihō*, p. 16.
126. Hassan bin Ahmad and Mohamad Kassim Kamiddin. At first the Army was reluctant to accept *Nantokusei* into the Military Academy, but in 1945 it changed the policy in order to prepare them immediately for military service. Forty-two students were admitted to the Academy.
127. Gotō, *Nippon Senryōki no Indoneshia*, p. 210.
128. Goodman, *An Experiment in Wartime Intercultural Relations*, p. 19. Suwa, *Nanpō Tokubetsu Ryūgakusei*, p. 24. Suwa received a number of letters from *Nantokusei* studying in Hiroshima, Miyazaki, Kumamoto, and Kyoto, complaining of poor quality food and troubles with dormitory supervisors and curriculum, particularly *shūshin* (ethics). See also Murakami, *Ajia ni Makareta Tani*, p. 242.
129. Following the adoption of *Principles for Educational Emergency Measures* by the cabinet on March 18, 1945, all university and college students were drafted into military service while middle-school students were mobilized for ammunition and aircraft factories. Egami, "Daitōa Sensō Makki ni okeru Ryūgakusei Gyōsei," pp. 142–4.
130. For the story of Omar's death, see Nakayama, *Ten no Hitsuji*.
131. For the story of Mansoor's death, see TV Nishi Nippon, "Nanpō Tokubetsu Ryūgakusei no Kiseki" ("The Life of A Special Student from the Southern Region"), February 1986.
132. Raja Nong Chik was arrested by British authorities upon his return to Singapore. He escaped from prison and joined the Indonesian independence struggle until 1947, when, following the Dutch police action, he made his way to China. He studied at Beijing University and Chungshan University for a while until the Communists seized power, and then he went to Taiwan and finished his education at Taipei University before returning home.
133. Correspondence with a former *Kōa Kunrenjo* trainee, September 7, 1976.
134. Interview with a former *Kōa Kunrenjo* trainee, November 23, 1976.
135. Interview with a former *Kōa Kunrenjo* trainee, March 3, 1986.
136. Correspondence with a former *Kōa Kunrenjo* trainee, September 27, 1976.
137. Correspondence with a former *Kōa Kunrenjo* trainee, September 23, 1976.
138. Correspondence with a former *Kōa Kunrenjo* trainee, October 2, 1976.
139. Correspondence with a former *Kōa Kunrenjo* trainee, September 7, 1976.
140. Interview with a former *Kōa Kunrenjo* trainee, October 15, 1976.
141. Interview with a former *Kōa Kunrenjo* trainee, October 10, 1976.
142. Correspondence with a former *Kōa Kunrenjo* trainee, October 20, 1976.

143. This opinion is a consensus of all former *Kōa Kunrenjo* trainees whom I interviewed in September and October 1976.
144. *The Syonan Sinbun*, April 21, 2603 (1943); Marai Kōa Kunrenjo, *Shin Marai*, pp. 17–18.
145. *The Syonan Sinbun*, April 21, 2603 (1943).
146. Interview with a former *Nantokusei*, November 1, 1983.
147. Tungku Abdullah's statement, June, 1977, quoted from Kadono, *Tōnan Ajia no Otōtotachi*, pp. 259–60.
148. Correspondence with a former *Kōa Kunrenjo* trainee, September 7, 1976.
149. Interview with a former *Kōa Kunrenjo* trainee, November 17, 1976.
150. Interview with a former *Kōa Kunrenjo* trainee, September 7, 1976.
151. Interview with a former *Kōa Kunrenjo* trainee, September 7, 1976. Interview with a former *Kōa Kunrenjo* trainee, November 1, 1983. For similar views expressed by Filipino students, see Goodman, *An Experiment in Wartime Intercultural Relations*, p. 22. Ages of *Kōa Kunrenjo* students ranged from 17 to 25 years old, while those of *Nantokusei* from 17 to 24 years old.
152. For instance, indigenous people were required to salute to or bow to Japanese soldiers. Failure to act accordingly often resulted in a slap in the face.
153. Ogata Shin'ichi, former Syonan police chief, was seized by a mob of protesters at Singapore Airport on his arrival on August 4, 1958. See *Yomiuri Shimbun* and *Tokyo Shinbun*, August 6, 1958. For detailed accounts of the incident, see *The Strait Times*, August 4, 5, 6, 1958.
154. 205 *Nantokusei* came to Japan, but nine Filipino students returned home on September 30, 1944 and one Filipino was assigned to the Philippine Embassy. Egami, *ISI Kaihō*, no. 46 (1985, II), p. 11.
155. Interview with former *Nantokusei*, November 1, 1983.
156. Interview with former *Nantokusei*, November 1, 1983.
157. *Yomiuri Shimbun*, November 1, 1983 (editorial).
158. Opinions expressed by former *Nantokusei* at a round table discussion with Japanese including the author, held at Hotel New Ōtani, October 31, 1983.
159. *Yomiuri Shimbun*, November 1, 1983.
160. See my article, "The Kōa Kunrenjo and Nanpō Tokubetsu Ryūgakusei," *Shakai Kagaku Tōkyū*, pp. 64–6. This article was prepared with responses to questionnaires and interviews I conducted.
161. Interview with Ungku Abdul Aziz, November 3, 1976.
162. *Bunkajin* in their thirties and forties were drafted into military service.
163. Takasaki Ryūji, *Sensō Bungaku Tsūshin* (War Literature Bulletin) (Tokyo: Fūbaisha, 1975), pp. 330–50.
164. *Jinshū Shimbun*, April 29, 1942 reproduced in Jimbo, *Syonan Nippon Gakuen*, pp. 260–1.
165. Ibuse, "Hana no Machi," *Ibuse Masuji Zenshū*, Vol. 3, pp. 52–3.
166. Nakajima, *Shōwa Jidai*, p. 169.
167. Nakajima, *Kaisō no Bungaku*, V, pp. 81–2.
168. Ibid., pp. 102–3.
169. Jimbo, *Fūdo to Aijō*, p. 259.

170. Nakajima Kenzō, Sakai Seiichirō, Ibuse Masuji, Sayama Tadao, Jimbo Kōtarō, "Shinsei Marai wo Kataru" ("A Round Table Discussion on New Born Malaya") *Chisei* (March 1943), p. 60.

171. Tanaka, "Maraya Gunsei to Sengo Nippon," *Kiyō* (*Chiiki Kenkyū*), 14, 1981, p. 77, quoted from Takasaki, *Sensō bungaku tsūshin*, no. 4, pp. 70–1.

172. Odagiri Susumu (ed.), *Nippon Kindai Bungaku Daijiten* (Dictionary of Modern Japanese Literature) (Tokyo: Kōdansha, 1984), pp. 770–1.

173. For the description of Jimbo's personality as seen by a Singaporean, see N. I. Low, *When Singapore Was Syonan-tō* (Singapore: Eastern Universities Press, 1973), p. 95. Low described Jimbo as a "fanatic and hot-gospeller of hate, full of malevolence."

174. Tanaka, "Maraya Gunsei to Sengo Nippon," *Kiyō*, p. 77, quoted from Takasaki, *Sensō Bungaku Tsūshin*, pp. 70–1.

175. Satō Haruo, Ozaki Shirō, Ōki Atsuo, Hibino Shirō, Hino Ashihei (all well known writers, essayists, and poets) were prolific writers who exalted the war spirit. As a result, they were severely criticized or purged like Hino in the postwar years. Terasaki Hiroshi was one of a few *sendenbu* members who criticized the *sendenbu* programs and Ōya Sōichi who served in Java was one *bunkajin* who did not write anything about his wartime experience.

176. For Tsurumi, see note 21. Miki published *Hitō Fudōki* (Philippine Culture) in 1943 and "Firippinjin no Tōyōteki Seikaku" (Oriental Characteristics in the Filipino). He did not join the *Genron Hōkokukai* (Patriotic Association of Writers) which many *bunkajin* joined. He was arrested in March 1945 for sheltering a Communist and died in September 1945 as a result of torture.

177. For example, Takami Jun, a former proletarian writer, who served in Burma in 1942 and in China in 1944 as a war correspondent, is a case in point. He confided his inner thoughts to his diary which was published in eight volumes in 1959–61.

Appendix I

Japanese Language Emphasis Week Slogans

Manabe Tukae Nippon-go (Learn Use, Nippon-go)

Manabe Tukae Nippon-go
All you who live in Syonan-to
Now you will see in every page
Are words in this language
Beautiful, graceful, refined.
The words so near at hand
Unfold the beauties of the island
Kind spirit of Nippon!
A culture that must win
Enshrined in heart of Nippon-zin
Now power will give to you
Instruction in our Nippon-go
Portal to a higher mind
Obey the call, I ask once more
Nippon-go o tukaimasyo [Let's use Nippon-go]!
Go study then and persevere
Onto the goal which is so near.

Source: The Syonan Times, June 1, 2602 (1942)

Why you Must Learn Nippon-go

Win these lines is a moral writ in language you must know
Here now to emphasize
Your future will be progress when you have mastered Nippon-go.
Yet here it is within your reach in moments you can spare
On these days and every day
Unending joy and profit too in higher gifts to share.
Manabe tukae Nippon-go – this from your mind do not erase
Unless you bend your will 'twill only mean an empty phrase
Success must come to those who try – this is the only way
There chance is here to learn and use this language all the day.
Let all who live in Syonan where Nippon hold unbounded sway
Embrace the chance to thoughts express in loyalty display
Always in Nippon-go
Rulers and subjects then meet, to understand and feel
No longer are there barriers for friendship true to seal.
Now the time to learn, to use this language in the home
In office, in the street, on bus – wherever you may roam;
Perceive the great importance before it is too late
Practice now and persevere, do not sit and wait
Only those who try can expect to gain the prize
Nippon-go to speak, in truth, will early make you wise
Good luck, to your success I humbly raise my glass
On ending line to add with wishes mine –*arigato gosaimasu*.

Source: The Syonan Times, July 16, 2602 (1942)

Appendix II

Biographical Data for *Nanpō Tokubetsu Ryūgakusei*

Abdul Razak bin Abdul Hamid was born in 1927 in Penang. Graduated from Kampong Bahru Malay *Kokumin Gakkō*. Appointed to the Malay *Kōa Kunrenjo* in the first group in May 1942, and his appointment was extended three more months for his academic excellence. Appointed as a Japanese language teacher by the Education Department of the Selangor State Government. Selected as *Nantokusei* in June 1944 and enrolled at Hiroshima University of Humanities and Sciences in April 1945. He became a victim of the atomic bomb (*hibakusha*). Returned to Malaya in September 1945. Became an instructor at Sultan Idris Teacher's College in Perak 1957 and later a lecturer at MARA. Operates a law firm in Kuala Lumpur.

Bostam bin Haji Mohamed Kurshi was born in 1922 in Singapore. Educated at Raffles Institution and Pitman's College. Enrolled in Syonan *Gunsei-kambu Kokugo* School for six months. Appointed as a *Nantokusei* in June 1943. Entered Hiroshima Higher Normal School in April 1945. Returned to Singapore in October 1946. Became a senior immigration officer, Immigration Office, Singapore.

Hashim bin Naemat was born in 1922 in Malacca. His father was a surveyor. Education at Malacca Preliminary English School and Malacca High School before being appointed to Syonan *Kōa Kunrenjo* in 1942. Appointed as a *Nantokusei* in 1943. Admitted to Kanagawa Police Training School in May 1944, where he stayed until late August before being transferred to Fukuoka Higher School in April 1945. Returned to Malaya in September 1945. Became Director General of Immigration Bureau, Malaysia.

Hassan bin Ahmad was born in 1928 in Malacca. His father was a contractor for the Malacca *Kōa Kunrenjo* and his mother, a Japanese, was a nurse. Studied at an English School and was appointed to the Malay *Kōa Kunrejo* in 1942. Employed as an interpreter at the Police Department, Malacca State Government before being selected as a *Nantokusei* in 1944. Admitted to the Military Academy in May 1945. Returned to Malaya in September 1945. Information about his postwar career is not available.

Ibrahim bin Mohamud was born in 1926 in Johore. His father was a judge of High Court, Johore. Studied at an English School for seven years before being admitted to the Malay *Kōa Kunrenjo* in 1942. Employed by the Johore State Government prior to his selection as a *Nantokusei* in 1944. Enrolled at Tokushima College of Engineering where he studied Civil Engineering from April 1945 until his departure for home in September 1945. Became Director General of Aviation Bureau, Malaysia.

Nik Yusof bin Nik Ali was born in 1924 in Kelantan. His father was a palm oil manufacturer. Studied at Ismail English School and Padang Gorong Malay School. Appointed to the Syonan *Kōa Kunrenjo* in 1942 and a *Nantokusei* in 1943. Admitted to Hiroshima Higher Normal School in April

1944 and transferred to Hiroshima University of Humanities and Sciences. Died of the radiation effects of the atomic bomb on August 6, 1945.

Raja Nong Chik bin Raja Ishak was born in 1924 in Selangor, a relative of the Sultan of Selangor. Selected as a *Nantokusei* in 1943 and admitted to Fukuoka Higher School and later transferred to the Imperial University of Kyoto. Before returning to Malaya, he joined the Indonesian national independence struggle. Appointed a Malaysian senator serving until 1985. President of a number of companies and a member of the executive board of ASCOJA (ASEAN Council of Japan Alumni) founded by former Prime Minister Fukuda Takeo.

Syed Omar bin Mohamed Alsagoff was born in 1926 in Johore. His father was a businessman. Studied at Medan Dutch School, Johore Bahru Primary School, and Middle School. Studied Japanese at Syonan *Nippon-go Gakkō* and selected as a *Nantokusei* in 1943. Admitted to Hiroshima Higher Normal School in April 1944 and transferred to Hiroshima University of Humanities and Sciences in April 1945. Died of the effects of atomic bomb radiation on September 3, 1945 in Kyoto. He was a brother-in-law of Ungku Abdul Aziz, former vice chancellor of the University of Malaya.

Raja Shaeran Shah bin Raja Abidin was born in 1921 in Perak. His father was a civil servant. Studied at Taiping Malay School and King Edward VII School. Appointed to the Syonan *Kōa Kunrenjo* in 1942 and employed as a Japanese language teacher by the Perak State Government. Selected as a *Nantokusei* in June 1943. Admitted to Miyazaki Higher School of Agriculture and Forestry in April 1944 and transferred to the Imperial University of Kyoto in April 1945. Returned home in September 1945. Became the Keeper of the Ruler's Seal, Malaysia.

Syed Mansoor was born in 1922 in Penang. His father was a postal service clerk. Studied at medical college in Singapore for two years. Appointed *Nantokusei* in 1943. Admitted to Kumamoto Medical College in April 1944. Died of tuberculosis at the Kyushu Imperial University Hospital in Fukuoka on 21 December 1946.

Tungku Abdullah bin Imanku Abdul Rahman was born in 1925 in Negri Sembilan. His father was the Sultan of Negri Sembilan. Studied at Kuala Kangsar Malay College for six years and also at Seremban Vocation School prior to his selection as a *Nantokusei* in 1943. Admitted to Miyazaki Higher School of Agriculture and Forestry and transferred to Fukuoka Higher School. Returned to Malaya in September 1945. Entered into the Malaysian civil service as a district officer in Selangor. After retiring from the civil service, he became manager of Duncan, Gilby, Murchison Co.

Yusof Abdul Kadir Rahman was born in 1926 in Penang. His father was a judge. Studied at Raffles College for one year. Admitted to the Syonan *Kōa Kunrenjo* in 1942. Selected as a *Nantokusei* in 1944 and admitted to the Law Faculty of the Imperial University of Kyoto in April 1945. Returned to Malaya in September 1945. Became a federal judge.

Mohamed Kassim Kamiddin was born in 1924 in North Borneo. Studied at English School for two years. Employed at Tawao District Office and selected as a *Nantokusei* in 1944. Enrolled at the Military Academy in May 1945. Returned home in September 1945. Postwar career is unknown.

Yusuf Pengiran was born in 1926 in North Borneo (Brunei). Studied at Malay Normal School. Appointed a teacher at Mili State *Kokumin Gakkō* prior to his selection as a *Nantokusei* in 1944. Admitted to Hiroshima University of Humanities and Sciences in April 1945. Became a victim of atomic bomb radiation but survived. Returned home in September 1945. Became Director General of the Information Bureau and later Prime Minister of Brunei. He is now the President of the Brunei Chamber of Commerce and Industry.

Appendix III

Biographical Data of Tokugawa Scholarship Students

Ungku Abdul Aziz was born in 1922 in Johore, a relative of the Sultan of Johore. Came to Japan as a Tokugawa Scholarship student in 1943 and studied at Waseda University. Returned home in early 1945. Became a Professor of Economics at the University of Malaya and appointed Vice Chancellor of the University serving in the post until his retirement in 1988. Awarded Royal Professorship by the Malaysian Government and also the First Order of Sacred Treasure by the Japanese Government in 1989. He is the principal planner of Malaysia's "Look East Policy" advocated by Prime Minister Mohamed Mahathir.

Ungku Mushin. His biographical information is unavailable.

Wan Abdul Hamid was born in Johore, a relative of the Sultan of Johore. As a Tokugawa Scholarship student, he studied at Tokyo College of Agriculture and returned in early 1945. Became the Director of PERNAS (*Perbadanan Nasional*), National Development Corporation.

Cheah binti Yahya. Her biographical information is unavailable.

Rosan Mahyuddin. Her biographical information is unavailable.

5 The Japanese Propaganda Corps in the Philippines: Laying the Foundation

Motoe Terami-Wada

INTRODUCTION

When Japan commenced hostilities against the United States of America in December 1941, the task of developing cultural propaganda to accompany the armed attack was naturally in the hands of the military, who had been preparing during the previous year at least for a possible future war. Based on the previous experiences of occupying Taiwan, Korea and Manchuria, the Japanese military keenly understood the importance of having cultural policies concurrent with military operations, a sentiment shared by some intellectuals.[1]

The office in charge of such cultural and propaganda activities in the would-be occupied areas was to be under the *Sanbō Hon'bu* (General Staff Office). Members of this office were recruited from among the graduates of military schools. Most of them had spent time abroad, mainly in Europe, England, China and Russia, as students or as military or naval attachés to the Japanese embassies.

Due to the nature of the office, its departments and sections since 1908 had been normally referred to by number. On the eve of the war, there were four departments, under which were sections. Their functions were as follows: First Department – maneuvers, tactics, organization; Second Department – information, propaganda, strategy; Third Department – ships, railroad, communications; Fourth Department – compilation of war history.

The Second Department had four sections, called by the numbers from 5 to 8. Section 5 was responsible for Russia; Section 6 for the US, England, France and Germany; Section 7 for China; and Section 8 for propaganda and strategy. Sometime in the 1930s, the Southern Area was added as a concern of Section 6.[2]

173

The Second Department's Section 8 was in charge of the planning and implementation of information gathering and analysis, propaganda, and strategy in foreign countries. In 1937, Section 8 began concentrating on China and the Southern Area.[3]

Around the middle of June, 1940, the *Sanbō Hon'bu* began discussion of plans for the cultural campaign in the four Southern Regions of the Southern Area, namely the Philippines, Singapore, Malaya and Burma. Accordingly, eight military personnel were sent to these regions for two months in order to collect the data necessary for the planning. By September, 1941, the *Sanbō Hon'bu* felt ready to commence hostilities against the U.S.[4]

Actual preparations meant first of all acquiring the personnel and materiel necessary for propaganda activities. One of the organizations that the *Sanbō Hon'bu* decided to establish was a Propaganda Corps, said to be patterned after the German model. There had been a previous Propaganda Corps, but its duty was limited to

accompanying the Imperial Army to persuade the inhabitants to return to their respective houses, to disseminate the true intention of the Imperial Army, to obtain the inhabitants' cooperation, and to establish peace and order.[5]

However, this time, the military wanted propaganda work to include the more difficult goal of leaving a lasting impact on the people they were about to conquer. Moreover, the new Propaganda Corps for the first time recruited a vast number of civilians for this type of work. The main duties of the Corps were to be the following: (1) engage in propaganda campaigns directed at the local people as well as enemy soldiers in the would-be occupied areas; (2) report to the Japanese at home on the state of the occupied areas so as to sustain morale; (3) heighten the fighting spirit of the Japanese soldiers in the field.

In order to achieve these purposes, it was believed that the best intellectuals were needed. The *Sanbō Hon'bu* started recruiting writers, painters, journalists, religious personnel, etc., as shall be described below. The office gathered some 150 for each of the Southern Regions. Each group was to have about 250 soldiers to assist them.[6]

The basic plan of the cultural operations was prepared by the *Sanbō Hon'bu*, but the Corps was given a free hand in some activities and its initiatives were encouraged. This was ostensibly to enable the Corps to adjust to the day-to-day changes in a war situation. It may be, however, that confusion reigned because nobody in the Propaganda Corps knew exactly what to do, a dilemma which will be illustrated below. This indicates that in the beginning at least, the *Sanbō Hon'bu* did not have a concrete plan for the Corps to follow.

In addition to the military, other government agencies which had been functioning as propaganda organs to control the thought of the Japanese at home were to be utilized. The Government Information Bureau, propaganda personnel of the Navy, the Ministry of Home Affairs, the Ministry of Education, the Ministry of Communication, *Dōmei* News Agency, the Japan Broadcasting Association or NHK, Japanese embassies abroad, and the future Greater East Asia Ministry, set up in November, 1942, were to assist the invading forces in the Southern Regions.[7] It was envisioned that after a return to "normal" conditions in the occupied areas had been achieved, overall cultural policies would ultimately be directed by the Greater East Asian Ministry. However, the Japanese occupations ended before the Ministry could attain full development.

Therefore, most of the propaganda operations in the Southern Regions at the initial stage were undertaken by the Propaganda Corps. It is the purpose of this essay to look into the Corps' activities and to discuss just how creative they were and how much initiative the Corps did have *vis-à-vis* the *Sanbō Hon'bu's* basic propaganda plan. The focus will be on the Corps' first year, from its entry into Manila until the end of 1942. This was the period in which the Propaganda Corps laid the foundation for future cultural propaganda activities.

THE PROPAGANDA CORPS OF THE 14TH ARMY

In the middle of November, 1941, the selected writers, poets, painters, photographers, actors, and the like received notices from the military to report to a designated place for interviews. They were asked such questions as "Do you know how to carry a canteen?" or "Have you ever worn a saber before?" After the interview, they underwent a simple physical examination. Those who passed both the interview and the examination were immediately divided into four groups, one for each Southern Region, by secret code. However, the successful examinees themselves did not come to know of their destination until much later.[8]

The Philippine group of the newly recruited Propaganda Corps, with the members neither knowing yet where they were headed nor what their duties were supposed to be, left Japan and arrived in Taiwan's Keelung Port on November 29. They did know vaguely that they would be working for the military to serve in the cultural field, but they were not aware that Japan would enter into a war against the U.S. In Taipei, they met their superior, Lieutenant-Colonel Katsuya Tomishige, who confirmed that they had been drafted into the Propaganda Corps of the 14th Army. Katsuya was assisted by Captain Hitomi Jun'suke, Second-Lieutenants Mochizuki Shigenobu and Kirito Takeo, among others. These officers turned out to be themselves neophytes in propaganda activities.[9]

For his part, Captain Hitomi, while on duty in Manchuria, received an order indicating that he had been drafted into the 14th Army Propaganda Corps. He had no idea what the Propaganda Corps was supposed to do, nor did he know where the 14th Army was destined to go. Nevertheless, he immediately proceeded to the Military Headquarters in Taiwan on 26 November, 1941, as the order had stipulated. Upon reaching Taipei, he was informed by a fellow military officer that the 14th Army was going to the Philippines and that their duty was to engage in propaganda activities. He never dreamed that he was to stay in the Philippines throughout the whole occupation as one of the leaders of these campaigns.

Colonel Katsuya, the first head of the Propaganda Corps, seemed to have some experience in this field, having been the head of the Department of Information assigned to Shanghai. However, his address to the Corps members was disappointing. He said: "It is true that I have worked in the Information Department, but I don't know anything about propaganda work. It is all up to you to do the job."

The group included 6 novelists and poets, 4 painters, 9 writers for newspapers and magazines, 5 cameramen, 2 broadcasting technicians, 4 printing technicians, 5 movie people including a cameraman, 14 Catholic priests, Catholic students and lay workers, and 12 Protestant ministers. These religious people were to have an independent organization after their entry into Manila. In the meantime, they worked together with the Propaganda Corps. Besides all the above, there were about 100 correspondents sent by various newspaper companies. All these amounted to some 300.[10]

After several days of rest, the group left Taipei on December 4 for a still undisclosed destination. On the morning of December 8, they learned via the radio that Japan had attacked Pearl Harbor and that war between the U.S. and Japan had begun. It was only then that they were told that they were headed for the Philippines.

Duties Prior to Reaching the Philippines

To acquaint them with the Philippines the group members were immediately given copies of a thin booklet of some 50 pages, describing the politics, economy, religions, and customs of the country, and the different ethnic groups and their characteristics. Copies, however, were so few in number that each one had to be shared by around ten people.[11]

These about-to-be propagandists were immediately divided into sub-groups responsible for interpreting, writing, and painting. The very first job of the Propaganda Corps was to come up with propaganda which would be used for leaflets or aired over loudspeakers. The writers' group developed these which were at once translated into English by the interpreters' group. Meanwhile, the painters' group had to design propaganda posters.[12]

The messages which were to be disseminated were the following:
1. That Japan had been compelled to start the war in order to establish peace in East Asia.
2. That Japan's true intentions in creating East Asia's New Order would be advantageous for the Philippines.
3. That the U.S. did not try to understand Japan's position and continued to harass her.[13]

Besides the above, updates on Japanese successes since the Pearl Harbor attack were given. This propaganda campaign also did not fail to mention that, based on Japan's war progress, it was just a matter of time before the Philippines would surrender. There were also special notes addressed to Philippine Commonwealth President Manuel L. Quezon, urging him to surrender.[14]

Meanwhile, the Religious Group made their own leaflets, dated December 25, addressed to the Filipino bishops and priests. The gist of the leaflets was that while Rome had been advocating peace, world brotherhood and coexistence based on justice and law, some of the European countries and the U.S. had not heeded Rome's wise counsel. Therefore, Japan had decided to establish a New Order in East Asia based on the spirit of the Way of the Emperor. In order to accomplish this, Japan was compelled to use the one remaining method, force. At the end of the message, gratitude to the Filipinos for honoring the Japanese Catholic martyrs, Takayama Ukon and Naitō Juan, as well as for the hospitality shown during the 33rd International Eucharistic Congress held in Manila in 1937 was expressed. The leaflet assured the Filipino religious that the Japanese military was sending Catholic priests and lay people to protect Filipino Catholics and the churches.[15]

Some of the leaflets had been produced beforehand in Taipei and others even before the war had started. The rank and file Corps members did not know that the General Staff Office, specifically Section 8, had set up an office to produce leaflets for the Southern Regions as early as August, 1940. The Office had commissioned five well-known cartoonists to draw pictures with propaganda lines written in one of eleven different languages – English, Malay, Tagalog, Visayan, Hindustani, Bengal, Tamil, Urdu, Burmese, Indonesian, and Vietnamese. In the making of the messages and drawings, political refugees as well as students from the countries involved were consulted not only for the language but also for the national costumes and customs. The total number of leaflets intended for the Southern Regions was in the millions.[16]

The ships carrying the Propaganda Corps members, called "*Bunka Senshi*" ("cultural warriors") left for the Philippines on December 18. The majority of them landed either at Lingayen Gulf or at Lamon Bay a few days before Christmas.[17]

From the Landing Points to Manila

The members of the Propaganda Corps who reached the Philippines via Lingayen Gulf landed in the middle of the night in the small village of Santiago, Bauan, La Union without much enemy resistance. They found Bauan a deserted town, nearly destroyed by the crossfire between the USAFFE and the Japanese Imperial Army, which had landed ahead of them.[18]

The very first duties that the Corps was given were to distribute the leaflets they had prepared beforehand and then to produce some more. In one day they were ordered to make 15,000 leaflets urging the town's inhabitants to come down from the nearby hills and mountains where they had sought refuge.[19]

This task was assigned to the writers' and interpreters' groups. The gist of the message they came up with was that the Japanese Army had no intention of harming those who cooperated, and therefore that the people should return to the town center immediately.

General Artemio Ricarte arrived from Japan the night before Christmas Eve by plane. Ricarte was one of the Filipino nationalists who had risen up against Spain in 1896. Even after the U.S. had taken over the Philippines as a result of the Philippine–American War, he refused to pledge allegiance to the U.S. He was exiled, and in 1915 he sought refuge in Japan, where he stayed until the outbreak of the war. After a long absence, he made his first speech on Philippine soil in front of captured Filipino soldiers in Bauan on Christmas Day.

While the others were busy writing what they hoped was appealing propaganda and translating these into English, the technical group went around looking for printing equipment. They were fortunate enough to find some in San Fernando, La Union. With the ink not yet dry, the leaflets were brought to the Naguilian Airport and loaded on planes that would scatter them.

The artists were not idle either. They used crayon to draw propaganda pictures, churning out 30–40 posters a day. Again the technical group had to look for the necessary materials such as paper and brushes, since the only materials they had brought with them were crayons and tube colors. Along with the rest of the leaflets, the posters were pasted on the walls of empty schools, churches, and other prominent buildings in the town plaza. The barrios, which were within a two–kilometer radius from Bauan town center, were also covered. Surprisingly, the local inhabitants did start to return to their homes the following day.

The Propaganda Corps members who had landed in Bauan did more or less the same things in the towns that they passed through *en route* to Manila. The Corps split up for this trip: some went through Binalonan, Cabanatuan, and Baliwag; others went via Binalonan, Tayug, Unigan, Lupao, San Jose, Talavera, San Miguel, and Baliwag; another group went through Tarlac and San Fernando.

The Religious Corps members also produced posters and announcements while six of them left for Baguio with the advancing military forces. Along the way they distributed safe conduct passes to those who were willing to cooperate with the Japanese military. In San Fernando, a mass which was attended by around 75 Filipinos was celebrated by a Japanese priest. In the same town, a friendly game of basketball was held between the best team in the town and the members of the Religious Corps.[20]

A smaller batch of Propaganda Corps members landed in Atimonan on December 24 and went through Malikboy, Pagbilao, Tayabas, and Lukban, distributing leaflets as they proceeded. In Lukban, a Filipino prisoner-of-war (POW) joined the Corps as an interpreter.

The first speech explaining the purpose of the Japanese occupation was delivered in Candelaria by Captain Hitomi in Japanese. This was translated by a Corps member into English, before being translated by the Filipino POW into Tagalog.

The Corps left Candelaria on December 28, and went through Sariaya and Tiaong. The members were accommodated by a sugar factory owner in Cabuyao, where they spent the first day of 1942. They proceeded to Biñan, where the local inhabitants lined up along the road and shouted "*Mabuhay*" ("Welcome"). The next day in Parañaque, they were treated with the traditional Japanese New Year's delicacy, rice cake, by the Japanese residents there. On the same day, they made their entry into Manila.[21]

IMPRESSIONS OF PHILIPPINE CULTURE AND THE PEOPLE

As mentioned earlier, one duty of the Propaganda Corps was to inform the Japanese at home and soldiers fighting in the field about the life and culture of the future members of the Greater East Asia Co-Prosperity Sphere (GEACPS). Thus the propagandists, especially those in the literary field, were encouraged to write their experiences in or impressions of the newly occupied areas. Indeed, their personal views could have influenced the cultural policy that they undertook afterward.

The first thing which struck the Propaganda Corps members was the hot, humid and monotonous tropical weather. For them this partly accounted for the perception that the Filipinos tended to be lazy physically as well as spritually, meaning that Filipinos showed little desire to engage in deep thinking or contemplation. Instead they seemed to the Japanese to be more sensuous and somewhat flippant. The fact that there were very few stores which sold only books was said to be a manifestation of these characteristics. Most of the stores carried all sorts of other merchandise besides books. However, beauty parlors could be seen everywhere, according to their observations.[22]

Nevertheless, the weather was not the only cause of these apparent tendencies. The Filipino's historical experience was seen as a major factor. Kon Hidemi, a novelist, remarked that the peasants had become lazy due to the exploitative *cacique* system, wherein tenants are charged exorbitant fees payable in cash or crops. Since the peasants had been forced into becoming semi-slaves, it seemed to him that they had lost the desire to strive for improvement. Therefore, he believed, solving the land problem would contribute greatly to eliminating Filipino indolence.[23]

Miki Kiyoshi, a philosopher, contended that the centuries of being under colonial rule had produced chronic malnutrition, which had resulted in physically and mentally inactive Filipinos. He suggested that a vigorous health program promoting correct diet and physical development was essential to the progress of the Philippines.[24]

Both men believed that before colonization the Filipinos were truly hardworking people. Miki pointed out that pre-Spanish proverbs and sayings were abundant with ideas on the importance of hard work and saving for a time of need. All of the propaganda writers attributed the seemingly negative Filipino characteristics – such as flippancy, dependency, and lack of nationalism or patriotism – to Western colonization, especially by the U.S. Kon lamented that the life-long ambitions of many Filipino youths were to work for a U.S. company and to buy a secondhand car payable in monthly installments.

He also noted that many Filipinos had asked what Japan had to offer, since Spain had given the Philippines religion and the U.S. had brought education. This indicated to Kon hopeless Philippine dependence on others. The Filipinos' master could be anybody as long as comfort was given, he wrote. Such a frame of mind was not suited to establishing an independent country. What Japan could give, he believed, was a spirit of self-reliance.

Kon noted that another negative product of Western colonization was that the Filipinos seemed to have the least pride in their "race" among the GEACPS members. Some of them were even proud of their mixed blood. It was very difficult, he argued, to make Filipinos, especially the mestizos, develop an "Oriental spirit."

For instance, according to Kon, Spanish mestizos did not even know about Spain. Therefore, they did not have any patriotic feelings toward that country. At the same time, they were not interested in the Philippines; they were only interested in themselves. Thus, they tended to be irresponsible, conceited, decadent, lazy and wary of hard work. The problem was, in Kon's view, that the educated people, who were supposed to work with the Japanese military to lead the masses, were mostly those mestizos.

But Miki pointed out that some Filipinos, the Ifugaos for instance, still possessed the Oriental virtue of endurance and self-pride. The myths proved that in the past, the Filipino people did have self-respect. Again Western colonization was the culprit. Loss of self-esteem had led to loss of Philippine identity, and Philippine culture had become an "imitation culture."

Miki also cited firm family ties as a strong existing Filipino tradition. However, he contended that this loyalty to and unity within the family never had the chance to develop on a national scale. Japan, on the other hand, had been successful in transferring family loyalty to national loyalty. *Hakkō Ichiu* (eight corners of the world under one roof) was the Japanese idea of expanding the concept of family, embodied in the GEACPS, to other "remote areas" like the Philippines. Miki stressed that the building of the GEACPS would bring the Philippines, which had been an orphan for so long, back into the original Oriental family.

Concomitant with this, Kon felt that the Japanese had to teach the Filipinos how to get rid of their dependency on others. It was Japan's privilege, even duty, to set a good example, according to Miki. It was not an accident but "historic inevitability" that Japan had come to liberate the Asians from the oppression of British and U.S. imperialism.

It was also the Japanese responsibility to search for the genuine Filipino culture and to help develop it. Hino Ashihei, a distinguished novelist who was also a member of the Propaganda Corps, wished to use the talent and energy of young writers such as N. V. M. Gonzalez and Manuel Arguilla for nation-building.[25]

All agreed, too, that the Filipinos did not know anything about Japan and its culture. Thus, the task of disseminating Japanese culture – language, traditions, customs, etc. – should be given the utmost priority in their cultural policy, since Japan would be the leader and should be emulated.

Based on observations of camps for Prisoners of War, the Corps members suggested that the use of movies and music would be effective means of disseminating Japanese culture. The prisoners appeared to be greatly impressed by Japanese news documentaries and were skillful musicians who could easily organize musical bands and quickly learn Japanese military songs.[26]

The above impressions were taken into consideration during the countless planning meetings among the Corps members as well as with military officials. The cultural campaign which unfolded thereafter was the brainchild of the Propaganda Corps, as approved by the military.

REBUILDING MANILA

As soon as the Propaganda Corps members had settled into the newly occupied capital, they held their first meeting in Manila. The Corps was reminded of the official decisions of the *Nanpō Senryōchi Gyōsei Jisshi Yōryo* (Summary for Administering the Occupied Southern Area). This document stated that the utmost importance should be given to efforts that would bring back normal conditions to the citizenry, since the purpose of the military power advancing toward the south was to obtain natural resources for Japan's survival as well as for supplies of the occupying forces.[27] Thus, the top priority for the moment was the task of capturing the hearts of the people, for this was the only way to secure material resources needed for pursuing the Greater East Asia War.[28] This was, in fact, the rationale for the anticipated maximum utilization by the Japanese of the press, radio and film in the Philippines.

To this end, the *Kikaku Han* or Planning Committee had been formed and was actually already functioning on the way to Manila. The *Kikaku Han* was to serve as a temporary nucleus for the entire Propaganda Corps. During one of its first meetings, the following priorities were listed:
1. Seize the newspaper companies and reopen them as soon as possible so that Japan's motives can be propagated.
2. Seize the radio stations and repair broadcasting equipment so that the stations can function again.
3. Immediately reopen all movie theaters to regain a normal atmosphere.[29]

The military authorities paid special attention to the press, radio and film because they regarded the Filipinos as relatively backward culturally since the only reading matter for the average Filipino was newspapers and magazines. The Filipinos, they felt, preferred to spend their time listening to the radio or watching movies, "swallowing whatever entered the eyes and ears." Thus the newspapers, magazines, radio programs and films were seen as potentially influential propaganda tools in the Philippines. The tendency among Filipinos to believe whatever the mass media dished out was also considered to be a reflection of the negative influence of the U.S.[30]

By this time, the Propaganda Corps had two Filipino USAFFE POWs who had surrendered to the Imperial Army on its way to Manila. One of them is on record known only as Andrew; both had volunteered to assist the Corps. Some expatriate Japanese also volunteered to assist. They were to be of great help, since the new arrivals had neither any geographical sense of the localities nor any knowledge of the local languages.

Radio

The radio team, led by Sasaka Shōhei, an NHK employee assigned to the Propaganda Corps, went around the city to visit four radio broadcasting stations, namely KZRH, KZND, KZRF, and KZRM. Afterward, they went to the RCA transmitting station in Quezon City. They were guided by an expatriate Japanese, a Mr Kamizuma of the Mitsui Bussan Kaisha, a trading company.[31]

The inspection team saw that all facilities had been destroyed except for the antennae. However, they later discovered that the USAFFE "destroy" orders given prior to the invasion had not been strictly followed. For they found the radio equipment of KZRH (Voice of the Philippines) hidden in the basement of the Heacock Building. It had been brought there by one of the store's managers, Bert H. Silen, in order to save it from Japanese air attack. He brought the radio team to the hiding place in exchange for his personal freedom.

The problem of securing transmitting equipment was solved with the information received by the Japanese authorities that two sets of mobile broadcasting equipment could be located somewhere in Manila. On January 9, they found one of the transmitters concealed at the Taft Avenue Jai Alai. Until its discovery, underground elements had been using it to communicate with Corregidor.

Personnel of the NHK immediately transferred this vital piece of equipment to the Manila Yacht Club. January 13 was spent setting up the test studio and installing cable for a transmitting station. Using the Yacht Club's flag pole as an antenna, the first broadcast in occupied Manila was out the next day, January 14. The broadcast consisted of news dispatched by the *Dōmei* News Agency.

The Japanese authorities continued to use the prewar call letter and frequency of KZRH for this temporary station. Broadcasting was in the evening from 7.00 p.m. to 11.58 p.m., with news in English, Tagalog, and Japanese. The very first program schedule was as follows:[32]

Time (p.m.)	Program	Announcer
7.00	Station identification	J. H.
7.02	News in Japanese	[Sasaka]
7.10	News in English	Y. P.
7.17	Music	
11.23	Special News	
11.30	Notification in Japanese regarding automobiles and gasoline	[Sasaka]
11.34	Music	
11.37	Notification in Japanese regarding automobiles and gasoline	[Sasaka]
11.39	Music	
11.44	Notifications in Japanese and English	[Sasaka] Y. P.
11.58	Sign off	

It is not known who J. H. was. Y. P. stands for Yay Panlilio, who was born in the U.S. of an Irish father and a Filipino mother. She was married to a Filipino by the name of Eduardo Panlilio, and had worked as a writer for a prewar English daily, the *Herald*. Panlilio was introduced as an announcer to Sasaka by Victor Takizawa, another Mitsui Bussan Kaisha employee. While on the air, she tried to communicate with Corregidor. Eventually, she left Manila and joined the Markings guerrilla unit in Tanay, Rizal, a Manila suburb.[33]

With the completion of repairs on the KZRH station four days from the first day of broadcasting (January 18), broadcasting time was extended, from 7.55 a.m. to 10.00 p.m. First on the schedule was the Domei-dispatched news in English, Tagalog, Spanish, and Japanese. Fifteen minutes were alloted for each language. Later on, news was also broadcast in Visayan. News reporting was on three times a day. The time 7.30–7.50 p.m. was reserved for the announcement of notices from the military.[34] Occasionally, messages appealing to the USAFFE soldiers in Bataan and Corregidor to surrender were aired.

Film and Theater

The movie team of the Propaganda Corps met strong opposition in their attempt to reopen movie theaters.[35] Those against this were the Manila Defense Headquarters, the military police (*Kempeitai*), the Public Peace Section of the Japanese Military Administration, and the Special Service Agency (*Tokkō*). Their objection hinged on two arguments. First, from the point of view of security, this was not advisable. Since a movie theater was a closed, dark place while a film was in progress, it would be difficult for only a few soldiers to suppress a disturbance should one occur. And it would be impossible to station enough soldiers at each movie house with 50 or more people. Second, they asked why U.S. films should be shown when there was a state of war between Japan and the U.S. After much persuasion, however, theaters were indeed allowed to reopen by the end of January, 1942.

Theaters which wanted to show films had to register first with the Japanese authorities. After checking the background of the owners as well as of their employees, permits were issued. Those who were granted permission showed censored U.S. or Filipino films and had to close at 6.00 p.m. By the end of January, at least the following Manila theaters were recorded as registered: Ideal, Avenue, Lyric, Times, State, Capitol, Life, Strand, and Radio for movies; and the Metropolitan Theater for stage shows. As of February 1, 1942, 16 of the 48 movie theaters in Manila had reopened.[36] For the month of February alone, the Propaganda Corps viewed at least 150 films for censorship.

While the films were being censored, local production of movies was temporarily suspended. Thus the same prewar U.S. and Tagalog films were shown over and over. The Propaganda Corps felt compelled to provide other forms of popular entertainment.

Meanwhile, the Propaganda Corps office was visited daily by the production managers of show groups, musicians, theater owners, and others inquiring about available job opportunities. Among them was a certain Carpi, an Italian national who owned the Carpi Opera Group. Due to the outbreak of the war, the group was stranded in the Philippines. Upon the entry of the Japanese into the Philippines, he had been detained as an enemy national by the U.S. authorities. He was released by Japanese troops soon after the latter entered Manila.

Kon Hidemi, who was in charge of entertainment, already knew of this show group, since it had previously performed in Japan. He urged Carpi to organize a revue company with the support of his office. Kon accompanied Carpi in going around Manila to gather performers. He relates:

> We went as far as Tondo where the poor and the scoundrels live, to
> talk to a girl singer who was taking care of her younger sister in bed

with tuberculosis. We met with an acrobat who worked as a blacksmith in Pasay, a Hungarian dancer who lived in a tenement house in Plaza Santa Cruz, a meter-tall dwarf who was the caretaker of a huge mansion, a Russian dance couple, and others.[37]

The group thus formed numbered nearly thirty, with several nationalities – among them German, Italian, Hungarian, Spanish, White Russian, Chinese, Indian, Filipino, Czechoslovakian – hence its name, "International Revue Company."

The Revue's first performance, advertised as a "Grand Stage Show," was held on February 23.[38] For the finale, all the players appeared on stage carrying a Japanese flag in each hand, and they sang the "*Aikoku Kōshinkyoku*" (Patriotic March). A total of 50,000 copies of the song's notes and lyrics in Romanized Japanese were printed, and these were distributed among the audience during each performance.[39]

Print

As soon as Manila was occupied, all publishing firms were ordered by the Japanese military authorities to stop printing, with the exception of a few prewar newspapers. The authorities likewise arrested those members of the press who were enemy nationals, mostly Americans. Among those who experienced arrest and subsequent detention were A. V. H. Hartendorp (*Philippine Magazine*), R. McCullogh Dick (*Philippines Free Press*), D. T. Boguslav (*Manila Tribune*), Bessie Hackett, and R. C. Bennett (both of the *Manila Daily Bulletin*).[40]

A military proclamation dated February 7, 1942 stated that anyone who wished to publish a newspaper, magazine, book, or pamphlet should first apply for and obtain a permit from the Japanese Military Administration, after which they would then be subject to censorship by the authorities.[41] On May 26 of the same year, the military issued police orders calling for the registration of mimeograph machines and any other apparatus which could use stencil paper for the printing of literature, correspondence, or illustrations.[42]

In March, all printed matter carried by Manila bookstores was inspected.[43] There were, according to the inspectors, nearly 40 bookstores. But if the stores which sold books along with other merchandise such as toys and office supplies were included, the number would be around 125.

It took the inspectors almost a month to go through all the printed matter in one store. Of all the published materials examined, 70 percent were in English, 10 percent in Spanish, 12 percent in Chinese, and 8 percent in Tagalog. Any printed item containing the following was confiscated: (1) anti-Japanese propaganda; (2) advocacy of democracy; (3) attempts to alienate the Axis powers from one another; (4) repudiation of the war; (5) opposition to the fundamental principles of the educational renovations in the Philippines; (6) exposure of alleged improper conduct of the Japanese Military Administration.

Using the above criteria, quite a few Chinese books were banned. Most English books were considered harmless, and Tagalog and Spanish books hardly offered any problems.[44] The Manila bookstores were allowed to reopen right after the Easter vacation of that year,[45] and the above guidelines continued to be in effect for future publications.

DUTIES IN BATAAN

While some Corps members were busy developing the propaganda machinery in Manila, others were involved in the very urgent task of persuading the enemy soldiers in the Bataan Peninsula to surrender. These Corps members left for San Fernando, Pampanga, site of the military headquarters. Upon reporting to the headquarters and procuring materials necessary for their propaganda work, some left for Dinalupihan, Morong, and Orani in Bataan, according to the town assigned to each. Before they started their assignment, they were advised by a General Staff member to study the psychological state of those who had surrendered so that they could produce leaflets that would effectively appeal to the USAFFE soldiers. According to Ozaki, the motives of those who surrendered had undergone changes. Early surrenders had been the result of hunger and fatigue; subsequent surrenders seemed to be due to a craving for cigarettes; and more recent ones were because of missed families and loved ones.[46]

The collaboration of writers, interpreters, and painters produced more leaflets. This time the leaflets and handbills targeted the USAFFE soldiers and tried to appeal to the emotions. Incidents of racial discrimination perpetrated by U.S. soldiers against Filipino soldiers were described. The leaflets likewise mentioned that the

Filipinos were merely being used as a shield by the former and that the cowardly MacArthur had escaped and forsaken them.

In addition, the leaflets sought to appeal to the soldiers' homesickness by saying that their parents, wives, and other loved ones were waiting for them. Some leaflets showed lewd pictures of naked women, carrying captions like "Why stay in that foxhole when you can enjoy life?"[47] Other leaflets touched on the Filipinos' national pride and patriotism. Some such leaflets said, "Remember the gallant Filipinos who fought America for the honor of Independence 45 years ago!" or "Now the Philippines rises again once [and] for all to put an end to the American atrocities!" There were also "armistice tickets" to encourage Filipino soldiers to surrender.

The leaflets were printed not only in English, Spanish and Tagalog, but also in Ilocano and Visayan. These were dropped two or three days a week.[48] After printing tens of thousands of these leaflets, some were immediately taken to the San Fernando airport, where planes dropped them over enemy front lines. Others were transported by trucks to the war fronts, where they were dropped by hydrogen balloons. These balloons likewise dropped letters from the soldiers' loved ones. Even the eldest son of Jorge B. Vargas, Chairman of the Japanese-appointed Executive Commission, received a letter from his mother. Someone managed to pick it up, and it eventually reached the Vargas boy.[49]

At the end of March, the Japanese air-dropped the ultimatum to surrender. The ultimatum was signed by Commander-in-Chief General Masaharu Honma. He urged General Jonathan Wainwright to be sensible and to follow "the defenders of Hong Kong, Singapore and the Netherlands East Indies in the acceptance of an honorable defeat." If Honma did not receive a reply by a certain date, he would consider himself at liberty to take any action whatsoever.[50] At the same time "surrender tickets" were dropped, containing the following captions:

1. Come towards our lines waving a white flag.
2. Strap your gun over your left shoulder muzzle down and pointed behind you. Show this ticket to the sentry.
3. Any number of you may surrender with this one ticket.[51]

Additional propaganda was carried by the balloons, and loudspeakers were used as well. In the afternoon of January 24, for instance, just before an all-out attack was to be launched against the USAFFE, a popular Bing Crosby song was heard over the loudspeaker. This was followed by other well-known U.S. songs. Then a voice called to the USAFFE in English: "We, the Japanese Imperial Army, are speaking to you, American soldiers. Abandon this useless struggle immediately . . ." After being repeated several times, a Tagalog *kundiman* (love song) by a female vocalist was aired. To the Filipino soldiers, this message was conveyed: "What do you, Filipino soldiers, fight for?" The announcer was hidden in a trench, with branches and leaves falling on top of his head every time bullets hit the trees. By the time the broadcast was finished, the loudspeaker had three bullet holes.[52]

Romantic music was sometimes aired in the middle of the night. To further exacerbate feelings of homesickness, a mother's voice would appeal to her son. Or an ex-USAFFE soldier would ask his fellow soldiers to surrender immediately. One of the USAFFE soldiers reminisced:

> Out of the night came a woman's voice, sweet and persuasive. In sentimental words, it announced the dedication of a program to "the brave and gallant defenders of Bataan." Songs followed, quivering through the forest. They were selected to arouse nostalgia to the breaking point in a boy facing death and longing for home. "Home, Sweet Home," "Old Folks at Home" – these were the kinds of songs the Japanese broadcast in the dead of the night, alternating heartbreak with horror. These sounds were being broadcast from Japanese sound trucks on the very front of the enemy soldiers' lines.[53]

The newly reopened radio station in Manila, KZRH, was utilized for this purpose as well. On January 28, KZRH aired a 20-minute message in English and Spanish urging the soldiers to surrender. Part of the message was as follows:

> Do you remember that hundreds of Filipino laborers were murdered right after the completion of the Fort? There were about 300 laborers engaged in this undertaking. However, all of them except for three were killed by the American soldiers. These three were saved after jumping into Manila Bay. The American Army committed this kind of atrocity because they did not wish the secret of the Fort to be known by outsiders. Twenty years have passed and today why do you still allow yourselves to be the slaves of the American imperialists who betrayed you? If you have any patriot-

ism and self-pride at all, you should leave the American Army and surrender to the Japanese who came here to assist the Philippines.[54]

Besides this kind of broadcast, the Propaganda Corps utilized well-known Filipinos such as General Emilio Aguinaldo and Jorge Vargas. The former addressed his speech specifically to General Douglas MacArthur on February 1. He spoke in Tagalog, which was translated into English. He said "My country had to take up arms against the Japanese Army for the simple reason that the Philippines was under the American flag," and then urged Wainright to stop resisting immediately to save the lives of the Filipinos.[55]

KZRH broadcasts addressing the soldiers continued. The destruction brought about by the war and the sufferings of the civilian victims were reported by a Filipino newspaperman. The military authorities vehemently denied that the Japanese did not take prisoners; instead, they insisted that enemy soldiers would be treated in the *Bushido* way.[56]

The radio broadcasts did not emanate only from Manila; NHK International reached Bataan and Corregidor as well. Tokyo Rose, a female announcer, poked fun at the enemy soldiers' predicament: "Get smart and give up. Why starve in the stinking jungle while the folks back home make a big profit?" She also announced the names of those who had left with MacArthur and those who were allegedly killed by the Japanese forces, so as to lower the soldiers' morale.[57]

DUTIES IN THE PROVINCES: GOODWILL MISSIONS

While an all-out propaganda war was being fought in Manila and Bataan, yet another effort was initiated by the Propaganda Corps. It was called the "Goodwill Mission." Its primary duty was to promote normal conditions in the provinces by informing the people about the "real" aims and purposes of the Japanese Army and asking them to return to their homes and resume their prewar peaceful pursuits.

Since the end of January, Goodwill Missions were sent to several places, among them Batangas, Bicol, Zambales, Southern Tagalog, Mountain Province, Ilocos Norte, and Mindoro.[58] The following are accounts of two such missions; one went around the Southern Tagalog region, and the other went to the Bicol region.

Goodwill Mission to the Southern Tagalog Region

This group left for Laguna on January 26, and was led by Captain Hitomi. He had a number of Filipino staff, one of whom was the novelist Manuel E. Arguilla. Arguilla was introduced to the Corps by Yay Panlilio, the radio announcer mentioned earlier. Among the speakers were Dr Julio Luz, a medical doctor who had studied in Nagoya, Japan for five years and could speak Japanese, and Francisco Villanueva, a *Tribune* staff writer. Arguilla himself did not make speeches; he distributed leaflets and observed how the people reacted.[59]

The first stop was Biñan. From Manila to Biñan, it was observed that life along the main road was rapidly returning to normal, according to Arguilla's report. The Corps distributed leaflets and copies of the *Sunday Tribune* and *Taliba* on the way. In Biñan, free movies were shown at the Cine Ligaya, which was packed full at night and again the following morning. Speeches were made between film showings.

The message of the speeches was that the people should resume their usual work and help encourage others to do likewise. The speakers gave full assurance of their protection by the Japanese forces. Whenever Dr Luz called for a *"Banzai Nippon"* cheer, the people responded willingly.

The next stop was Lipa, Batangas. People in the province seemed to be hungry for news, since everybody scrambled for the leaflets and newspapers being distributed. All through Tanauan and Malvar, and until Lipa, the Propaganda Corps saw empty houses along the road. Only a few men were to be seen, but no women were about. The following morning, they went around the Lipa town center and its outskirts to look for those who were hiding. The people they managed to find were urged to return to the town center. Captain Hitomi spoke twice to those who had gathered, with Dr Luz translating into Tagalog. At least 750 men and a few women applied for and obtained the safe conduct passes, which were issued free of charge by the Corps.[60]

Goodwill Mission to the Bicol Region

The Goodwill Mission sent to the Bicol region was one of the largest, with over 50 members, seven of whom were from the Propaganda

Corps. It made a 20-day tour covering the entire Bicol region and traveling as far as Sorsogon. Again Captain Hitomi was the head. Also with the group were two from the Religious Corps of the Military Administration, namely Reverend Father Francis Ito, a Catholic priest, and Reverend John Fujita, a Protestant minister. By this time, the Religious Section was no longer under the Propaganda Corps but was under the supervision of the Japanese Military Administration. The Propaganda Corps, on the other hand, received orders directly from the Commanding General through the General Staff member in charge of Information.[61]

Some Filipino government officials also came along, such as an assistant director of the Bureau of Local Government and two representatives of the National Rice and Corn Corporation (NARIC). In addition, press people accompanied the group as participants and observers. And military police were there to protect them from guerrilla attacks.[62]

Public speaking was a main feature of this trip, aside from the distribution of leaflets and newspapers. Among the Filipino speakers were the following: Minviluz Dominguez, granddaughter of General Artemio Ricarte; Nene Moreno, Dominguez's cousin; Fruto R. Santos, a revolutionary figure who later joined the Sakdal Movement, which was a prewar peasant-based anti-U.S. movement that subsequently developed its own political party; and Bibiana Tuazon, a former member of that Sakdalista Party. They all spoke in Tagalog. The Japanese speakers were Hitomi and the two religious personnel. Other propaganda activities included showing movies and putting up posters.

The group left Manila for Bicol on February 17 and made a stop in Biñan for lunch. The next day, they were in Lucena distributing leaflets and newspapers, and delivering speeches at the plaza and market place. On the 19th, they arrived in Atimonan.

Each speaker stressed a different point. Dominguez, Ricarte's granddaughter, talked about the independence movement at the turn of the century. At the same time, she exposed the "deceptive" and "hypocritical" actions of the U.S. regarding the Philippines. She concluded that real independence would be achieved through the establishment of the GEACPS.

It was Ricarte whom the Propaganda Corps had first approached to join the Goodwill Mission. However, due to his old age and asthma, he declined. Instead he sent his eldest granddaughter, Minviluz, who spoke good Japanese, since she had resided in Yokohama for ten years. Grandfather Ricarte coached her on what to say and which points to emphasize. These were:

1. Japan is not our enemy and will recognize our independence in due time.
2. Japan's military force is so strong that it defeated Russia in 1905.
3. Therefore, we must cooperate with Japan.[63]

In Atimonan, a man in his late fifties cried upon seeing Dominguez, saying that he was a Ricartista. An old woman approached her after the speech and introduced herself as a former acquaintance of the General. Ricarte had stayed in her house when he had visited the area during the revolution.

Tuazon talked about Filipino women. She declared that the Filipina should shed superficial U.S. influences and become a real Asian woman with lofty morals and virtues. She added that women should participate in the establishment of an Asia for Asians and a Philippines for the Filipinos.[64]

Bibiana Tuazon, to the Japanese Corps members, seemed to be typical of Japanese women. She hardly wore make-up and was usually quiet and soft-spoken. Once on stage, however, she spoke with passion and strength. When the Propaganda Corps happened to pass through Gapan on the way to Manila after landing on the Lingayen Gulf, Bibiana, with her father's encouragement, joined them along with the elderly Santos. She was glad to join the pacification campaign so that she would be able to tell the people that it was time to achieve under Japan the much-awaited independence. Therefore, she urged people not to be afraid of the Japanese and to cooperate with them.[65]

Santos shared with the audience a historical background of the struggle for Philippine independence. He said that defeating the Anglo-U.S. powers was necessary in order to obtain real independence. Therefore, the Filipinos should cooperate with Japan so as to win the war. Finally, Hitomi spoke of Japan's sincere intentions in waging the war, and he asked for the Filipinos' understanding and cooperation.

These public-speaking engagements were usually sponsored by the provincial governor and held at the town plaza in the evenings. On these occasions, Filipino folk dances, songs, and even plays were performed not only by the Corps members but also by local talent. For instance, a play presented in Naga City showed a greedy merchant taking advantage of the situation by hoarding food items. In the play, he was arrested and executed by the Japanese Army.

The speeches usually attracted audiences as large as 3,000. On one occasion, a young local Indian male joined the throng and spoke of the plight of his countrymen under the British. During the speaking engagements, designated Propaganda Corps members who were Filipinos circulated among the audience to note the people's reactions. They reported that some listeners felt as if they were listening to a sermon by Jesus.[66]

But people also complained about the soaring prices of commodities, especially after the Japanese had landed in the country. Other complaints were the rising unemployment rate and the hoarding of food items by Chinese merchants. These problems were brought up in the meetings with local politicians, religious figures, and expatriate Japanese residents.

The films which the group brought were all documentaries, such as "Heavy Industry of Japan" and "Japanese Navy." Occasionally, Tagalog films were shown if these happened to be available in the towns visited.

AN ALL OUT CULTURAL CAMPAIGN

Religion

While Corps members were occupied with persuading USAFFE soldiers to surrender, going to the provinces on Goodwill Missions, and reconstructing the mass-media organs, the Religious Corps were busy meeting with church people in Manila.

As early as January 7, the Chief of the Japanese Army's Religious Section, who was a Catholic, called on Manila Archbishop Michael J. O'Doherty at his Palace. In the meeting, he explained the aim of the Japanese occupation and urged a more intimate relationship between the Catholic Churches of Japan and the Philippines.[67] On January 18, a conference participated in by a Religious Corps representative and the heads of religious orders was held. The newspaper reported that during the conference, the Catholic Church agreed to cooperate with Japan.[68] The head of the Religious Corps started to visit each of the twelve monasteries and met with the heads.[69] And starting January 11 and every Sunday thereafter, Japanese priests gave sermons and celebrated Masses at various Manila churches.[70] On the part of the Japanese military, they released U.S. and British Protestant leaders as an act of good will.[71]

Indeed, there was an equally active effort to impress the Protestant Churches, especially in the emphasis on Filipinization of the Church. This operation sought the creation of a federation of all Protestant sects under Filipino, not Western, leaders. The federation was to follow the unification pattern of the 42 small Protestant denominations, which grouped together into the "Church of Christ in Japan." It was urged that services be conducted mainly in Tagalog.[72] Finally on October 10, a two-day church meeting was held at the United Church of Manila. And eventually all the Protestant churches were organized into the Federation of Evangelical Churches. Its constitution and by-laws were also taken up during the meeting.[73] The Religious Corps likewise did not fail to meet with the members of the non-Catholic indigenous Aglipayan Church's higher echelon.[74]

The matter of Takayama Ukon, a Japanese Catholic who in the seventeenth century had sought refuge from persecution in the Philippines, was exploited. A memorial service in his honor was held at the San Marcelino Church on September 20. Aside from Reverend Gregorio Tsukamoto's mass being broadcast over KZRH, Colonel Katsuya of the *Hōdōbu* and Jorge B. Vargas were there. They stressed the fullest support and cooperation of the Filipino Catholic Church. Vargas urged that the "the spirit of self-abnegation and other virtues that constituted the moral greatness of Takayama" be stimulated.[75] In November, a monument to Takayama was erected on the eastern part of the Fuji Barracks in Intramuros.[76]

On 4 December, the Blessed Virgin of the Immaculate Conception was proclaimed patroness and protector of the Philippines by a papal bull.[77] This signified that the Vatican officially and openly recognized the Japanese occupation of the Philippines.

To further enhance the close ties between the Japanese and Filipino Catholics, the Nippon-Filipino Catholic Association was organized on December 6. Later it published *Tagapagturo* (The Guide) as its organ. The magazine was printed in English and Tagalog.[78]

Besides giving sermons and officiating at masses in Manila churches, Japanese priests often spoke over KZRH to reach more Christians. Although the Religious Corps was independent of the Propaganda Corps, they worked together closely. Instances of cooperation were exemplified whenever Religious Corps members accompanied the Goodwill Missions to the provinces.

They also sent their own missions to the provinces, aside from accompanying the Propaganda Corps. During their stay in the Philippines until the end of December 1942, they practically covered the whole Philippines: Baguio, Central Luzon (Pampanga and Tarlac Provinces, and Cabanatuan City), Southern Luzon (Batangas and Tayabas Provinces), Mindoro Island, Bicol region (Naga and Legaspi Cities), and the islands of Masbate, Mindanao, and the Visayas.[79]

The Issue of Language

The "Six Basic Principles of Education" which came out on February 17, 1942 called for the teaching of the Japanese language and the eradication "in due course" of the use of English. For the Japanese authorities, this was one way of erasing the idea of reliance on the West, on the U.S. and Great Britain. However, the "due course" never came about. For practical reasons, English remained as a means of communication throughout the occupation period.[80]

It was into the dissemination of the Japanese language that the Propaganda Corps poured most of its effort after the gunsmoke over Corregidor had subsided. The Corps members believed that the best way of making the Filipinos understand the Japanese Spirit was through their language. Teaching started at some schools, churches, government offices and other organizations and institutions. The very first Japanese lesson was started by a Japanese Protestant minister at the YMCA and YWCA on February 24.[81] Mass media such as the radio and newspapers were utilized to propagate Japanese.

Contests were held to promote the language. In August, as one of the features of the Japanese Language Week, a slogan contest in Japanese was held. The slogan had to emphasize the importance of Japanese as a common language in the GEACPS and the importance of popularizing it in the Philippines. Another contest was the writing of an essay either in Japanese or Roman characters. The subject was "The Philippines within the Greater East Asia Co-Prosperity Sphere."[82] Various kinds of contests – essay, slogan, song, poster, novel, *katakana*, etc. – continued to be held throughout the occupation period.

As a move toward the preservation of Filipino culture, Tagalog became the official language along with the Japanese language. Spanish was banned in court, and Tagalog was used for the first time at the Court of Appeals in July. But the ban on Spanish was lifted within two months due to the resulting confusion.[83]

Still, the attempt to use Tagalog in official papers continued. The graduation diplomas of the police training school in Tarlac were in Tagalog. A copy of this diploma was received by the Department of Agriculture and Commerce. The official communication in Tagalog attached to the copy was the first of its kind.[84] The Federation of Filipino Retailers' Association started using Tagalog in their announcements.[85]

To further promote the language, the Department of Education, Health and Public Welfare through the National Language Institute prepared Tagalog-English vocabulary lists. They included phrases and terms commonly used in government, business transactions, and judicial procedures.[86]

Music

Recognizing Filipinos' interest in music, Japanese songs were introduced. They were aired over the radio and the lyrics published in the newspapers. However, a closer look at the cultural activities in the field reveals that music was used also to try to inject a Filipino identity in the minds of the people; to try to make them realize the uniqueness of their heritage. First, Nicanor Abelardo, a Filipino composer, was honored over radio station KZRH.[87] The following month, a Music Festival was held in conjunction with the traditional floral and religious festivals of May. The presentation included classical symphony music, Philippine folk songs from various regions, the Japanese song "Sakura Sakura," and Igorot dance music.[88]

In July, the New Philippines Symphony Society was inaugurated. Kon Hidemi, who was responsible for the music program, was also the man behind the birth of the first all-Filipino orchestra.[89] Moreover, preservation of primitive Filipino folk music was encouraged, while Japanese songs were taught in public schools. It was at the end of the year that Japanese patriotic marches and songs began to be played at all the local theaters and during concerts.

Health Advocacy

To promote health and to build healthy physiques, health consciousness was invoked by exhibiting the prize winners of a health poster contest. More posters were produced by civilian health agencies, assisted by the Medical Corps of the Imperial Army. Radio *Taisō* (a calisthenics program) was first broadcast over KZRH on September 1 and continued to be broadcast every morning at 7:50 a.m. The first Radio *Taisō* Week was held in October. Toward the end of the year, the "*Taisō* Society," headed by Commissioner of Education, Health and Public Welfare Claro M. Recto, was organized in order to popularize this form of aerobic exercise.[90]

Another health promotion activity was the Child Health Day at the year's end. One feature of the program was the awarding of prizes by the wife of Artemio Ricarte to the healthiest war babies. Before the ceremony, a short talk in Tagalog about the life of Mrs Ricarte was given. One other feature of the program was the radio *Taisō* contest attended by various elementary schools in Manila.[91]

The New Cultural Movement

In September, the *Hōdōbu* formally launched the New Cultural Movement. The Movement aimed to "revive the hidden qualities of the Filipinos" and to "create and accelerate the general cultural movement in the New Philippines." This was declared by Marquis Tokugawa Yorisada, President of the Philippine Society of Japan, who had been sent to the Philippines as an adviser to the Japanese Military Administration.

A conference sponsored by the *Hōdōbu* was held and among those who attended were the following Japanese: Tokugawa; Colonel Katsuya, head of the *Hōdōbu*; Ozaki Shirō, Hino Ashihei, and Miki Kiyoshi, all of whom were not only members but were also the brains of the *Hōdōbu*; and Hisashi Enosawa, an expatriate Japanese who had been active before the war in disseminating Japanese culture through publications. The Filipinos were represented by the following: Jorge Vargas, Chairman of the Executive Commission; Claro M. Recto, Commissioner of Education, Health, and Public Welfare; Pedro Aunario, writer in Spanish; Francisca Benitez, then President of the Philippine Women's University; and Bienvenido Gonzales, President of the University of the Philippines.[92]

Katsuya spoke for the Japanese side: the Filipinos should "dissolve once and for all every vestige of their past reliance on Occidental ideas and outlook on life." Instead, they should build up their own new culture based essentially on the "racial" characteristics of the Filipinos. Part of the process was increasing their knowledge and understanding of the spiritual culture of Japan. The literature, art, and music of the New Philippines should permeate to the masses, and this new culture should promote the virtues of simplicity and vigor in life.

The other *Hōdōbu* members had the following to say: Ozaki declared that through the New Cultural Movement the Filipino would willingly become the stepping stone for the next generation of the Oriental race; Hino wondered why the Filipinos conveyed their ideas in English, and he urged them to realize that they were Filipinos and to be proud of it; Miki pointed out that the social development in the Philippines should be shared by everyone and not confined to the wealthy alone, and he stressed that the peasant culture should be looked into and developed; Enosawa maintained that in order to understand a nation, for instance Japan, one should understand its spiritual background, such as the existence of the *Tenno*, *Hakkō Ichiu* etc.

Among the Filipino participants Vargas agreed that in building the New Philippines culture, the first thing to be done was to discard the weaknesses acquired from Spain and the U.S. The next step was to conserve and embellish the ancient native culture. He believed that the assimilation of the culture of other Oriental nations, particularly Japan, was important, and that the most effective means of promoting such a movement was to popularize the Japanese language. Aunario, while agreeing with Vargas that the Japanese language should be promoted, stressed that developing the national language was equally important. He did say, however, that learning Japanese would enrich the native idioms and would strongly bind the entire Asian family. He suggested that in order to further promote Japanese culture, selected intellectuals should be sent to Japan to absorb it.

Recto expressed appreciation for the efforts of the Japanese Military Administration. He praised the effort to develop a Filipino culture under the principles of "the Philippines for Filipinos," a welcome nationalism.

Benitez, the sole woman participant, pointed out that the Filipino woman's high position, a factor to be reckoned with, was ingrained in the native culture and not merely created by foreign influence. She understood the spiritual regeneration in the Movement to mean the revival and strengthening of Oriental virtues and Filipino traits, and the weeding out of Occidental ways and attitudes.

These cultural efforts took on a more concrete shape as time went by. Propaganda was disseminated through newly organized institutions like the Neighborhood Association, *Kanmin Renrakusho* (Liaison and Public Assistance Service), and KALIBAPI (*Kapisanan sa Paglilingkod sa Bagong Pilipinas* or Association in the Service of the New Philippines), which were established in August, October and December of 1942, respectively.

CONCLUDING REMARKS

It has been said that the military did not give that much importance to cultural operations and therefore did not have a concrete cultural policy. However, the military personnel, particularly those who were in Section 8 of the *Sanbō Hon'bu*, should have had certain basic knowledge on the matter if they had graduated from the *Nakano Gakkō*.

There is a pamphlet entitled *Chōhō Senden Kinmu Shishin* (A Guide to Intelligence and Propaganda Duty), published in 1928 as a textbook for use in that school. The pamphlet recommended the following basic policy: agitating national pride, "racial" traditions and religious beliefs can move the emotions of the majority. Therefore, the recruiting of ideologists, educators, and religious missionaries for propaganda purposes was suggested.

This pamphlet proves that the military did have a basic propaganda policy as early as the end of the 1920s, and, accordingly, in the Philippines it was implemented vigorously and forcefully by the members of the Propaganda Corps. As far as timing and technique were concerned, these were left to the members' creativity and ability.

In the actual implementation, the following fields were considered vital: (1) newspapers and telegraphic communications; (2) wireless communication and broadcasting; (3) books, periodicals, pamphlets and leaflets; (4) word-of-mouth communication; (5) painting and photography; (6) art objects, stage plays, movies, songs, and music; (7) slogans and emblems; (8) schools, institutes, and exhibitions; and (9) activities for POWs.[93]

The military's overall cultural propaganda policy was indeed very basic. As mentioned at the beginning of this essay, the original policy had come from the *Sanbō Hon'bu*. The ones who developed the policy so as to fit the Philippine situation were the "cultural warriors" of the Propaganda Corps and other civilians. Policies could have been transmitted from the Tokyo headquarters or adopted upon suggestions from the Corps members. Whichever was the case, the implementation was undertaken by the handpicked intellectuals of the Propaganda Corps. The Propaganda Corps members' impressions of and ideas about the Philippines and its culture eventually were fleshed out in their cultural propaganda policies.

Until the middle of May 1942, the Propaganda Corps had concentrated on bringing back normal conditions to the citizenry and at the same time persuading the USAFFE soldiers in Bataan and Corregidor to surrender. This must have been the order of the General Staff Office in Tokyo, transmitted to the General Headquarters in Manila, which in turn was conveyed to the Propaganda Corps. However, the Corps members themselves concretized this basic order so as to reach out to the people and soldiers. For instance, the Corps was ordered to describe the aims of the GEACPS. The members thought such an abstract idea was difficult to explain. Instead, they pointed out that

> the skin color of the Filipinos and the Japanese is the same. Therefore we should be friends. The white-skinned Americans are our common enemies, and together we shall get rid of them.[94]

In another instance, Corps members were ordered to highlight the fall of Singapore so as to make people realize the strength of the Japanese military. But they felt that the most important and urgent task at that time was not to emphasize the power of the Army. Instead, they concentrated on persuading the anti-Japanese guerrillas to surrender in order to prevent innocent civilians from being caught in the crossfire.[95]

They also realized the effectiveness of making speeches in the local dialect. So they hired Tagalog interpreters, among whom were Japanese expatriates as well as Filipinos who had studied in Japan. Their choice of speakers was also correct from the Japanese point of view, given the official policy of accentuating the independence and patriotism of the Filipinos. Among the speakers, most of whom volunteered, were General Ricarte's granddaughter, and former members of the Sakdal movement, all of whom were staunch advocates of Philippine independence and possessed a historic strong anti-US and pro-Japanese sentiment.

The above examples illustrate that Hitomi Junsuke, who stayed in the Philippines throughout the occupation, and Akiyama Kunio, head of the Department of Information in 1944, were justified in emphasizing the Propaganda Corps' initiative and creativity. This point was reiterated by Utsunomiya Naokata, then head of the Department of General Affairs of the Military Administration and

General Staff officer who later became the military attaché of the Japanese embassy under the Republic. Utsunomiya had himself once served as principal of the Nakano School.[96]

Were creativity, adaptability and initiative the only merits that the Corps members displayed? They were a unique entity within the military establishment because they were intellectual civilians who could have had a different outlook on the war. For instance, one of the most active Propaganda Corps members was Kon Hidemi. He persuaded the military to open movie theaters in Manila as early as February 1942 as a part of the normalization plan. He busied himself in censoring all the existing motion pictures to be shown. He organized the first stage show called "International Revue" at the Metropolitan Theater. He was also behind the establishment of the first all-Filipino orchestra.

Kon was a graduate of Tokyo University and majored in French literature. While studying, he had organized a couple of theater groups. He stayed behind one extra year at the University to study the history of European art. Kon introduced the works of the French novelist André Gide by translating the latter's work into Japanese, and he taught French literature at Meiji University from 1933 until the outbreak of the war.[97]

Ozaki Shirō was one of the best selling prewar novelists and was a leader of the student movement at Waseda University. He had been blacklisted and arrested by the government's Security Bureau due to his radical views and social commitment. Eventually he was attracted to socialism and introduced it through his writings. In 1920, he published *On the History of the Development of Modern Socialism*. At one point, he joined a proletarian literary organization, which he later left. His novels were made into movies and performed on the stage.

Miki Kiyoshi was unique among the Propaganda Corps members because in a sense he was sent to the war front as punishment for his liberal political ideas. After majoring in philosophy at Kyoto University, he went to Paris to acquaint himself more with the works of Blaise Pascal. In France, he was attracted to Marxism. Upon his return to Japan, he wrote on various philosophies, including Marxism, and these works had a profound influence on the intellectuals and youths of the 1920s. In 1929, he became the editor of the magazine *Proletarian Science*, a Marxist-oriented publication. In the same year, he was arrested and imprisoned for six months on the charge of extending financial support to the Japanese Communist

Party. When Japan was under the strong influence of anti-democratic political elements, he tried his best to oppose them. Upon returning to Japan after serving in the Propaganda Corps in the Philippines, he was rearrested on charges of hiding a Communist friend. The harsh treatment he received in prison weakened his health, and he died shortly after the end of the war.[98]

Most of the core members of the Propaganda Corps were "liberals" of the time, as their background indicates. They were not particularly for the war and some of them were rather cynical about it. However, most of them felt proud when they found out that they would be serving in the military. When they were thrown into the actual battle-field where there was a life-or-death situation, their patriotism was greatly stimulated. Being intellectuals and unaccustomed to combat, they naturally wished that the war would end soon, but with Japan's victory.

They understood that their duty as "cultural warriors" was to persuade the hearts and the minds of the Filipinos to their side. While on the one hand they believed that Japanese culture was superior and therefore to be emulated by the conquered, on the other hand they apparently really wanted to build a New Philippines which was filled with patriotism and dignity. Some of them felt that it was their mission to lead the Filipinos in that direction. Therefore, they emphasized the upgrading of the people's health and physical strength (e.g. radio *Taisō*) and the indigenous culture including the national language. For some, nurturing Filipino culture could have been a manifestation of defiance against Japanese militarism, as seen in Miki Kiyoshi's essays or in his statement at the cultural conference as mentioned earlier.

The Commonwealth government on the eve of the Japanese invasion was preparing the nation politically, economically, militarily and culturally for the advent of Philippine independence in 1946. On the literary scene, for instance, the Philippine Writers' League was established in 1939 and a Commonwealth Literary Contest was held in 1940. Through these moves, Filipino writers were urging the government to publish selected and collected works of great Filipino writers, especially the writers of the revolutionary period, hence encouraging nationalism.[99] They also stressed strong support for a national language based on Tagalog since it would be instrumental in fostering national unity.[100] At the same time, they were appealing to fellow writers to take an interest in the Pan-Malayan movement (organized by then governor of Sorsogon province Wenceslao Vinzons, who was executed by the Japanese for being a guerrilla). The movement advocated closer ties with other Southeast Asian countries, through some kind of co-prosperity sphere.[101]

The above indicates that the Filipino cultural scene on the eve of the Pacific War and the cultural policies of the Japanese Imperial Army had significant common ground. In this light, the propaganda policy followed and implemented by the Japanese Propaganda Corps was impressively correct and tactful. However, the economic disaster, physical destruction and totalitarian order brought about by the Japanese occupation of the Philippines certainly obliterated any positive outcome *vis-à-vis* propaganda which might have resulted from the activities of the Propaganda Corps.

Notes and References

1. To reflect this sentiment, the military established in 1938 an organization known as the *Nakano Gakkō* (Nakano School) to train military personnel for information-gathering activities as well as for propaganda. Utsunomiya Naokata, *Amerika "S" Haken Tai* (The US Army's "S" Detachment) (Tokyo: Fuyo Shobō, 1983), p. 28; and Kusakabe Ichirō, *Rikugun Nakano Gakkō Jitsuroku* (A True Record of the Nakano Military School) (Tokyo: Besuto Bukku, 1980), p. 9. For a detailed discussion on the intellectuals' views, see Chua Ser-koon, "Research on the Japanese Cultural Policy on the Eve of Japan's Southward Invasion," *Southeast Asia: History and Culture*, May 16, 1987: pp. 122–45.
2. Nihon Kindaishiryō Kenkyūkai (Study Committee of Japanese Modern History) (ed.), *Nihon Rikukaigun no Seido Soshiki Jinji* (System, Organization and Personnel of the Japanese Military and Navy) (Tokyo: Tokyo Daigaku Shuppan Kai, 1984), p. 382. Also see Hiragushi Takashi, *Dai Hon'ei Hōdōbu* (The Department of Information of the Imperial Headquarters) (Tokyo: Toshoshuppan, 1980), p. 47; and Tsuneishi Shigetsugu, *Shinri Sakusen no Kaisō* (Recollection of Psychological Strategy) (Tokyo: Tōsen Shuppan, 1978), p. 5.
3. Tsuneishi, *Shinri Sakusen no Kaisō*, p. 5. Also see Hiragushi, *Dai Hon'ei Hōdōbu*, p. 47; Utsunomiya, *Amerika "S" Haken Tai*, p. 47; and Machida Keiji, *Tatakau Bunka Butai* (Fighting Cultural Corps) (Tokyo: Hara Shobō, 1967), p. 21.
4. The first point stressed that Japan is prepared to go to war against the U.S., Great Britain and the Netherlands, for reasons of survival and self-protection. It added that preparations for the war would be over by the end of October. As of November, 1941, a month prior to the Pearl Harbor attack, the policy makers were still trying to negotiate with the U.S., in the hope that a peaceful solution would be worked out. The

step-by-step decision-making process is seen in National Defense Institute, "Teikoku Kokusaku Suikō Yōryō" (Points for the Execution of the Imperial National Policy), in *Daitōa Sensō Kaisen Keii* (Details on How the Greater East Asia War Was Started), (Tokyo: Asagumo Shuppan, 1973), vol. 4, pp. 505–6.

Regarding the people sent abroad, see Tsuneishi, *Shinri Sakusen no Kaisō*, p. 56. The two sent to the Philippines were Lieutenant Shimamura Noriyasu and Captain Iwakoshi Shinroku. See Sugita Ichiji, *Jōhō Naki Sensō Shidō* (Leading the War without Information) (Tokyo: Hara Shobō, 1988), p. 146.

5. *Shūhō* (Weekly periodical of the Newspaper Corps of the military and Department of Information), no. 76, March 30, 1938, p. 8.

6. Machida, *Tatakau Bunka Butai*, p. 22; and Tsuneishi, *Shinri Sakusen no Kaisō*, p. 110. Terashita Tatsuo and Ozaki Shirō say there were only 100 civilians for each region. See Terashita Tatsuo, *Sanpagita Saku Sensende* (At the War Front Where Sampaguitas Bloom) (Tokyo: Dorimu Shuppan, 1967), p. 74; and Ozaki Shirō, *Jinsei Gekijō* (Theater of Life) (Tokyo: Shinchō-sha, 1953), p. 325.

7. Tsuneishi, *Shinri Sakusen no Kaisō*, pp. 155–64; and Peter de Mendelssohn, *Japan's Political Warfare* (London: George Allen and Unwin, 1944), pp. 20–30.

8. Based on the memoirs of former Corps members such as the following: Ishizaka Yōjirō, *Mayon no Kemuri* (Smoke of Mount Mayon) (Tokyo: Shūei-sha, 1977); Hamano Kenzaburō, *Senjō* (The Battlefield) (Tokyo: Sekibundō, 1977); Kon Hidemi, *Hitō Jūgun* (Serving with the Forces in the Philippines) (Tokyo: Sōgensha, 1944); and Terashita, *Sanpaguita Saku Sensende*.

9. The rest of this section comes from the following source, unless otherwise indicated: Hitomi Jun'suke, "Hitō Sensen ni Okeru Mochizuki Shigenobu-kun" (Mr Shigenobu Mochizuki at the Philippine War Front), in Mochizuki Nobuo (ed.), *Hitō no Kunibashira* (The Pillars of the Philippines) (Nagano: privately published, 1980), pp. 8 and 65–6. Also, interviews with Hitomi at his residence in Kyoto, July 2, 1981, and in Manila, March 12, 1989.

10. Ozaki, "Nihon no PK Butai" ("Japanese Propaganda Corps"), *Kaizō*, May, 1953, p. 217.

11. Hitomi to Motoe Terami-Wada, undated letter, received on February 20, 1989.

12. Kon, *Hitō Jūgun*, pp. 82 and 87.

13. Ibid., p. 101. These points must have been based in the "Teikoku Kokusaku Suikō Yōryō," which emphasized that the war's purpose was to protect Japan and to establish Greater East Asia's New Order. For more details, see National Defense Institute, *Daitōa Sensō Kaisen Keii*, vol. 4, pp. 505–6.

14. Kon, *Hitō Jūgun*, p. 94.

15. Ono Toyoaki, *Hitō Senbu to Shūkyōhan* (Propaganda in the Philippines and the Religious Corps) (Tokyo: Chūō Shuppan, 1945), pp. 20–2. See also Tsukamoto Shōji, *Jūgun Shisai no Shuki* (Notes of a Priest Who Served in the Army) (Tokyo: Chūō Shuppan, 1945), pp. 9–11.

16. For details see Tsuneishi, *Shinri Sakusen no Kaisō*, pp. 7, 89, 92 and 94; and Sugita, *Jōhō Naki Sensō Shidō*, p. 164. Hitomi revealed in his letter that there were half a dozen sealed wooden boxes labeled "Military Secret." He was allowed to open these after the ship had left Taiwan. Carlos P. Romulo himself was impressed by the neatly printed leaflets he and his comrades received later. See Carlos P. Romulo, *I Saw the Fall of the Philippines* (Garden City, N.Y.: Doubleday, Doran, 1943), pp. 109 and 146.

17. Some members, especially the religious personnel, had left earlier to accompany the advance troops. Ono, *Hitō Senbu to Shūkyōhan*, p. 17.

18. Kon, *Hitō Jūgun*, p. 110; Ozaki, *Senki, Bata'an Hantō* (War Record, Bataan Peninsula) (Tokyo: Keibun Kan, 1962), p. 12; and Hitō Haken Hōdō-bu (Department of Information Sent to the Philippines) (ed.), *Hitō Senki* (The Philippine War Record) (Tokyo: Bungei Shunju Sha, 1943), p. 23. A second batch of members of the Propaganda Corps arrived in March 1942. Included among them were Miki Kiyoshi, Hino Ashihei, and Shibata Kenjirō.

19. Their activities between Bauan and Manila related here are based on the accounts found in Kon, *Hitō Jūgun*; Ozaki, *Senki, Bata'an Hantō*; and Department of Information, *Hitō Senki*.

20. Ono, *Hitō Senbu to Shūkyōhan*, pp. 15 and 32–3. See also Tsukamoto, *Jūgun Shisai no Shuki*, pp. 23 and 118.

21. The group's travel from Atimonan to Manila is related in Kinoshita Jirō, "Achimonan Jōriku Butai" (The Unit which Landed in Atimonan") in Hitō Haken Hōdō-bu (ed.), *Hitō Senki*, pp. 45–50.

22. The impressions of the Corps members are culled from Miki Kiyoshi, (ed.), *Hitō Fudōki* (Record of the Natural Features of the Philippine Islands) (Tokyo: Koyama Shoten, 1943).

23. Kon's impressions are from the following articles by him: "Bunka Sensen Nite" ("At the Cultural War Front"), *Bungei*, October, 1942, pp. 46–51; and "Firipin no Nomin to Gakusei" ("Peasants and Students in the Philippines"), *Bungei*, January, 1943, pp. 111–13.

24. Miki's impressions are from Miki, "Hitōjin no Tōyōteki Seikaku" ("Oriental Characteristics of the Filipinos"), in *Hitō Fudōki*, pp. 4–41. This originally appeared from July to October, 1942 in eight parts in the *Minami Jūjisei* (Southern Cross), a newspaper for Japanese soldiers. The eight installments were later compiled into a book together with articles of other Corps members.

25. Hino, "Hitō no Bunka" ("The Philippine Culture"), in *Hitō Fudōki*, p. 88.

26. Kon, "Bunka Sensen Nite," p. 48, and *Hitō Jūgun*, p. 136; Hino, "Hitō no Bunka," pp. 62–3; and Kimura Ki, "Hitō Bunkasen no Genjitsu" ("The Reality of Cultural Warfare in the Philippines"), *Gendai*, June, 1942, pp. 185–7.

27. Approved by the Liaison Council on November 20, 1942. Ministry of Foreign Affairs ed., *Nihon Gaikō Nenpyō Oyobi Shuyō Bunsho* (A Chronological table for Japanese Diplomacy and Important Documents, 1840–1945) (Tokyo: Hara Shobō, 1980), p. 562.

28. Takeda Mitsuji, *Nanpō no Gunsei* (Military Administration in the Southern Area) (Tokyo: Senryō Sha, 1943), p. 28.

29. Hitomi, "Mochizuki," p. 71. The members of the Planning Committee were well-known novelists, poets, and painters. Among them were Ozaki Shirō, Ishizaka Yojirō, Kon Hidemi, Mukai Junkichi, Ikeda Teiji, and Terashita Tatsuo. See Hitomi, "Hitō Sensen ni Okeru," p. 71.
30. Takeda, *Nanpō no Gunsei*, pp. 803–4.
31. The accounts of how the radio stations were reopened in the newly occupied city were based on a diary kept by Sasaka. Part of the diary is in Kimura Ki, *Minami no Shinju*, pp. 189–209. Another source is an interview with Sasaka Shōhei at his residence in Yokohama, Japan, August 5, 1987.

    Mitsui Bussan Kaisha was one of the eleven cooperatives and organizations which had been supplying information to the military. See Sugita, *Jōhō Naki Sensō Shidō*, p. 147.
32. From the "Daily Record of KZRH," found in Satō Katsuzō, "Hitō Hōsō Kanri Kyōkai no Ayumi" ("The Development of the Broadcast Control Bureau in the Philippines"), NHK Broadcast Control Culture Research, Annual Report 18 (1972), p. 222.
33. Colonel "Yay," *Marking* (Manila: Venceremos Enterprise, 1979), pp. 1–9. Also see a personal letter addressed to Sasaka Shōhei in Kimura, *Minami no Shinju*, pp. 212–14.
34. *Tribune*, January 18, 1942.
35. For this section, information came from Kon, "Hitō no Eiga Kōsaku Byoten" ("A Sketch of Movie Strategy in the Philippines"), *Sunday Mainichi*, January 24, 1943; as well as Kon, *Hito Jūgun*, pp. 189–93.
36. *Tribune*, February 28, 1942. In May 1943, the number of movie theaters in Manila had grown to 54, according to the *Tribune*, May 26, 1943.
37. Kon, *Hitō Jūgun*, p. 215.
38. *Tribune*, February 25, 1942.
39. Kon, *Hitō Jūgun*, p. 215.
40. A. V. H. Hartendorp, *The Japanese Occupation of the Philippines* (Manila: Bookmark, 1967), vol. 2, p. 50.
41. *Official Journal of the Japanese Military Administration (OJJMA)*, (Manila: Niti Niti Shinbun Sha, March 1942–July 1943), vol. 1, p. 14.
42. *Tribune*, May 27, 1942.
43. Based on Instruction No. 16, in *OJJMA*, vol. 1, p. 11.
44. Shibata Kenjirō, "Tosho Shuppan Kenetsu Shidō Kachō no Ki" ("Record of an Officer Who Censored Printing Materials"), *Weekly Mainichi*, March 14, 1943, pp. 27–9. See also *OJJMA*, vol. 4, p. 11.
45. Kimura, *Minami no Shinju*, p. 173.
46. Ozaki, *Jinsei Gekijō*, p. 186.
47. Hitomi, "Mochizuki," p. 74; and Terashita, p. 297. One of the soldiers recalls that some leaflets had pictures of *adobo*, a popular Filipino dish, as well as those of beautiful women. Interview with Leocadio de Asis, December 7, 1988. Other examples of leaflets and handbills are seen in Uldarico S. Baclagon, *Last 130 Days of the USAFFE* (Metro Manila: privately published, 1982), pp. 146, 159–72; and Romulo, *I Saw the Fall of the Philippines*. These illustrations were said to be taken from *Esquire* magazine. A picture of some of the leaflets can be seen between pages 138 and 139 in Teodoro A. Agoncillo, *The Fateful Years: Japan's*

Adventure in the Philippines, 1941–1945 (Quezon City: R. P. Garcia Publishing Co., 1965), vol. 1.

48. Romulo, *I Saw the Fall of the Philippines*, pp. 109 and 146. The author was impressed by the thoroughness of the Japanese preparations.

49. The invitation to the public to send letters to Filipino soldiers in Bataan and Corregidor came out in the *Tribune*, such as on March 11, 1942. For the incident regarding Vargas's son, see Kon, *Hitō Jūgun*, p. 219. The young Vargas indeed received the letter, as confirmed by his brother, Ramon (Nene) Vargas. Interview with him on August 22, 1988.

50. See Louis Morton, *The Fall of the Philippines* (Washington, D.C.: Office of the Chief of Military History, Department of the Army, 1953), p. 418; Celedonio A. Ancheta (ed.), *The Wainright Papers*, (Quezon City: New Day Publishers, 1980), vol. 2, p. 24; and Donald Knox, *Death March: The Survivors of Bataan* (New York: Harcourt Brace Jovanovich, 1981), pp. 90–1. See also Manuel A. Buenafe, *Wartime Philippines* (Manila: Philippine Education Foundation, Inc., 1950) p. 103.

51. Agoncillo, *The Fateful Years*, vol. 7, p. 177.

52. Department of Information, *Hitō Senki*, pp. 65–6. See also Buenafe, *Wartime Philippines*, p. 96.

53. Romulo, *I Saw the Fall of the Philippines*, p. 158.

54. Kimura, *Minami no Shinju*, pp. 132–3.

55. Douglas MacArthur, *Reminiscenses* (New York: McGraw-Hill, 1964), pp. 134–5. For the date and content of Aguinaldo's speech, see *Tribune*, February 2, 1942.

56. *Tribune*, April 15 and 16, 1942.

57. Stephen M. Mellnik, *Philippine War Diary, 1939–1945* (New York: Van Nostrand, 1981), pp. 99 and 102. Also see Carlos Quirino, *Chick Parsons: America's Master Spy in the Philippines* (Quezon City: New Day Publishers, 1980), p. 69.
    There were a number of counter attacks made by the USAFFE soldiers in the field of propaganda. They set up a radio station called "The Voice of Freedom" and published world news and entitled it "The International News Summary." They utilized the Japanese-Americans in the USAFFE to translate messages into Japanese. These broadcasts appealed to the occupying soldiers to surrender.

58. The Goodwill Missions were reported in the following *Tribune* issues of 1942:

Topic	Issues
To Batangas	February 5
To Bicol	March 11, 15–19, 21–23
To Zambales and Southern Tagalog	May 3, 17
To Bontoc	June 7
To Mindoro	June 10
To Ilocos	July 19
To Nueva Ecija and Bulacan	August 17

59. Kon, *Hitō Jūgun*, p. 207. The account of this trip is also related in Ozaki,

Jinsei Gekijō, pp. 146–59. Ozaki says that Dr Julio Luz volunteered as interpreter for the Corps.

60. This is according to Arguilla, whose reports on the mission appeared in the *Tribune* issues for February 5, and of March 15–17 and 19.
61. Sugita, *Jōhō Naki Sensō Shidō*, p. 215.
62. *Tribune*, March 11, 1942.
63. Tape-recorded reminiscenses of her experience with the Goodwill Mission sent by Ms Minviluz Dominguez, who currently resides in California, to Motoe Terami-Wada on April 24, 1989, and telephone interview with her on July 7, 1989.
64. Ishizaka, *Mayon no Kemuri*, pp. 150–1.
65. Interview with Ms Bibiana Tuazon-Ihita, at her residence in Osaka, April 15, 1989. Also see Horikawa Shizuo, *Manila e no Michi* (The Road to Manila) (Tokyo: Tokyo Shiryū-sha, 1961), pp. 203–4.
66. The source of the rest of this section is Ishizaka, *Mayon no Kemuri*, pp. 168–9.
67. *Tribune*, January 11, 1942.
68. Ibid., January 20, 1942.
69. Ono, *Hitō Senbu to Shūkyōhan*, p. 183.
70. *Tribune*, January 15 and 23, March 8 and 13, 1942.
71. Ibid., January 29, 1942.
72. Ibid., May 10, 1942.
73. Ibid., October 10, 1942.
74. April 7, 1942, "Diary," in Ono, *Hitō Senbu to Shūkyōhan*.
75. *Tribune*, September 21 and 22, 1942.
76. Ibid., November 14, 1942.
77. Ibid., December 7, 1942.
78. Ibid., December 24, 1942.
79. Ono, *Hitō Senbu to Shūkyōhan*, pp. 183–90.
80. *Tribune*, February 18, 1942.
81. Ono, *Hitō Senbu to Shūkyōhan*, p. 184.
82. *Tribune*, August 19 and 26, 1942.
83. Ibid., July 25 and 31, September 3, 1942.
84. Ibid., September 3, 1942.
85. Ibid., September 8, 1942.
86. Ibid., September 9, October 14, 1942.
87. Ibid., April 24, 1942.
88. Ibid., May 3 and 24, 1942.
89. Ibid., July 23, 1942.
90. Ibid., August 25, September 4, October 11, December 14, 1942.
91. Ibid., December 18, 19 and 27, 1942.
92. Ibid., November 12 and 13, 1942.
93. See *Chōhō Senden Kinmu Shishin* (A Guide to Intelligence and Propaganda Duty) (n.p., 1928). This pamphlet is among the documents of the Military History Department of the National Institute for Defense Studies in Tokyo.
94. Interview with Hitomi, March 12, 1989.
95. Ibid.

96. Based on an undated letter of Hitomi received on February 26, 1989 and letter of Akiyama to Utsunomiya, who quoted parts to Terami-Wada in a letter dated February 12, 1989. For Utsunomiya's background, see Utsunomiya, *Amerika "S" Hakentai*, p. 23.

97. He became the first head of the Board of Culture under the Ministry of Education in 1968. He later became chairman of the Board of Directors of the Japan Foundation. For the information on the Propaganda Corps members mentioned here, see *Nihon Kindai Bungaku Jiten No. 3* (Encyclopedia of Japanese Modern Literature No. 3) (Tokyo: Kōdansha, 1977).

98. Ibid.

99. Elmer Ordoñez, "Literature under the Commonwealth," in *Lectures on the Culture of the Philippines* (Quezon City: University of the Philippines Press, 1963), p. 406.

100. Agoncillo, Arguilla, and Esteban Nedruda, *Literature under the Commonwealth* (Manila: Philippine Writers' League, 1940); reprint (Manila: Alberto Florentino, 1973), p. 61.

101. Ordoñez, "Literature under the Commonwealth," p. 406.

Index